Visualforce Development Cookbook

Second Edition

Discover over 70 real-world examples to overcome the most complex concepts you will face developing with Visualforce

Keir Bowden

PACKT enterprise
PUBLISHING
professional expertise distilled

BIRMINGHAM - MUMBAI

Visualforce Development Cookbook

Second Edition

First edition: September 2013

Second edition: August 2016

Production reference: 1260816

Published by Packt Publishing Ltd.

Livery Place

35 Livery Street

Birmingham B3 2PB, UK.

ISBN 978-1-78646-808-6

www.packtpub.com

Credits

Author

Keir Bowden

Reviewer

Rahul Sharma

Commissioning Editor

Aaron Lazar

Acquisition Editor

Chaitanya Nair

Content Development Editor

Nikhil Borkar

Technical Editor

Hussain Kanchwala

Copy Editor

Safis Editing

Project Coordinator

Suzanne Coutinho

Proofreader

Safis Editing

Indexer

Tejal Daruwale Soni

Production Coordinator

Aparna Bhagat

Cover Work

Aparna Bhagat

About the Author

Keir Bowden is a 30-year veteran of the IT industry from the United Kingdom. After spending the early part of his career in the defence industry, he moved into investment banking systems, implementing systems for Banque Nationale de Paris, CitiGroup, and Deutsche Bank. In the late 1990s, Keir moved into Internet technologies, leading to a development of the order management and payment handling systems of one of the first European Internet shopping sites.

Keir started working with Force.com in late 2008 and has been recognized multiple times by Salesforce as an MVP for his contribution and leadership in the community. In 2012, he became the first certified technical architect outside of Salesforce in EMEA, and he has served as a judge on several EMEA Technical Architect Certification Review Boards. Keir is also a prominent blogger on Apex, Visualforce and Lightning Components solutions; and a regular speaker at events such as Dreamforce, Cloud World Forum, and Salesforce World Tour.

Keir is a chief technical officer of BrightGena—a Salesforce.com Platinum Cloud Alliance Partner in the United Kingdom, where he is responsible for the present and future technical strategies.

Keir acted as a technical reviewer for the *CRM Admin Cookbook* before accepting the challenge of authoring this book, which also happens to be his first.

I would like to thank my partner, Marie, for putting up with me spending even more time than usual on my laptop, something that neither of us had previously thought possible. I'd also like to thank my reviewers, whose tireless efforts and attention to detail ensure that the recipes are correct and perform as expected.

About the Reviewer

Rahul Sharma has been working on the Force.com platform since 2010 and is a certified advanced developer and administrator. Currently, he is working with Cognizant and has worked on most of the areas in Salesforce. He is an active contributor to the Salesforce developer community (he holds the Pro position) and Stack Exchange. He holds a bachelors degree in electronics engineering based out of Mumbai, India. His areas of interest are UI and mobile development, along with Salesforce. He can be reached at
`about.me/rahuls91221`.

He was a technical reviewer for the following books:

- *Learning Force.com Application Development*
- *Visualforce Developer's Guide*
- *Mastering Application Development with Force.com*

I would like to thank my family & friends for support , and Packt Publishing for giving me another opportunity to review an excellent book by our Salesforce MVP Keir Bowden.

www.PacktPub.com

eBooks, discount offers, and more

Did you know that Packt offers eBook versions of every book published, with PDF and ePub files available? You can upgrade to the eBook version at www.PacktPub.com and as a print book customer, you are entitled to a discount on the eBook copy. Get in touch with us at customercare@packtpub.com for more details.

At www.PacktPub.com, you can also read a collection of free technical articles, sign up for a range of free newsletters and receive exclusive discounts and offers on Packt books and eBooks.

https://www2.packtpub.com/books/subscription/packtlib

Do you need instant solutions to your IT questions? PacktLib is Packt's online digital book library. Here, you can search, access, and read Packt's entire library of books.

Why subscribe?

- Fully searchable across every book published by Packt
- Copy and paste, print, and bookmark content
- On demand and accessible via a web browser

Free access for Packt account holders

Get notified! Find out when new books are published by following @PacktEnterprise on Twitter or the Packt Enterprise Facebook page.

Table of Contents

Preface   1

Chapter 1: General Utilities   7

  Introduction   7

  Overriding standard buttons   8

    Getting ready   8

    How to do it…   8

    How it works…   9

  Data-driven styling   11

    How to do it…   11

    How it works…   11

    See also   13

  Turning off an action poller   13

    Getting ready   13

    How to do it…   13

    How it works…   14

    See also   15

  Visualforce in the sidebar   15

    Getting ready   16

    How to do it…   16

    How it works…   18

    There's more…   19

  Passing parameters to action methods   19

    Getting ready   19

    How to do it…   19

    How it works…   20

  Reacting to URL parameters   22

    Getting ready   22

    How to do it…   22

    How it works…   23

    See also   24

  Passing parameters between Visualforce pages   25

    How to do it…   25

    How it works…   27

    See also   29

Opening a pop-up window   29
   How to do it…   29
   How it works…   30
   See also   32
Adding a launch page   32
   How to do it…   33
   How it works…   34
Testing a custom controller   35
   Getting ready   36
   How to do it…   36
   How it works…   36
   See also   38
Testing a controller extension   38
   How to do it…   39
   How it works…   39
   See also   41
Chapter 2: Custom Components   43
Introduction   43
Passing attributes to components   44
   How to do it…   44
   How it works…   45
   See also   47
Updating attributes in component controllers   47
   Getting ready   47
   How to do it…   48
   How it works…   49
   See also   51
Passing action methods to components   51
   How to do it…   52
   How it works…   53
   There's more…   54
   See also   54
Data-driven decimal places   54
   How to do it…   55
   How it works…   55
   See also   56
The custom iterator component   57
   Getting ready   57
   How to do it…   57

How it works…   59
Setting a value into a controller property   61
Getting ready   61
How to do it…   62
How it works…   63
See also   64
Multiselecting related objects   65
Getting ready   65
How to do it…   67
How it works…   68
Notifying the containing page controller   71
Getting ready   71
How to do it…   71
How it works…   72
See also   75

Chapter 3: Capturing Data Using Forms   77

Introduction   77
Editing a record in Visualforce   78
Getting ready   78
How to do it…   78
How it works…   79
See also   80
Adding error messages to field inputs   80
Getting ready   81
How to do it…   81
How it works…   81
See also   83
Adding error messages to non-field inputs   83
Getting ready   83
How to do it…   83
How it works…   84
See also   86
Using field sets   86
Getting ready   86
How to do it…   88
How it works…   88
Adding a custom lookup to a form   90
Getting ready   90
How to do it…   90

How it works…	91
See also	94
Adding a custom datepicker to a form	94
Getting ready	95
How to do it…	95
How it works…	96
See also	97
Retrieving fields when a lookup is populated	97
Getting ready	98
How to do it…	98
How it works…	98
Breaking up forms with action regions	99
Getting ready	100
How to do it…	100
How it works…	101
See also	102
The Please wait spinner	103
How to do it…	103
How it works…	104
Action chaining	105
Getting ready	105
How to do it…	106
How it works…	106
Chapter 4: Managing Records	109
Introduction	109
Styling fields as required	109
Getting ready	110
How to do it…	110
How it works…	111
See also	112
Styling table columns as required	112
Getting ready	113
How to do it…	113
How it works…	113
See also	115
Attaching an image to a record	115
Getting ready	116
How to do it…	116
How it works…	118

There's more…   119
See also   119
Managing attachments   119
Getting ready   120
How to do it…   120
How it works…   121
There's more…   122
See also   122
Maintaining custom settings   123
Getting ready   123
How to do it…   124
How it works…   125
Refreshing record details from embedded Visualforce   126
Getting ready   127
How to do it…   127
How it works…   129
Using wrapper classes   130
Getting ready   130
How to do it…   131
How it works…   131
See also   133
Changing options based on the user input   133
Getting ready   134
How to do it…   134
How it works…   135
See also   137
Changing page layout based on the user input   137
Getting ready   137
How to do it…   138
How it works…   138
See also   140
Form-based searching   141
Getting ready   141
How to do it…   141
How it works…   142
See also   143
Chapter 5: Managing Multiple Records   145
Introduction   145
Editing a record and its parent   146

Getting ready	146
How to do it…	146
How it works…	147
See also	148
Managing a list of records	**148**
Getting ready	149
How to do it…	149
How it works…	150
See also	151
Converting a lead	**152**
Getting ready	152
How to do it…	152
How it works…	153
There's more…	156
Managing a hierarchy of records	**156**
Getting ready	157
How to do it…	157
How it works…	158
See also	161
Inline editing a record from a list	**161**
Getting ready	161
How to do it…	162
How it works…	162
See also	165
Creating a Visualforce report	**165**
Getting ready	165
How to do it…	166
How it works…	166
Displaying report data in Visualforce	**169**
Getting ready	170
How to do it…	170
How it works…	171
Loading records asynchronously	**173**
Getting ready	173
How to do it…	174
How it works…	174
Chapter 6: Visualforce Charts	**177**
Introduction	**177**
Creating a bar chart	**178**

Getting ready	178
How to do it…	178
How it works…	179
See also	181
Creating a line chart	**181**
Getting ready	182
How to do it…	182
How it works…	182
See also	185
Customizing a chart	**185**
Getting ready	185
How to do it…	186
How it works…	186
Adding multiple series	**189**
Getting ready	189
How to do it…	189
How it works…	190
See also	193
Creating a stacked bar chart	**193**
Getting ready	193
How to do it…	193
How it works…	194
See also	198
Adding a third axis	**198**
Getting ready	198
How to do it…	199
How it works…	199
See also	203
Embedding a chart in a record view page	**203**
Getting ready	203
How to do it…	203
How it works…	206
Multiple charts per page	**208**
Getting ready	209
How to do it…	210
How it works…	210
Chapter 7: Enhancing the Client with JavaScript	**215**
Introduction	**215**
Using action functions	**216**

Getting ready	217
How to do it…	217
How it works…	217
Avoiding race conditions	219
Getting ready	220
How to do it…	220
How it works…	220
See also	222
The confirmation dialog	222
Getting ready	222
How to do it…	223
How it works…	223
See also	224
Pressing Enter to submit	225
Getting ready	225
How to do it…	225
How it works…	226
See also	227
The onload handler	227
How to do it…	228
How it works…	228
See also	230
Collapsible list elements	230
Getting ready	231
How to do it…	231
How it works…	232
Trapping navigation away	234
Getting ready	234
How to do it…	234
How it works…	235
See also	236
Creating a record using JavaScript remoting	237
Getting ready	237
How to do it…	237
How it works…	238
See also	239
Chapter 8: Force.com Sites	241
Introduction	241
Creating a site	242

Getting ready	242
How to do it…	243
How it works…	244
See also	245
Record and field access	245
Getting ready	246
How to do it…	246
How it works…	248
See also	248
Retrieving content from Salesforce	249
Getting ready	249
How to do it…	251
How it works…	251
See also	253
Web to lead form	253
Getting ready	253
How to do it…	254
How it works…	255
See also	257
Creating a website template	257
Getting ready	257
How to do it…	257
How it works…	258
See also	260
Adding a header menu to a template	260
Getting ready	260
How to do it…	261
How it works…	262
See also	264
Adding a sidebar to a template	264
Getting ready	265
How to do it…	265
How it works…	266
See also	268
Conditional rendering in templates	269
Getting ready…	269
How to do it…	269
How it works…	270
See also	272

Chapter 9: Visualforce in Salesforce1   273

   Introduction   273
   Navigating between pages   274
     How to do it…   275
     How it works…   277
   Lightning forms   280
     Getting ready   281
     How to do it…   281
     How it works…   283
   Capturing the user's location   285
     Getting ready   285
     How to do it…   286
     How it works…   287
   Saving an image when creating a record   289
     Getting ready   290
     How to do it…   290
     How it works…   291
     See also   295
   Capturing a signature when creating a record   295
     Getting ready   295
     How to do it…   296
     How it works…   297
     See also   299
   Displaying a location in a map   300
     Getting ready   300
     How to do it…   301
     How it works…   302
     See also   303
   Scanning the QR code to access the record   303
     Getting ready   303
     How to do it…   304
     How it works…   304

Chapter 10: Troubleshooting   307

   Introduction   307
   Avoiding validation errors with action regions   308
     Getting ready   308
     How to do it…   308
     How it works…   309

See also | 310
Surfacing errors | 310
Getting ready | 311
How to do it… | 311
How it works… | 311
See also | 313
Multiple bindings to the same record | 313
Getting ready | 314
How to do it… | 314
How it works… | 315
There's more … | 317
Reducing view state size 1 – the transient keyword | 317
Getting ready | 318
How to do it… | 319
How it works… | 320
There's more … | 322
Reducing view state size 2 – HTML vs Visualforce components | 323
Getting ready | 323
How to do it… | 323
How it works… | 324
There's more … | 327
Debugging Visualforce | 327
How to do it… | 328
How it works… | 328
There's more … | 330
Logging messages in a Visualforce page | 331
Getting ready | 332
How to do it… | 332
How it works… | 333
There's more | 334

Index | 335

Preface

The Visualforce framework allows developers to build highly customized, personalized, and branded user interfaces for their Salesforce, Force.com, and Salesforce1 applications. Hosted natively on the Salesforce platform, Visualforce gives developers complete control over all areas of the user interface, allowing them to satisfy complex business requirements and support multiple devices.

Visualforce pages use a mixture of HTML and Visualforce components, which are processed server-side and delivered to the browser as HTML. This allows the use of standard web technologies, such as CSS and JavaScript, to provide an enriched and dynamic user experience.

The *Visualforce Development Cookbook* provides solutions for a variety of challenges faced by the Salesforce developers and demonstrates how easy it is to build rich interactive pages for both desktop and mobile devices using Visualforce. Each recipe contains clear, step-by-step instructions along with detailed explanations of the key areas of Visualforce, Apex or JavaScript code, that deliver the solution.

Whether you are looking to make a minor addition to the standard page functionality or override it completely, this book will provide you with practical examples that can be readily adapted to a number of scenarios.

What this book covers

Chapter 1 , *General Utilities*, covers enhancing or replacing standard functionality with Visualforce, systemizing business processes, guiding users through the creation and ongoing management of data, and writing effective tests.

Chapter 2, *Custom Components*, demonstrates how to create custom Visualforce components to encapsulate functionality for reuse across multiple pages and techniques to allow communication between component and page controllers.

Chapter 3, *Capturing Data Using Forms*, describes how to capture data entered in a Visualforce page and send this to the server for processing.

Chapter 4, *Managing Records*, offers techniques to streamline and enhance the management of Salesforce data using Visualforce pages, using styling to indicate required fields and changing pages in response to user actions.

Chapter 5, *Managing Multiple Records*, covers recipes to manage multiple records in a single page, ranging from editing parent and child records to managing a deep and wide hierarchy.

Chapter 6, *Visualforce Charts*, presents a series of recipes to create charts of increasing complexity, embed a chart into a standard Salesforce page, and add multiple charts to a single page in a similar style to a Salesforce dashboard.

Chapter 7, *Enhancing the Client with JavaScript*, shows how to use JavaScript to provide a variety of client-side enhancements, including confirmation of user actions, instant feedback on user inputs, and speeding up pages that access server-side data via remote methods.

Chapter 8, *Force.com Sites*, provides step-by-step instructions to configure a publicly accessible website styled with the Lightning Design System, allowing visitors to access the Salesforce records and extract boilerplate content to reusable templates.

Chapter 9, *Visualforce in Salesforce1*, demonstrates how Visualforce can be used to enhance the user experience on the Salesforce1 mobile device, including capturing the user's location and attaching images when creating records.

Chapter 10, *Troubleshooting*, covers some common error scenarios and how to avoid them, along with tips to improve performance by reducing the size of the Visualforce viewstate and page load time in general.

What you need for this book

In order to build the recipes from this book, you will need an Enterprise, Unlimited or Developer (recommended) Edition of Salesforce, and System Administrator access. You will also need a supported browser, such as the latest version of Google Chrome, Mozilla Firefox, Apple Safari 8+, Internet Explorer 9+, or Microsoft Edge. Use the **Setup** menu to cut and paste the code samples rather than the developer console, as it may report visibility errors when the organization has a custom namespace.

Who this book is for

This book is intended for intermediate Visualforce developers who are familiar with the basics of Visualforce and Apex development on the Salesforce platform. An understanding of the basics of HTML, CSS and JavaScript is also useful for some more advanced recipes.

Sections

In this book, you will find several headings that appear frequently (Getting ready, How to do it, How it works, There's more, and See also).

To give clear instructions on how to complete a recipe, we use these sections as follows:

Getting ready

This section tells you what to expect in the recipe, and describes how to set up any software or any preliminary settings required for the recipe.

How to do it...

This section contains the steps required to follow the recipe.

How it works...

This section usually consists of a detailed explanation of what happened in the previous section.

There's more...

This section consists of additional information about the recipe in order to make the reader more knowledgeable about the recipe.

See also

This section provides helpful links to other useful information for the recipe.

Conventions

In this book, you will find a number of text styles that distinguish between different kinds of information. Here are some examples of these styles and an explanation of their meaning.

Code words in text, database table names, folder names, filenames, file extensions, pathnames, dummy URLs, user input, and Twitter handles are shown as follows: "Once the payment reaches the state `Complete` the action poller will be disabled."

A block of code is set as follows:

```
<apex:column style="color:
    {!IF(AND(NOT(ISNULL(campaign.ActualCost)),
    campaign.ActualCost<=campaign.BudgetedCost),
  "lawngreen", "red")}" value="{!campaign.ActualCost}"/>
```

New terms and **important words** are shown in bold. Words that you see on the screen, for example, in menus or dialog boxes, appear in the text like this: "Click on the **New** button."

Warnings or important notes appear in a box like this.

Tips and tricks appear like this.

Reader feedback

Feedback from our readers is always welcome. Let us know what you think about this book-what you liked or disliked. Reader feedback is important for us as it helps us develop titles that you will really get the most out of. To send us general feedback, simply e-mail feedback@packtpub.com, and mention the book's title in the subject of your message. If there is a topic that you have expertise in and you are interested in either writing or contributing to a book, see our author guide at www.packtpub.com/authors.

Customer support

Now that you are the proud owner of a Packt book, we have a number of things to help you to get the most from your purchase.

Downloading the example code

You can download the example code files for this book from your account at `http://www.p acktpub.com`. If you purchased this book elsewhere, you can visit `http://www.packtpub.c om/support` and register to have the files e-mailed directly to you.

You can download the code files by following these steps:

1. Log in or register to our website using your e-mail address and password.
2. Hover the mouse pointer on the **SUPPORT** tab at the top.
3. Click on **Code Downloads & Errata**.
4. Enter the name of the book in the **Search** box.
5. Select the book for which you're looking to download the code files.
6. Choose from the drop-down menu where you purchased this book from.
7. Click on **Code Download**.

Once the file is downloaded, please make sure that you unzip or extract the folder using the latest version of:

* WinRAR / 7-Zip for Windows
* Zipeg / iZip / UnRarX for Mac
* 7-Zip / PeaZip for Linux

The code bundle for the book is also hosted on GitHub at `https://github.com/PacktPubl ishing/Visualforce-Development-Cookbook-2e`. We also have other code bundles from our rich catalog of books and videos available at `https://github.com/PacktPublishing/`. Check them out!

Downloading the color images of this book

We also provide you with a PDF file that has color images of the screenshots/diagrams used in this book. The color images will help you better understand the changes in the output. You can download this file from `https://www.packtpub.com/sites/default/files/down loads/VisualforceDevelopmentCookbook_ColorImages.pdf`.

Errata

Although we have taken every care to ensure the accuracy of our content, mistakes do happen. If you find a mistake in one of our books-maybe a mistake in the text or the code-we would be grateful if you could report this to us. By doing so, you can save other readers from frustration and help us improve subsequent versions of this book. If you find any errata, please report them by visiting http://www.packtpub.com/submit-errata, selecting your book, clicking on the **Errata Submission Form** link, and entering the details of your errata. Once your errata are verified, your submission will be accepted and the errata will be uploaded to our website or added to any list of existing errata under the Errata section of that title.

To view the previously submitted errata, go to https://www.packtpub.com/books/content/support and enter the name of the book in the search field. The required information will appear under the **Errata** section.

Piracy

Piracy of copyrighted material on the Internet is an ongoing problem across all media. At Packt, we take the protection of our copyright and licenses very seriously. If you come across any illegal copies of our works in any form on the Internet, please provide us with the location address or website name immediately so that we can pursue a remedy.

Please contact us at copyright@packtpub.com with a link to the suspected pirated material.

We appreciate your help in protecting our authors and our ability to bring you valuable content.

Questions

If you have a problem with any aspect of this book, you can contact us at questions@packtpub.com, and we will do our best to address the problem.

1
General Utilities

In this chapter, we will cover the following recipes:

- Overriding standard buttons
- Data-driven styling
- Turning off an action poller
- Visualforce in the sidebar
- Passing parameters to action methods
- Reacting to URL parameters
- Passing parameters between Visualforce pages
- Opening a pop-up window
- Adding a launch page
- Testing a custom controller
- Testing a controller extension

Introduction

This chapter provides solutions for a variety of situations that Visualforce developers are likely to encounter on a regular basis. Enhancing or replacing standard functionality with Visualforce enriches the user experience, improving user productivity and adoption. Visualforce also allows business processes to be highly systematized, guiding users through the creation and the ongoing management of data. Writing effective tests for Visualforce controllers is a key skill that allows developers to deploy Visualforce pages to production, and be confident that they will work as intended.

Overriding standard buttons

Two common complaints from users are that the information they are interested in requires a number of clicks to access, or that there is too much information on a single page, resulting in a cluttered layout that requires significant scrolling. This is an area where a Visualforce override can make a significant difference by traversing relationships to display information from a number of records on a single page.

Salesforce allows the standard pages associated with sObject record actions, such as view and edit, to be overridden with Visualforce pages. This is typically used to display the record in a branded or customized format; for example, to display details and related lists in separate tabs.

In this recipe, we will override the standard page associated with viewing an account record with a Visualforce page that not only provides a tabbed user interface but also lifts up additional activity information from the related contact list and line item information from the related opportunity lists. Furthermore, the related opportunities displayed will be limited to those that are open.

 Only Visualforce pages that use the standard controller for the sObject can override standard pages.

Getting ready

This recipe makes use of a standard controller, so we only need to create the Visualforce page.

How to do it...

1. Navigate to the Visualforce setup page by clicking on **Your Name|Setup|Develop|Visualforce Pages**.
2. Click on the **New** button.
3. Enter AccViewOverride in the **Label** field.
4. Accept the default **AccViewOverride** that is automatically generated for the **Name** field.
5. Paste the contents of the AccViewOverride.page file from the code download into the **Visualforce Markup** area and click on the **Save** button.

6. Then, navigate to the Visualforce setup page by clicking on **Your Name|Setup|Develop|Visualforce Pages**.

7. Locate the entry for the **AccViewOverride** page and click on the **Security** link.

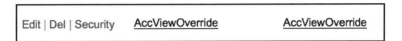

8. On the resulting page, select which profiles should have access and click on the **Save** button:

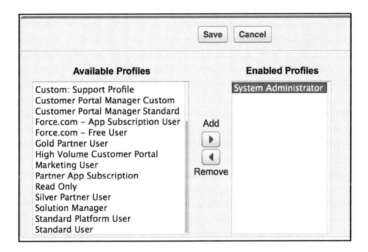

 As the record view override applies to all users, ensure that all profiles are given access to the Visualforce page. Any user with a profile that does not have access will receive an Insufficient Privileges error when attempting to view an account record.

9. Now that the Visualforce page is complete, configure the account view override. Navigate to **Your Name|Setup | Customize|Accounts|Buttons, Links and Actions**.

10. Locate the **View** entry on the page and click on the **Edit** link.

11. On the following page, locate the **Override With** entry, check the **Visualforce Page** radio button, and choose **AccViewOverride** from the list of available pages.

12. Click on the **Save** button.

How it works...

When a user clicks on an account record link anywhere in Salesforce, the tabbed page with details from related records is displayed, as shown in the following screenshot:

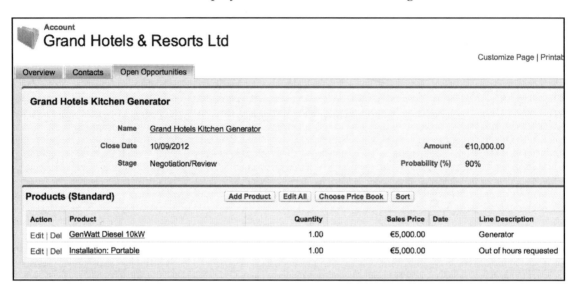

The key areas of the code are the tabs for the related records. The **Open Opportunities** tab iterates the opportunities related list, and generates an `<apex:pageblock />` for each opportunity that is currently open by encapsulating this inside a conditionally rendered `<apex:outputPanel />`:

```
<apex:repeat value="{!Account.Opportunities}" var="opp">
  <apex:outputPanel rendered="{!NOT(opp.IsClosed)}">
    <apex:pageBlock >
```

Then, the standard `<apex:relatedList />` component is used to generate the opportunity product list by specifying the current value of the opportunity iterator as the subject of the component:

```
<apex:relatedList subject="{!opp}" list="OpportunityLineItems" />
```

Data-driven styling

A useful technique when creating a custom user interface with Visualforce is to conditionally style important pieces of information to draw the user's attention to them as soon as a page is rendered.

Most Visualforce developers are familiar with using `merge` fields to provide `sObject` field values to output tags, or to decide if a section of a page should be rendered. In the tag shown next, the `merge` field, `{!account.Name}`, will be replaced with the contents of the `Name` field from the account `sObject`:

```
<apex:outputField value="{!account.Name}"/>
```

The `merge` fields can also contain formula operators and be used to dynamically style data when it is displayed.

In this recipe, we will display a table of campaign records and style the campaign cost in green if it was within-budget, or red if it was over-budget.

How to do it...

1. Navigate to the Visualforce setup page by clicking on **Your Name|Setup|Develop|Visualforce Pages**.
2. Click on the **New** button.
3. Enter `ConditionalColour` in the **Label** field.
4. Accept the default **ConditionalColour** that is automatically generated for the **Name** field.
5. Paste the contents of the `ConditionalColour.page` file from the code download into the Visualforce Markup area and click on the **Save** button.
6. Navigate to the Visualforce setup page by clicking on **Your Name|Setup|Develop|Visualforce Pages**.
7. Locate the entry for the **ConditionalColour** page and click on the **Security** link.
8. On the resulting page, select which profiles should have access and click on the **Save** button.

How it works...

Opening the following URL in your browser displays the **ConditionalColour** page: `https://<instance>/apex/ConditionalColour`. Here, `<instance>` is the Salesforce instance specific to your organization, for example, `na6.salesforce.com`.

A list of campaigns is displayed, with the campaign cost rendered in red or green depending on whether it came in on- or over-budget:

Campaigns

Campaign Name	Budgeted Cost	Actual Cost
DM Campaign to Top Customers - Nov 12-23, 2001	€25,000	€23,500
GC Product Webinar - Jan 7, 2002	€10,000	€11,400
International Electrical Engineers Association Trade Show - Mar 4-5, 2002	€50,000	
User Conference - Jun 17-19, 2002	€100,000	

The page makes use of a standard list controller by defining the `recordSetVar` attribute on the `<apex:page />` standard component:

```
<apex:page StandardController="Campaign" recordSetVar="Campaigns">
```

Standard list controllers allow a Visualforce page to manage a collection of records without the need for Apex code. The collection of records, by default, is from the last list view accessed by the user. Specifying the `filterId` property in the page allows the records from a particular list view to be used.

For more information on standard list controllers, see: `https://developer.salesforce.com/docs/atlas.en-us.pages.meta/pages/pages_controller_sosc_about.htm`.

Conditional styling is applied to the **Actual Cost** column by comparing the actual cost with the budgeted cost.

```
<apex:column style="color:
   {!IF(AND(NOT(ISNULL(campaign.ActualCost)),
   campaign.ActualCost<=campaign.BudgetedCost),
 "lawngreen", "red")}" value="{!campaign.ActualCost}"/>
```

See also

- The *Data-driven decimal places* recipe in `Chapter 2`, *Custom Components* shows how to format numeric values to a specified number of decimal places.

Turning off an action poller

The standard Visualforce `<apex:actionPoller/>` component sends AJAX requests to the server based on the specified time interval. An example use case is a countdown timer that sends the user to another page when the timer expires. But what if the action poller should stop when a condition in the controller becomes true, for example, when a batch apex job completes or an update is received from a third-party system?

In this recipe, we will simulate the progression of a payment through a number of states. An **action poller** will be used to retrieve the latest state from the server and display it to the user. Once the payment reaches the state `Complete`, the action poller will be disabled.

Getting ready

This recipe makes use of a custom controller, so this will need to be created before the Visualforce page.

How to do it...

1. Navigate to the **Apex Classes** setup page by clicking on **Your Name|Setup|Develop|Apex Classes**.
2. Click on the **New** button.
3. Paste the contents of the `PollerController.cls` Apex class from the code download into the **Apex Class** area.

Note that there is nowhere to specify a name for the class when creating it through the setup pages; the class name is derived from the Apex code.

4. Click on the **Save** button.

5. Next, create the Visualforce page by navigating to the Visualforce setup page, clicking on **Your Name|Setup|Develop|Visualforce Pages**.

6. Click on the **New** button.

7. Enter `ActionPoller` in the **Label** field.

8. Accept the default **ActionPoller** that is automatically generated for the **Name** field.

9. Paste the contents of the `ActionPoller.page` file from the code download into the Visualforce Markup area.

10. Click on the **Save** button to save the page.

11. Navigate to the Visualforce setup page by clicking on **Your Name|Setup|Develop|Visualforce Pages**.

12. Locate the entry for the **ActionPoller** page and click on the **Security** link.

13. On the resulting page, select which profiles should have access and click on the **Save** button.

How it works...

Opening the following URL in your browser displays the **ActionPoller** page: `https://<instance>/apex/ActionPoller`.

Here, `<instance>` is the Salesforce instance specific to your organization, for example, `na6.salesforce.com`.

The page polls the server for the current state, displaying the message **Polling ...** when the action poller executes, as shown in the following screenshot:

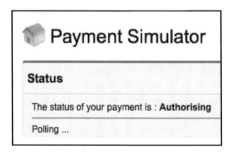

Once the current state reaches `Complete`, the action poller terminates.

The key to this recipe is the `enabled` attribute on the `actionPoller` component:

```
<apex:actionPoller action="{!movePayment}"
        rerender="payment" interval="5" status="status"
        enabled="{!paymentState!='Complete'}"/>
```

This `merge` field references the `paymentState` property from the custom controller, which is evaluated each time the action poller executes until it becomes false. At that point, the action poller is permanently disabled.

The **Polling ...** message is generated by the `actionStatus` component associated with the action poller. This component has a `startText` attribute but not a `stopText` attribute, which means that the text will only be displayed while the AJAX request is in progress:

```
<apex:actionStatus startText="Polling ..." id="status"/>
```

See also

- The *Using action functions* recipe in Chapter 7, *Enhancing the Client with JavaScript* shows how to execute a controller action method from JavaScript.

Visualforce in the sidebar

Visualforce is commonly used to produce custom pages that override or supplement standard platform functionality. Visualforce pages can also be incorporated into any HTML markup through the use of an `iframe`.

 An `iframe`, or `inline frame`, nests an HTML document inside another HTML document. For more information, visit http://reference.sitepo int.com/html/iframe.

In this recipe, we will add a Visualforce page to a Salesforce sidebar component. This page will display the number of currently open cases in the organization, and will be styled and sized to fit seamlessly into the sidebar.

Getting ready

This recipe makes use of a custom controller, so this will need to be created before the Visualforce page.

How to do it...

1. Navigate to the **Apex Classes** setup page by clicking on **YourName|Setup|Develop|Apex Classes**.
2. Click on the **New** button.
3. Paste the contents of the CasesSidebarController.cls Apex class from the code download into the **Apex Class** area.
4. Next, create the Visualforce page by navigating to the Visualforce setup page, clicking on **Your Name|Setup|Develop|Visualforce Pages**.
5. Click on the **New** button.
6. Enter CasesSidebar in the **Label** field.
7. Accept the default **CasesSidebar** that is automatically generated for the **Name** field.
8. Paste the contents of the CasesSidebar.page file from the code download into the **Visualforce Markup** area.
9. Click on the **Save** button to save the page.
10. Navigate to the Visualforce setup page by clicking on **Your Name|Setup|Develop|Visualforce Pages**.
11. Locate the entry for the **CasesSidebar** page and click on the **Security** link.
12. On the resulting page, select which profiles should have access and click on the **Save** button.

 Ensure that all profiles whose sidebar will display the Visualforce page are given access. Any user with a profile that does not have access will see an Insufficient Privileges error in their sidebar.

13. Next, create the home page component by navigating to the **Home Page Components** setup page, clicking on **Your Name|Setup|Customize|Home|Home Page Components**.
14. Scroll down to the **Custom Components** section and click on the **New** button.

15. If the **Understanding Custom Components** information screen appears, as shown in the following screenshot, click on the **Next** button:

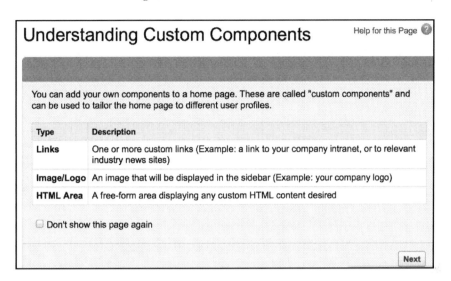

To stop this information screen appearing each time you create a home page component, select the **Don't show this page again** box before clicking on the Next button.

16. On the next page, titled **Step 1. New Custom Components**, enter **Case Count by Status** in the **Name** field, select the **Visualforce Area** option, and click on the **Next** button.

17. On the next page, titled **Step 2. New Custom Components**, select the **Narrow (Left) Column** option.

18. Select **CasesSidebar** from the **Visualforce Page** select list.

19. Enter 200 in the **Height (in pixels)** field.

20. Click on the **Save** button.

21. Next, add the new component to one or more home page layouts. Navigate to **Your Name | Setup | Customize | Home | Home Page Layouts**.

22. Locate the name of the home page layout you wish to add the component to and click on the **Edit** link.

23. On the resulting page, titled **Step 1. Select the Components to show**, select the **Case Count by Status** box in the **Select Narrow Components to Show** section and click on the **Next** button.

24. On the next page, titled **Step 2. Order the Components**, use the arrow buttons to move the **Case Count by Status** component to the desired position in the **Narrow (Left) Column** list and click on the **Save** button.

25. Repeat steps 22 to 24 for any other home page layouts that will contain the sidebar component.

This will add the component to the sidebar of the home page only. To add it to the sidebar of all pages, a change must be made to the user interface settings.

26. Navigate to **Your Name | Setup | Customize | User Interface** and locate the **Sidebar** section.

27. Select the **Show Custom Sidebar Components on All Pages** box, as shown in the following screenshot, and click on the **Save** button:

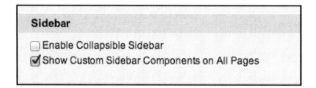

How it works...

The component appears in the sidebar on all pages, showing the number of cases open for each non-closed status, as shown in the following screenshot:

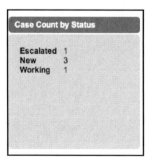

There's more...

The case counts displayed in the sidebar will be retrieved when the page is displayed, but will remain static from that point. An action poller can be used to automatically refresh the counts at regular intervals. However, this will introduce a security risk, as each time the poller retrieves the updated information it will refresh the user's session. This means that, if a user leaves their workstation unattended, the Salesforce session will never expire. If this mechanism is used, it is important to remind users of the importance of locking their workstation should they leave it unattended.

Passing parameters to action methods

When developers move to Apex/Visualforce from traditional programming languages, such as Java or C#, a concept many struggle with is how to pass parameters from a Visualforce page to a controller action method.

Passing parameters to an action method is key when a Visualforce page allows a user to manage a list of records and carry out actions on specific records. Without this, the action method cannot determine which record to apply the action to.

In this recipe, we will output a list of opportunities and for each open opportunity, provide a button to update the opportunity status to **Closed Won**. This button will invoke an action method to remove the list element and will also send a parameter to the controller to identify which opportunity to update.

Getting ready

This recipe makes use of a custom controller, so this will need to be created before the Visualforce page.

How to do it...

1. Navigate to the **Apex Classes** setup page by clicking on **Your Name|Setup|Develop|Apex Classes**.
2. Click on the **New** button.
3. Paste the contents of the `ActionParameterController.cls` Apex class from the code download into the **Apex Class** area.
4. Click on the **Save** button.

5. Next, create the Visualforce page by navigating to the Visualforce setup page, clicking on **Your Name|Setup|Develop|Visualforce Pages**.

6. Click on the **New** button.

7. Enter `ActionParameter` in the **Label** field.

8. Accept the default **ActionParameter** that is automatically generated for the **Name** field.

9. Paste the contents of the `ActionParameter.page` file from the code download into the **Visualforce Markup** area.

10. Click on the **Save** button to save the page.

11. Navigate to the Visualforce setup page by clicking on **Your Name|Setup|Develop|Visualforce Pages**.

12. Locate the entry for the **ActionParameter** page and click on the **Security** link.

13. On the resulting page, select which profiles should have access and click on the **Save** button.

How it works...

Opening the following URL in your browser shows the list of currently open opportunities: `https://<instance>/apex/ActionParameter`.

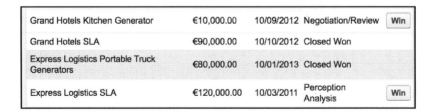

Here, `<instance>` is the Salesforce instance specific to your organization, for example, `na6.salesforce.com`.

Clicking on the **Win** button for the **Grand Hotels Kitchen Generator** opportunity updates the status to **Closed Won** and redraws the list of opportunities:

Grand Hotels Kitchen Generator	€10,000.00	10/09/2012	Closed Won
Grand Hotels SLA	€90,000.00	10/10/2012	Closed Won
Express Logistics Portable Truck Generators	€80,000.00	10/01/2013	Closed Won
Express Logistics SLA	€120,000.00	10/03/2011	Perception Analysis	Win

The page markup to send the parameter to the controller is as follows:

```
<apex:commandButton value="Win" action="{!winOpp}" status="status"
        rerender="opps_pb"
        rendered="{!opp.StageName!='Closed Won'}">
    <apex:param name="oppIdToWin" value="{!opp.Id}"
assignTo="{!oppIdToWin}" />
</apex:commandButton>
```

The `<apex:param />` component defines the value of the parameter, in this case the ID of the opportunity, and the controller property that the parameter will be assigned to – `oppIdToWin`.

Note that there is a `rerender` attribute on the command button. If this attribute is omitted, making the button a simple postback request, the parameter will not be passed to the controller. This is a known issue with Visualforce, as documented in the following knowledge article: .

The property is declared in the controller in the normal way:

```
public Id oppIdToWin {get; set;}
```

Finally, the action method is invoked when the button is pressed:

```
public PageReference winOpp()
{
    Opportunity opp=new Opportunity(Id=oppIdToWin,
                            StageName='Closed Won');
    update opp;
    return null;
}
```

The ID of the opportunity to update is assigned to the `oppIdToWin` controller property *before the action method is invoked*; thus, the action method can simply access the property to get the parameter value.

The `rerender` attribute on the `<apex:commandButton />` causes the `<apex:pageBlockTable />` containing the opportunities to be rerendered. This will implicitly execute the `getOpps()` method to populate the `opps` property that the table iterates with the latest information from the database:

```
<apex:pageBlockTable value="{!opps}" var="opp">
...
<apex:commandButton value="Win" action="{!winOpp}" status="status"
rerender="opps_pb" ... >
```

Reacting to URL parameters

The URL parameters are used to pass information to Visualforce pages that the page or controller can then react to. For example, setting a record `ID` parameter into the URL for a page that uses a standard controller causes the controller to retrieve the record from the database and make it available to the page.

In this recipe, we will create a Visualforce search page to retrieve all accounts where the name contains a string entered by the user. If the parameter name is present in the page URL, a search will be run against the supplied value prior to the page being rendered for the first time.

Getting ready

This recipe makes use of a custom controller, so this will need to be created before the Visualforce page.

How to do it...

1. Navigate to the **Apex Classes** setup page by clicking on **Your Name|Setup|Develop|Apex Classes**.
2. Click on the **New** button.
3. Paste the contents of the `SearchFromURLController.cls` Apex class from the code download into the **Apex Class** area.

4. Click on the **Save** button.
5. Next, create the Visualforce page by navigating to the Visualforce setup page, clicking on **Your Name|Setup|Develop|Visualforce Pages**.
6. Click on the **New** button.
7. Enter `SearchFromURL` in the **Label** field.
8. Accept the default **SearchFromURL** that is automatically generated for the **Name** field.
9. Paste the contents of the `SearchFromURL.page` file from the code download into the **Visualforce Markup** area.
10. Click on the **Save** button to save the page.
11. Navigate to the Visualforce setup page by clicking on **Your Name|Setup|Develop|Visualforce Pages**.
12. Locate the entry for the **SearchFromURL** page and click on the **Security** link.
13. On the resulting page, select which profiles should have access and click on the **Save** button.

How it works...

Opening the following URL in your browser retrieves all accounts where the **Name** field contains the text `ni`: `https://<instance>/apex/SearchFromURL?name=ni`.

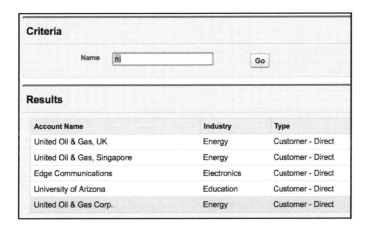

Here, `<instance>` is the Salesforce instance specific to your organization, for example, `na6.salesforce.com`.

The constructor of the custom controller is the first method to be called when a Visualforce page is retrieved. This attempts to extract a value for the parameter `Name` from the page URL, and if one has been supplied, executes the search:

```
public SearchFromURLController()
{
  searched=false;
  String nameStr=
    ApexPages.currentPage().getParameters().get('name');
  if (null!=nameStr)
  {
      name=nameStr;
      executeSearch();
  }
}
```

Note that the constructor also sets the value retrieved from the URL in the `Name` property. This property is bound to the `input` field on the page, and causes the input field to be prepopulated with the value retrieved from the URL when the page is first rendered.

The action method that executes the search is as follows:

```
public PageReference executeSearch()
{
  searched=true;
  String searchStr='%' + name + '%';
  accounts=[select id, Name, Industry, Type from Account where name LIKE
:searchStr];
  return null;
}
```

Note that `searchStr` is constructed by concatenating the search term with the `%` wildcard characters; this allows the user to enter a fragment of text rather than full words. Also, note that the concatenation takes place outside the SOQL query and the resulting variable is included as a bind expression in the query. If the concatenation takes place directly in the SOQL query, no matches will be found. This approach also helps to defend against SOQL injection attacks, as any text input by the user is surrounded by characters that stop embedded database commands from being executed.

See also

- The *Passing parameters between Visualforce pages* recipe in this chapter shows how URL parameters can be used to maintain the state across pages that do not share the same controller.

Passing parameters between Visualforce pages

If a user is redirected from one Visualforce page to another and they both share the same controller and extensions, the controller instance will be retained and re-used, allowing the second page to access any information captured by the first.

If the pages do not share the same controller and extensions, the controller instance will be discarded and the second page will have no access to any information captured by the first. If the state needs to be maintained across the pages in this case, it must be encapsulated in the parameters on the URL of the second page.

In this recipe, we will build on the example from the previous recipe to create a Visualforce search page to retrieve all accounts where the name contains a string entered by the user, and provide a way for the user to edit selected fields on all the accounts returned by the search. The record IDs of the accounts to edit will be passed as parameters on the URL to the edit page.

How to do it...

As the search page makes reference to the edit page, the edit page and associated custom controller must be created first:

1. Navigate to the **Apex Classes** setup page by clicking on **Your Name|Setup|Develop|Apex Classes**.
2. Click on the **New** button.
3. Paste the contents of the `EditFromSearchController.cls` Apex class from the code download into the **Apex Class** area.
4. Click on the **Save** button.
5. Next, create the edit Visualforce page by navigating to the Visualforce setup page, clicking on **Your Name|Setup|Develop|Visualforce Pages**.

6. Click on the **New** button.

7. Enter `EditFromSearch` in the **Label** field.

8. Accept the default **EditFromSearch** that is automatically generated for the **Name** field.

9. Paste the contents of the `EditFromSearch.page` file from the code download into the **Visualforce Markup** area.

10. Click on the **Save** button to save the page.

11. Navigate to the Visualforce setup page by clicking on **Your Name|Setup|Develop|Visualforce Pages**.

12. Locate the entry for the **EditFromSearch** page and click on the **Security** link.

13. On the resulting page, select which profiles should have access and click the **Save** button.

14. Next, create the search page by navigating to the **Apex Classes** setup page, clicking on **Your Name|Setup|Develop|Apex Classes**.

15. Click on the **New** button.

16. Paste the contents of the `SearchAndEditController.cls` Apex class from the code download into the **Apex Class** area.

17. Click on the **Save** button.

18. Next, create the Visualforce page by navigating to the Visualforce setup page, clicking on **Your Name|Setup|Develop|Visualforce Pages**.

19. Click on the **New** button.

20. Enter `SearchAndEdit` in the **Label** field.

21. Accept the default **SearchAndEdit** that is automatically generated for the **Name** field.

22. Paste the contents of the `SearchAndEdit.page` page from the code download into the **Visualforce Markup** area.

23. Click on the **Save** button to save the page.

24. Navigate to the Visualforce setup page by clicking on **Your Name|Setup | Develop|Visualforce Pages**.

25. Locate the entry for the **SearchAndEdit** page and click on the **Security** link.

26. On the resulting page, select which profiles should have access and click on the **Save** button.

How it works...

Opening the following URL in your browser retrieves all accounts where the name field contains the string United:

https://<instance>/apex/SearchAndEdit?name=United.

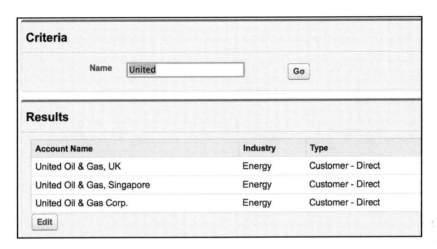

Here, <instance> is the Salesforce instance specific to your organization, for example, na6.salesforce.com.

Notice that the page contains an **Edit** button, and clicking on this executes the following action method:

```
public PageReference edit()
{
  PageReference pr=Page.EditFromSearch;
  Integer idx=1;
  for (Account acc : accounts)
  {
    pr.getParameters().put('account' + idx, acc.id);
    idx++;
  }
  return pr;
}
```

This method initially creates a page reference for the edit page-**EditFromSearch**. It then iterates the accounts in the search results and adds an entry to the page reference parameters for the account ID. Each parameter has the name account, concatenated with the index of the result, starting from 1. This will result in a URL of the form

```
https://<instance>/apex/EditFromSearch?account1=001i0000006OVLIAA4&acco
unt2=001i0000006OVLJAA4.
```

The **EditFromSearch** page then renders a form with an editable row per account:

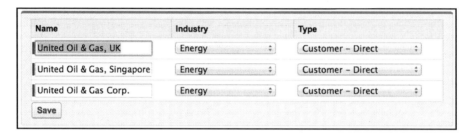

The constructor of `EditFromSearchController` that manages the data for the page extracts the IDs from the URL and adds them to a list, starting with `account1`, until it hits a parameter index that is not present in the URL:

```
Integer idx=1;
String accStr;
do
{
   accStr=ApexPages.currentPage().getParameters().
get('account' + idx);
   if (accStr!=null)
   {
     ids.add(accStr);
   }
   idx++;
}
while (null!=accStr);
```

The action method that saves the user's edits redirects them to the standard account tab once the save is complete:

```
return new PageReference('/001/o');
```

 Note that accessing the standard tab via this URL is not supported by Salesforce, and if the URL scheme or three-character prefix for account (001) were to change, this redirection would stop working.

See also

- The *Reacting to URL parameters* recipe in this chapter shows how a controller can process URL parameters prior to rendering a Visualforce page.

Opening a pop-up window

Pop-up browser windows have received mixed reviews in recent years. Originally created, before tabbed browsers existed, to display additional information without interfering with the page the user had navigated to, they were quickly hijacked and used to display advertisements and spam. Pop-ups should be used sparingly in applications and wherever possible in response to an action by the user.

The target attribute can be specified as **_blank** on HTML hyperlink tags to open the link in a new window, but all modern browsers allow the user to specify that new windows should be opened as new tabs instead. Also, if the browser does open the URL in a new window, it will be of the same size as the existing window and block most of it. Opening a window in JavaScript allows for fine-grained control over many aspects of the pop-up window, for example, the size and whether to display a toolbar.

In this recipe, we will create a page that renders a list of accounts, displaying a very small subset of fields per row. A link will be provided on each row to allow the user to view full details of the account in a pop-up window.

 Note that there is no way to ensure that a browser will display a pop-up window. Pop-up blockers generally allow windows to be opened in response to an action by the user, such as clicking on a link, but it is possible for users to configure their browser to block all pop-ups regardless of how they were triggered.

How to do it...

This recipe requires two Visualforce pages to be created: the main page containing the list of accounts and the pop-up window page. The pop-up page is referenced by the main page, so this will be created first:

1. Navigate to the Visualforce setup page by clicking on **Your Name | Setup | Develop | Visualforce Pages**.
2. Click on the **New** button.

3. Enter `Popup` in the **Label** field.

4. Accept the default **Popup** that is automatically generated for the **Name** field.

5. Paste the contents of the `Popup.page` file from the code download into the **Visualforce Markup** area.

6. Click on the **Save** button to save the page.

7. Navigate to the Visualforce setup page by clicking on **Your Name|Setup|Develop|Visualforce Pages**.

8. Locate the entry for the **Setup** page and click on the **Security** link.

9. On the resulting page, select which profiles should have access and click on the **Save** button.

10. Next, create the main account list page by navigating to the Visualforce setup page, clicking on **Your Name|Setup|Develop|Visualforce Pages**.

11. Click on the **New** button.

12. Enter `PopupMain` in the **Label** field.

13. Accept the default **PopupMain** that is automatically generated for the **Name** field.

14. Paste the contents of the `PopupMain.page` file from the code download into the **Visualforce Markup** area.

15. Click on the **Save** button to save the page.

16. Navigate to the Visualforce setup page by clicking on **Your Name|Setup|Develop|Visualforce Pages**.

17. Locate the entry for the **PopupMain** page and click on the **Security** link.

18. On the resulting page, select which profiles should have access and click on the **Save** button.

How it works...

Opening the following URL in your browser displays a list of accounts:
`https://<instance>/apex/PopupMain`.

Action	Account Name	Industry	Type
Details	Aethna Home Products		
Details	American Banking Corp.		
Details	BrightGen		
Details	Burlington Textiles Corp of America	Apparel	Customer - Direct
Details	Contactless Account	Technology	Channel Partner / Reseller
Details	Dickenson plc	Consulting	Customer - Channel
Details	Edge Communications	Electronics	Customer - Direct
Details	Express Logistics and Transport	Transportation	Customer - Channel
Details	Farmers Coop. of Florida	Agriculture	
Details	GenePoint	Biotechnology	Customer - Channel
Details	Grand Hotels & Resorts Ltd	Hospitality	Customer - Direct

Here, `<instance>` is the Salesforce instance specific to your organization, for example, `na6.salesforce.com`.

 Note that, as this page uses a standard list controller, the list of accounts displayed will be that of the last list view that the user accessed.

The detail link markup is as follows:

```
<apex:outputLink
    onclick="return openPopup('{!acc.Id}');">
    Details
</apex:outputLink>
```

The `onclick` attribute defines the JavaScript function to be invoked when the link is clicked; note the `{!acc.id}`merge field, which passes the ID of the chosen account to the function.

The JavaScript function uses the `window.open` function to open the new window:

```
var newWin=window.open   ('{!$Page.Popup}?id=' + id, 'Popup',      '
height=600,width=650,left=100,top=100,resizable=no,
scrollbars=yes,toolbar=no,status=no');
```

The final parameter details the features required for the new window as a comma-separated list of `name=value` pairs.

Clicking on the **Details** link displays the full account details in a pop-up window:

Account				
Burlington Textiles Corp of America				

Account Detail		Edit	Delete	Include Offline
Account Owner	Keir Bowden [Change]		Rating	Warm
Account Name	Burlington Textiles Corp of America [View Hierarchy]		Phone	(336) 222-7000
Parent Account			Fax	(336) 222-8000
Account Number	CD656092		Website	http://www.burlington.com
Account Site			Ticker Symbol	BTXT

See also

- The *Adding a custom lookup to a form* recipe in `Chapter 3`, *Capturing Data Using Forms* shows how information can be captured in a pop-up window and passed back to the main window to populate `input` fields.

Adding a launch page

When a Visualforce page is deployed to production, only users whose profiles have been given access via the security settings will be able to access the page. Any user with a profile that does not have access will receive an `Insufficient Privileges` error, which is not a good experience and can lead users to think that the page is crashing.

A better solution is to check whether the user has access to the page and if they do not, present a user-friendly message that explains the situation and directs them to where they can get more help.

In this recipe, we will create a launch page accessible to all profiles that checks whether the user has access to the protected page. If the user has access, they will be transferred to the protected page, while if they don't, they will receive an explanatory message.

How to do it...

This recipe requires a second user login. Ensure that this is not created with the System Administrator profile, as that profile has access to all Visualforce pages regardless of the security settings:

1. Navigate to the Visualforce setup page by clicking on **Your Name|Setup|Develop|Visualforce Pages**.
2. Click on the **New** button.
3. Enter `ProtectedContent` in the **Label** field.
4. Accept the default **ProtectedContent** that is automatically generated for the **Name** field.
5. Paste the contents of the `ProtectedContent.page` file from the code download into the **Visualforce Markup** area.
6. Click on the **Save** button to save the page.
7. Navigate to the Visualforce setup page by clicking on **Your Name|Setup|Develop|Visualforce Pages**.
8. Locate the entry for the **ProtectedContent** page and click on the **Security** link.
9. On the resulting page, ensure that the profile of your second user does not have access to the **ProtectedContent** page.
10. Log in using your second user credentials and attempt to access any account record. You will receive an error message, as shown in the following screenshot:

Insufficient Privileges

You do not have the level of access necessary to perform the operation you requested. Please contact the owner of the record or your administrator if access is necessary.

---

11. Next, create the launch page controller by navigating to the **Apex Classes** setup page, clicking on **Your Name|Setup|Develop|Apex Classes**.
12. Click on the **New** button.
13. Paste the contents of the `LaunchController.cls` Apex class from the code download into the **Apex Class** area.
14. Click on the **Save** button.

15. Navigate to the Visualforce setup page by clicking on **Your Name|Setup|Develop|Visualforce Pages**.
16. Click on the **New** button.
17. Enter Launch in the **Label** field.
18. Accept the default **Launch** that is automatically generated for the **Name** field.
19. Paste the contents of the Launch.page file from the code download into the **Visualforce Markup** area.
20. Click on the **Save** button to save the page.
21. Navigate to the Visualforce setup page by clicking on **Your Name|Setup|Develop|Visualforce Pages**.
22. Locate the entry for the **Setup** page and click on the **Security** link.
23. On the resulting page, give access to all of the profiles and click on the **Save** button.

How it works...

Log in using your second user credentials and open the following URL in your browser: https://<instance>/apex/Launch.

Here, <instance> is the Salesforce instance specific to your organization, for example, na6.salesforce.com.

The resulting page displays a friendly error message announcing that your user does not have access to the page, and renders a clickable link to request access.

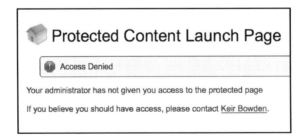

The Launch page declaration contains an `action` attribute:

```
<apex:page controller="LaunchController" action="{!allowAccess}">
```

This invokes the `allowAccess` action method in the controller before the page is rendered:

```
public PageReference allowAccess()
{
    PageReference pr=Page.ProtectedContent;
    try
    {
        pr.getContent();
        }
    catch (Exception e)
    {
        pr=null;
    }
    return pr;
}
```

The `allowAccess` method attempts to retrieve the contents of the protected page programmatically. If the contents are retrieved successfully, it returns the page reference for the **Protected** page, which redirects the user to that page. If an exception occurs, the method returns `null`, which leaves the user on the **Launch** page and displays the friendly error message.

Testing a custom controller

Writing unit tests for Visualforce page controllers is often a source of confusion for developers new to the technology. A common mistake is to assume that the page must somehow be rendered and interacted with in the test context, whereas in reality, the page is very much a side issue. Instead, tests must instantiate the controller and set its internal state as though the user interaction has already taken place, and then execute one or more controller methods and confirm that the state has changed as expected.

In this recipe, we will unit test `SearchFromURLController` from the Reacting to URL parameters recipe.

Getting ready

This recipe requires that you have already completed the Reacting to URL parameters recipe, as it relies on `SearchFromURLController` being present in your Salesforce instance.

How to do it…

1. Create the unit test class by navigating to the **Apex Classes** setup page and by clicking on **Your Name|Setup|Develop| Apex Classes**.
2. Click on the **New** button.
3. Paste the contents of the `SearchFromURLControllerTest.cls` Apex class from the code download into the **Apex Class** area.
4. Click on the **Save** button.
5. On the resulting page, click on the **Run Tests** button.

How it works…

The tests successfully execute, as shown in the following screenshot:

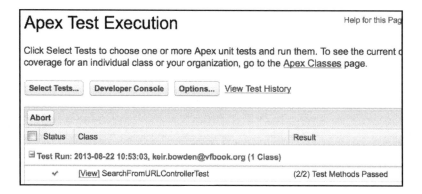

Open the **Developer Console** by clicking on your name at the top right of the screen and selecting **Developer Console** from the resulting drop-down menu:

Select the **Tests** tab and you will see the test coverage information on the right-hand side, showing 100% code coverage for the `SearchFromURLController` class:

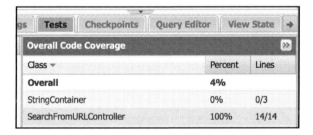

 Percentage coverage is important as at least 75 % coverage across all code must be achieved before classes may be deployed to a production organization.

The test class contains two unit test methods. The first method tests that the search is correctly executed when the search term is passed on the page URL. As unit tests do not have access to organization data, the first task for the test is to set up three test accounts:

```
List<Account> accs=new List<Account>();
accs.add(new Account(Name='Unit Test'));
accs.add(new Account(Name='Unit Test 2'));
accs.add(new Account(Name='The Test Account'));
insert accs;
```

As the controller is reacting to parameters on the URL, the page reference must be set up and populated with the `name` parameter:

```
PageReference pr=Page.SearchFromURL;
pr.getParameters().put('name', 'Unit');
Test.setCurrentPage(pr);
```

Finally, the controller is instantiated, which causes the action method that executes the search to be invoked from the constructor. The test method then confirms that the search was executed and the actual number of matches equals the expected number:

```
SearchFromURLController controller=new
        SearchFromURLController();
System.assertEquals(true, controller.searched);
System.assertEquals(2, controller.accounts.size());
```

The second unit test method tests that the search is correctly executed when the user enters a search term. In this case, there is no interaction with the information on the page URL, so the test simply instantiates the controller and confirms that no search has been executed by the constructor:

```
SearchFromURLController controller=new SearchFromURLController();
System.assertEquals(false, controller.searched);
```

The test then sets the search term, executes the search method, and confirms the results:

```
controller.name='Unit';
System.assertEquals(null, controller.executeSearch());
System.assertEquals(2, controller.accounts.size());
```

See also

- The *Testing a controller extension* recipe in this chapter shows how to write unit tests for a controller that extends a standard or custom controller.

Testing a controller extension

Controller extensions provide additional functionality for standard or custom controllers. The contract for a controller extension is that it provides a constructor that takes a single argument of the standard or custom controller that it is extending. Testing a controller extension introduces an additional requirement that an instance of the standard or custom controller, with appropriate internal state, is constructed before the controller extension.

In this recipe, we will create a controller extension to retrieve the contacts associated with an account managed by a standard controller and unit test the extension.

How to do it...

As the test class makes reference to the controller extension, this must be created first:

1. Navigate to the **Apex Classes** setup page by clicking on **Your Name|Setup|Develop|Apex Classes**.
2. Click on the **New** button.
3. Paste the contents of the `AccountContactsExt.cls` Apex class from the code download into the **Apex Class** area.
4. Click on the **Save** button.
5. Create the unit test class by navigating to the **Apex Classes** setup page, clicking on **Your Name|Setup|Develop|Apex Classes**.
6. Click on the **New** button.
7. Paste the contents of the `AccountContactsExtTest.cls` Apex class from the code download into the **Apex Class** area.
8. Click on the **Save** button.
9. On the resulting page, click on the **Run Tests** button.

How it works...

The tests successfully execute, as shown in the following screenshot:

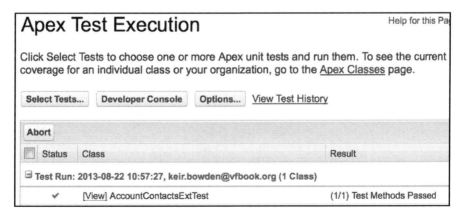

Open the **Developer Console** by clicking on your name at the top right of the screen and selecting **Developer Console** from the resulting drop-down menu.

Select the **Tests** tab and you will see the test coverage information on the right-hand side, showing **100%** code coverage for the `AccountContactsExt` class:

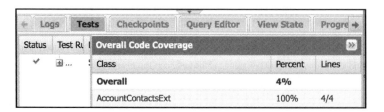

The test class contains one unit test method. As unit tests do not have access to the organization data, the first task for the test is to set up the account and contact information:

```
Account acc=new Account(Name='Unit Test');
insert acc;
List<Contact> contacts=new List<Contact>();
contacts.add(new Contact(FirstName='Unit',
    LastName='Test', Email='Unit.Test@Unit.Test',
    AccountId=acc.id));
contacts.add(new Contact(FirstName='Unit',
    LastName='Test 2', Email='Unit.Test2@Unit.Test',
    AccountId=acc.id));
insert contacts;
```

Next, the instance of the standard controller is instantiated:

```
ApexPages.StandardController std=
   new ApexPages.StandardController(acc);
```

Note that the `StandardController` requires the record that it is managing as a parameter to the constructor. As this is the record that will be made available to the controller extension, it must have the fields populated that the extension relies upon. In this case, the only field used by the extension is the ID of the account, and this is automatically populated when the account is inserted.

 In this recipe, the records to be tested are created in the test classes. In the real world, this is likely to lead to a lot of repetition and a maintenance overhead. In that case, a utility class to handle the setup of test data would be a more robust solution.

Finally, the controller extension is instantiated, taking the standard controller as a `constructor` parameter, and the test verifies that the extension has successfully retrieved the associated contacts:

```
AccountContactsExt controller=new AccountContactsExt(std);
System.assertEquals(2, controller.contacts.size());
```

See also

- The *Testing a custom controller* recipe in this chapter shows how to write unit tests for a custom controller that does not extend or rely upon another controller.

2
Custom Components

In this chapter, we will cover the following recipes:

- Passing attributes to components
- Updating attributes in component controllers
- Passing action methods to components
- Data-driven decimal places
- The custom iterator component
- Setting a value into a controller property
- Multiselecting related objects
- Notifying the containing page controller

Introduction

Custom components allow custom Visualforce functionality to be encapsulated as discrete modules, which provide two main benefits:

1. **Functional decomposition**: where a lengthy page is broken down into custom components to make it easier to develop and maintain.
2. **Code reuse**: where a custom component provides common functionality that can be reused across a number of pages.

A custom component may have a controller, but unlike Visualforce pages, only custom controllers may be used. A custom component can also take attributes, which can influence the generated markup or set property values in the component's controller to alter the business logic.

Custom components do not have any associated security settings; a user with access to a Visualforce page has access to all custom components referenced by the page.

Passing attributes to components

Visualforce pages can pass parameters to components via attributes. A component declares the attributes that it is able to accept, including information about the type and whether the attribute is mandatory or optional. Attributes can be used directly in the component or assigned to properties in the component's controller.

 Note that since the Spring 13 release of Salesforce (API version 27.0) you may not assign an attribute to a controller property with the same name. Attempting to do this results in the following error when saving the component:
```
Error: <apex:attribute assignTo> cannot be same as the
<apex:attribute name>
```

In this recipe, we will create a Visualforce page that provides contact edit capability. The page utilizes a custom component that allows the name fields of the contact, `Salutation`, `First Name`, and `Last Name`, to be edited in a three-column page block section. The contact record is passed from the page to the component as an attribute, allowing the component to be reused in any page that allows editing of contacts.

How to do it...

This recipe does not require any Apex controllers, so we can start with the custom component:

1. Navigate to the **Visualforce Components** setup page by clicking on **Your Name** | **Setup** | **Develop** | **Components**.
2. Click on the **New** button.
3. Enter `ContactNameEdit` in the **Label** field.
4. Accept the default **ContactNameEdit** that is automatically generated for the **Name** field.

5. Paste the contents of the `ContactNameEdit.component` file from the code downloaded into the **Visualforce Markup** area and click on the **Save** button.

Once a custom component is saved, it is available in your organization's component library, which can be accessed from the development footer of any Visualforce page. For more information visit `http://www.salesforce.com/us/developer/docs/pages/Content/pages_quick_start_component_library.htm`.

6. Next, create the Visualforce page by navigating to the Visualforce setup page by clicking on **Your Name | Setup | Develop | Visualforce Pages**.
7. Click on the **New** button.
8. Enter `ContactEdit` in the **Label** field.
9. Accept the default **Contact Edit** that is automatically generated for the **Name** field.
10. Paste the contents of the `ContactEdit.page` file from the code downloaded into the **Visualforce Markup** area and click on the **Save** button.
11. Navigate to the Visualforce setup page by clicking on **Your Name | Setup | Develop | Visualforce Pages**.
12. Locate the entry for the **Contact Edit** page and click on the **Security** link.
13. On the resulting page, select which profiles should have access and click on the **Save** button.

How it works...

Opening the following URL in your browser displays the `ContactEdit` page:
`https://<instance>/apex/ContactEdit`.

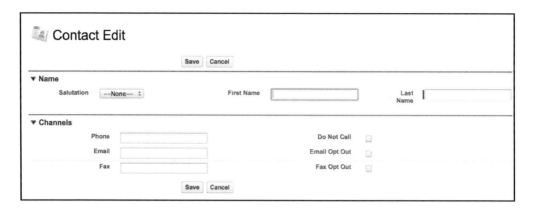

Here, `<instance>` is the Salesforce instance specific to your organization, for example, `na6.salesforce.com`:

The custom component that renders the input fields in the **Name** section defines a single, required attribute of type `Contact`:

```
<apex:attribute name="Contact" type="Contact"
    description="The contact to edit" required="true" />
```

The description of the attribute must always be provided, as this is included in the component reference. The type of the attribute must be a primitive, sObject, one-dimensional list, map, or custom Apex class.

The `Contact` attribute can then be used in the merge syntax inside the component:

```
<apex:inputField value="{!Contact.Salutation}"/>
<apex:inputField value="{!Contact.FirstName}"/>
<apex:inputField value="{!Contact.LastName}"/>
```

The page passes the contact record being managed by the standard controller to the component via the `Contact` attribute:

```
<c:ContactNameEdit contact="{!Contact}"/>
```

See also

- The *Updating attributes in component controllers* recipe in this chapter shows how a custom component can update an attribute that is a property of the enclosing page controller.

Updating attributes in component controllers

Updating fields of sObjects passed as attributes to custom components is straightforward, and can be achieved through simple merge syntax statements. This is not so simple when the attribute is primitive and will be updated by the component controller, as parameters are passed by value, and thus any changes are made to a copy of the primitive. For example, passing the name field of a contact sObject, rather than the contact sObject itself, would mean that any changes made in the component would not be visible to the containing page.

In this situation, the primitive must be encapsulated inside a containing class. The class instance attribute is still passed by value, so it cannot be updated to point to a different instance, but the properties of the instance can be updated.

In this recipe, we will create a containing class that encapsulates a Date primitive and a Visualforce component that allows the user to enter the date via day/month/year picklists. A simple Visualforce page and controller will also be created to demonstrate how this component can be used to enter a contact's date of birth.

Getting ready

This recipe requires a custom Apex class to encapsulate the Date primitive. To do so, perform the following steps:

1. First, create the class that encapsulates the Date primitive by navigating to the **Apex Classes** setup page by clicking on **Your Name | Setup | Develop | Apex Classes**.
2. Click on the **New** button.

3. Paste the contents of the `DateContainer.cls` Apex class from the code downloaded into the **Apex Class** area.

4. Click on the **Save** button.

How to do it...

1. First, create the custom component controller by navigating to the **Apex Classes** setup page by clicking on **Your Name** | **Setup** | **Develop** | **Apex Classes**.

2. Click on the **New** button.

3. Paste the contents of the `DateEditController.cls` Apex class from the code downloaded into the **Apex Class** area.

4. Click on the **Save** button.

5. Next, create the custom component by navigating to the Visualforce Components setup page by clicking on **Your Name** | **Setup** | **Develop** | **Components**.

6. Click on the **New** button.

7. Enter `DateEdit` in the **Label** field.

8. Accept the default **DateEdit** that is automatically generated for the **Name** field.

9. Paste the contents of the `DateEdit.component` file from the code downloaded into the **Visualforce Markup** area and click on the **Save** button.

10. Next, create the Visualforce page controller extension by navigating to the **Apex Classes** setup page by clicking on **Your Name** | **Setup** | **Develop** | **Apex Classes**.

11. Click on the **New** button.

12. Paste the contents of the `ContactDateEditExt.cls` Apex class from the code downloaded into the **Apex Class** area.

13. Click on the **Save** button.

14. Finally, create a Visualforce page by navigating to the Visualforce setup page by clicking on **Your Name** | **Setup** | **Develop** | **Visualforce Pages**.

15. Click on the **New** button.

16. Enter `ContactDateEdit` in the **Label** field.

17. Accept the default **ContactDateEdit** that is automatically generated for the **Name** field.

18. Paste the contents of the `ContactDateEdit.page` file from the code downloaded into the **Visualforce Markup** area and click on the **Save** button.

19. Navigate to the Visualforce setup page by clicking on **Your Name | Setup | Develop | Visualforce Pages**.

20. Locate the entry for the `ContactDateEdit.page` file and click on the **Security** link.

21. On the resulting page, select which profiles should have access and click on the **Save** button.

How it works...

Opening the following URL in your browser displays the `ContactDateEdit` page:
`https://<instance>/apex/ContactDateEdit?id=<contact_id>`.

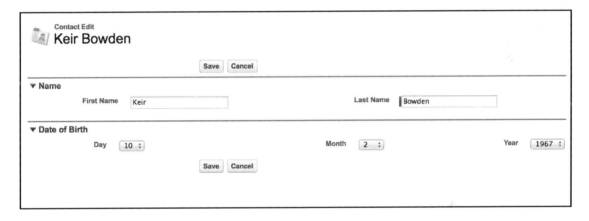

Here, `<instance>` is the Salesforce instance specific to your organization, for example, `na6.salesforce.com`, and `<contact_id>` is the ID of any contact in your Salesforce instance:

The Visualforce page controller declares a `DateContainer` property that will be used to capture the contact's date of birth:

```
public DateContainer dob {get; set;}
private Contact cont;
private ApexPages.StandardController stdCtrl {get; set;}
public ContactDateEditExt(ApexPages.StandardController std)
{
  stdCtrl=std;
  cont=(Contact) std.getRecord();
```

```
    dob=new DateContainer(cont.BirthDate);
}
```

Note that as `DateContainer` is a class, it must be instantiated when the controller is constructed.

The custom component that manages the **Date of Birth** section defines the following two attributes:

- A required attribute of type `DateContainer`, which is assigned to the `dateContainer` property of the controller
- The title of the page block section that will house the picklists; as this is a reusable component, the page supplies an appropriate title

Note that this component is not tightly coupled with a contact date of birth field; it may be used to manage a date field for any `sObject`:

```
<apex:attribute type="DateContainer"     name="dateContainerAtt"
    description="The date" assignTo="{!dateContainer}"
    required="true" />
<apex:attribute type="String"
    description="Page block section title" name="title" />
```

The component controller defines properties for each of the day, month, and year elements of the date. Each setter for these properties attempts to construct the date if all of the other elements are present. This is required as there is no guarantee of the order in which the setters will be called when the **Save** button is clicked and the postback takes place:

```
public Integer year {get;
    set {
            year=value;
            updateContainer();
            }
    }
private void updateContainer()
{
  if ( (null!=year) && (null!=month) && (null!=day) )
  {
    Date theDate=Date.newInstance(year, month, day);
    dateContainer.value=theDate;
  }
}
```

When the contained `Date` primitive is changed in the `updateContainer` method, this is reflected in the page controller property, which can then be used to update a field in the contact record:

```
public PageReference save()
{
  cont.BirthDate=dob.value;
  return stdCtrl.save();
}
```

See also

- The *Passing attributes to components* recipe in this chapter shows how an `sObject` may be passed as an attribute to a custom component.
- The *Adding a custom datepicker to a form* recipe in `Chapter 3`, *Capturing Data Using Forms* presents an alternative solution to capturing a date outside of the standard Salesforce range.

Passing action methods to components

A controller action method is usually invoked from the Visualforce page that it is providing the logic for. However, there are times when it is useful to be able to execute a page controller action method directly from a custom component contained within the page. One example is for styling reasons, in order to locate the command button that executes the `action` method inside the markup generated by the component.

In this recipe, we will create a custom component that provides contact edit functionality, including command buttons to save or cancel the edit, and a Visualforce page to contain the component and supply the `action` methods that are executed when the buttons are clicked.

How to do it...

This recipe does not require any Apex controllers, so we can start with the custom component:

1. Navigate to the Visualforce Components setup page by clicking on **Your Name | Setup | Develop | Components**.
2. Click on the **New** button.
3. Enter ContactEdit in the **Label** field.
4. Accept the default**ContactEdit** that is automatically generated for the **Name** field.
5. Paste the contents of the ContactEdit.component file from the code downloaded into the **Visualforce Markup** area and click on the **Save** button.
6. Next, create the Visualforce page by navigating to the Visualforce setup page by clicking on **Your Name | Setup | Develop | Visualforce Pages**.
7. Click on the **New** button.
8. Enter ContactEditActions in the **Label** field.
9. Accept the default **ContactEditActions** that is automatically generated for the **Name** field.
10. Paste the contents of the ContactEditActions.page file from the code downloaded into the **Visualforce Markup** area and click on the **Save** button.
11. Navigate to the Visualforce setup page by clicking on **Your Name | Setup | Develop | Visualforce Pages**.
12. Locate the entry for the ContactEditActions page and click on the **Security** link.
13. On the resulting page, select which profiles should have access and click on the **Save** button.

How it works...

Opening the following URL in your browser displays the `ContactEditActions` page:
`https://<instance>/apex/ContactEditActions?id=<contact_id>`.

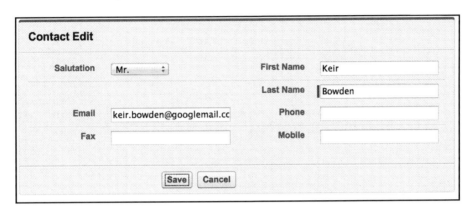

Here, `<instance>` is the Salesforce instance specific to your organization, for example, `na6.salesforce.com`, and `<contact_id>` is the ID of any contact in your Salesforce instance:

The Visualforce page simply includes the custom component, and passes the `Save` and `Cancel` methods from the standard controller as attributes:

```
<apex:page standardController="Contact">
  <apex:pageMessages />
  <apex:form >
    <c:ContactEdit contact="{!contact}" saveAction="{!save}"
    cancelAction="{!cancel}" />
  </apex:form>
</apex:page>
```

The `ContactEdit` custom component declares attributes for the action methods of type `ApexPages.Action`:

```
<apex:attribute name="SaveAction"
    description="The save action method from the page controller"
    type="ApexPages.Action" required="true"/>
<apex:attribute name="CancelAction"
    description="The cancel action method from the page controller"
    type="ApexPages.Action" required="true"/>
```

These attributes can then be bound to the command buttons in the component in the same way as if they were supplied by the component's controller:

```
<apex:commandButton value="Save" action="{!SaveAction}" />
<apex:commandButton value="Cancel" action="{!CancelAction}"
    immediate="true" />
```

There's more...

While this example has used `action` methods from a standard controller, any `action` method can be passed to a component using this mechanism, including methods from a custom controller or controller extension.

See also

- The *Updating attributes in component controllers* recipe in this chapter shows how a custom component can update an attribute that is a property of the enclosing page controller.

Data-driven decimal places

Attributes passed to custom components from Visualforce pages can be used wherever the merge syntax is legal. The `<apex:outputText />` standard component can be used to format numeric and date values, but the formatting is limited to literal values rather than merge fields. In this scenario, an attribute indicating the number of decimal places to display for a numeric value cannot be used directly in the `<apex:outputText />` component.

In this recipe, we will create a custom component that accepts attributes for numeric value and the number of decimal places to display for the value. The decimal places attribute determines which optional component is rendered to ensure that the correct number of decimal places is displayed, and the component will also bracket negative values. A Visualforce page will also be created to demonstrate how the component can be used.

How to do it...

This recipe does not require any Apex controllers, so we can start with the custom component:

1. Navigate to the Visualforce Components setup page by clicking on **Your Name | Setup | Develop | Components**.
2. Click on the **New** button.
3. Enter DecimalPlaces in the **Label** field.
4. Accept the default **DecimalPlaces** that is automatically generated for the **Name** field.
5. Paste the contents of the DecimalPlaces.component file from the code downloaded into the **Visualforce Markup** area and click on the **Save** button.
6. Next, create the Visualforce page by navigating to the Visualforce setup page by clicking on **Your Name | Setup | Develop | Visualforce Pages**.
7. Click on the **New** button.
8. Enter DecimalPlacesDemo in the **Label** field.
9. Accept the default **DecimalPlacesDemo** that is automatically generated for the **Name** field.
10. Paste the contents of the DecimalPlacesDemo.page file from the code downloaded into the **Visualforce Markup** area and click on the **Save** button.
11. Navigate to the Visualforce setup page by clicking on **Your Name | Setup | Develop | Visualforce Pages**.
12. Locate the entry for the DecimalPlacesDemo page and click on the **Security** link.
13. On the resulting page, select which profiles should have access and click on the **Save** button.

How it works...

Opening the following URL in your browser displays the **DecimalPlacesDemo** page:
https://<instance>/apex/DecimalPlacesDemo.

Opportunity Name	Name
Burlington Textiles Weaving Plant Generator	235,000.0000
Dickenson Mobile Generators	15,000.00
Edge Emergency Generator	35,000.0000
Edge Emergency Generator	75,000.000
Edge Installation	50,000
Edge SLA	60,000.0
Express Logistics Portable Truck Generators	80,000.000
Express Logistics SLA	120,000.00
Express Logistics Standby Generator	220,000.00
GenePoint Lab Generators	60,000.0
GenePoint SLA	30,000.000

Here, `<instance>` is the Salesforce instance specific to your organization, for example, `na6.salesforce.com`.

The Visualforce page iterates a number of opportunity records and delegates to the component to output the opportunity amount, deriving the number of decimal places from the amount:

```
<c:DecimalPlaces dp="{!TEXT(ROUND(MOD(opp.Amount/10000, 5), 0))}"
                 value="{!opp.Amount}" />
```

The component conditionally renders the appropriate output panel, which contains two conditionally rendered `<apex:outputText />` components, one to display a positive value to the correct number of decimal places and another to display a bracketed negative value:

```
<apex:outputPanel rendered="{!dp=='1'}">
  <apex:outputText rendered="{!AND(NOT(ISNULL(VALUE)), value>=0)}"
              value="{0, number, #,##0.0}">
    <apex:param value="{!value}"/>
  </apex:outputText>
  <apex:outputText rendered="{!AND(NOT(ISNULL(VALUE)), value<0)}"
              value="({0, number, #,##0.0})">
    <apex:param value="{!ABS(value)}"/>
  </apex:outputText>
</apex:outputPanel>
```

See also

- The *Data-driven styling* recipe in `Chapter 1`, *General Utilities* shows how to conditionally color a numeric value based on whether it is positive or negative.

The custom iterator component

The Visualforce standard component `<apex:repeat />` iterates a collection of data and outputs the contained markup once for each element in the collection. In the scenario where this is being used to display a table of data, the markup for the table headings appears before the `<apex:repeat />` component and is rendered regardless of whether the collection contains any records or not.

Custom iterator components may contain additional markup to be rendered outside the collection, for example, the headings markup in the scenario mentioned earlier. This allows the component to avoid rendering any markup if the collection is empty through the logic implemented in a custom controller.

In this recipe, we will create a custom component that takes a collection of data and renders a containing page block and a page block section for each element in the collection. If the collection is empty, no markup will be rendered. We will also create a containing page that displays the details of an `sObject` account and utilizes the custom component to display contact and opportunity information, if present.

Getting ready

This recipe makes use of a custom controller, so this will need to be present before the custom component can be created.

How to do it...

1. Navigate to the **Apex Classes** setup page by clicking on **Your Name | Setup | Develop | Apex Classes**.
2. Click on the **New** button.
3. Paste the contents of the `AllOrNothingController.cls` Apex class from the code downloaded into the **Apex Class** area.
4. Click on the **Save** button.

5. Navigate to the Visualforce Components setup page by clicking on **Your Name | Setup | Develop | Components**.

6. Click on the **New** button.

7. Enter `AllOrNothingPageBlock` in the **Label** field.

8. Accept the default **AllOrNothingPageBlock** that is automatically generated for the **Name** field.

9. Paste the contents of the `AllOrNothingPageBlock.component` file from the code downloaded into the **Visualforce Markup** area and click on the **Save** button.

10. Next, create the custom controller for the Visualforce page by navigating to the **Apex Classes** setup page by clicking on **Your Name | Setup | Develop | Apex Classes**.

11. Click on the **New** button.

12. Paste the contents of the `AllOrNothingListsExt.cls` Apex class from the code downloaded into the **Apex Class** area.

13. Click on the **Save** button.

14. Next, create the Visualforce page by navigating to the Visualforce setup page by clicking on **Your Name | Setup | Develop | Visualforce Pages**.

15. Click on the **New** button.

16. Enter `AllOrNothingLists` in the **Label** field.

17. Accept the default **AllOrNothingLists** that is automatically generated for the **Name** field.

18. Paste the contents of the `AllOrNothingLists.page` file from the code downloaded into the **Visualforce Markup** area and click on the **Save** button.

19. Navigate to the Visualforce setup page by clicking on **Your Name | Setup | Develop | Visualforce Pages**.

20. Locate the entry for the **AllOrNothingLists** page and click on the **Security** link.

21. On the resulting page, select which profiles should have access and click on the **Save** button.

How it works…

Opening the following URL in your browser displays the `AllOrNothingLists` page:
`https://<instance>/apex/AllOrNothingLists?id=<account_id>`.

Here, `<instance>` is the Salesforce instance specific to your organization, for example, `na6.salesforce.com`, and `<account_id>` is the ID of an account from your Salesforce instance.

The page displays brief details of the account and page blocks for the account's contacts and opportunities:

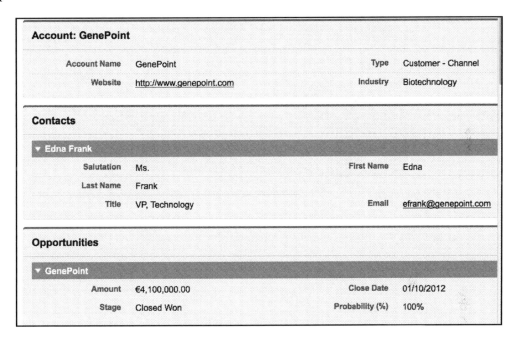

If the account does not have any opportunities or contacts, the appropriate page block is omitted:

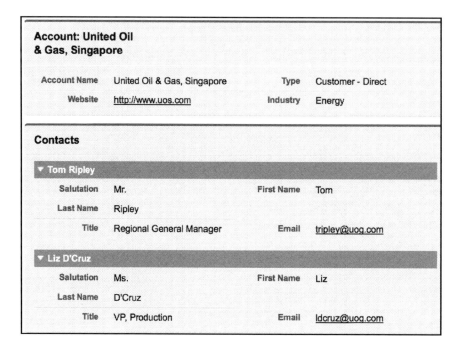

The `AllOrNothingPageBlock` custom component accepts a list of generic `sObjects` and wraps its content in an output panel that is only rendered if the list is not empty:

```
<apex:outputPanel rendered="{!render}">
    <apex:pageBlock >
      <apex:repeat value="{!list}" var="ele">
        <apex:componentBody >
          <apex:variable var="{!var}" value="{!ele}"/>
        </apex:componentBody>
      </apex:repeat>
    </apex:pageBlock>
  </apex:outputPanel>
```

The `<apex:componentBody />` defines where the content from the Visualforce page will be inserted. As this is inside the `<apex:repeat />` component, this insertion will take place for each element in the collection.

The Visualforce page passes attributes to the component of the list to iterate the title of the page block, and the variable name representing an element in the list. The contained markup can reference the variable name to access fields or properties of the element:

```
<c:AllOrNothingPageBlock list="{!opportunities}" var="opp"
      >
<apex:pageBlockSection >
      <apex:outputField value="{!opp.Amount}" />
      <apex:outputField value="{!opp.CloseDate}" />
      <apex:outputField value="{!opp.StageName}" />
      <apex:outputField value="{!opp.Probability}" />
</apex:pageBlockSection>
</c:AllOrNothingPageBlock>
```

Setting a value into a controller property

Visualforce controllers are often reused across pages with minor variations in behavior specific to the page, for example, displaying accounts of a particular type. While the controller can detect the page that it is being used by and alter its behavior accordingly, this is not a particularly maintainable solution, as use of the controller in any new page would require changes to the Apex code and renaming a page would break the functionality.

A better mechanism is for the page to set the values of properties in the controller to indicate the desired behavior. In this recipe, we will create a custom component that takes two attributes: a value and the controller property to set the value into. Two Visualforce pages with a common controller will also be created to demonstrate how the component can be used to change the behavior of the controller to suit the page.

Getting ready

This recipe does not require any Apex controllers, so we can start with the custom component.

How to do it...

1. Navigate to the Visualforce Components setup page by clicking on **Your Name | Setup | Develop | Components**.

2. Click on the **New** button.

3. Enter `SetControllerProperty` in the **Label** field.

4. Accept the default **SetControllerProperty** that is automatically generated for the **Name** field.

5. Paste the contents of the `SetControllerProperty.component` file from the code downloaded into the **Visualforce Markup** area and click on the **Save** button.

6. Next, create the custom controller for the Visualforce pages by navigating to the **Apex Classes** setup page by clicking on **Your Name | Setup | Develop | Apex Classes**.

7. Click on the **New** button.

8. Paste the contents of the `AccountsTypeController.cls` Apex class from the code downloaded into the **Apex Class** area.

9. Click on the **Save** button.

10. Next, create the first Visualforce page by navigating to the Visualforce setup page by clicking on **Your Name | Setup | Develop | Visualforce Pages**.

11. Click on the **New** button.

12. Enter `AccountsType1` in the **Label** field.

13. Accept the default **AccountsType1** that is automatically generated for the **Name** field.

14. Paste the contents of the `AccountsType1.page` file from the code downloaded into the **Visualforce Markup** area and click on the **Save** button.

15. Navigate to the Visualforce setup page by clicking on **Your Name | Setup | Develop | Visualforce Pages**.

16. Locate the entry for the **AccountsType1** page and click on the **Security** link.

17. On the resulting page, select which profiles should have access and click on the **Save** button.

18. Finally, create the second Visualforce page by navigating to the Visualforce setup page by clicking on **Your Name | Setup | Develop | Visualforce Pages**.

19. Click on the **New** button.

20. Enter `AccountsType2` in the **Label** field.

21. Accept the default **AccountsType2** that is automatically generated for the **Name** field.

22. Paste the contents of the `AccountsType2.page` file from the code downloaded into the **Visualforce Markup** area and click on the **Save** button.

23. Navigate to the Visualforce setup page by clicking on **Your Name | Setup | Develop | Visualforce Pages**.

24. Locate the entry for the **AccountsType2** page and click on the **Security** link.

25. On the resulting page, select which profiles should have access and click on the **Save** button.

How it works...

Opening the first Visualforce page in your browser displays a list of accounts whose type is **Customer – Direct**: `https://<instance>/apex/AccountsType1`.

Accounts: Customer - Direct

Account Name	Billing State/Province	Phone
United Oil & Gas, UK	UK	+44 191 4956203
United Oil & Gas, Singapore	Singapore	(650) 450-8810
Edge Communications	TX	(512) 757-6000
Burlington Textiles Corp of America	NC	(336) 222-7000
Grand Hotels & Resorts Ltd	IL	(312) 596-1000

Here, `<instance>` is the Salesforce instance specific to your organization, for example, `na6.salesforce.com`.

Opening the second Visualforce page displays a list of accounts whose type is **Customer – Channel**: `https://<instance>/apex/AccountsType2`.

Accounts: Customer - Channel		
Account Name	**Billing State/Province**	**Phone**
GenePoint	CA	(650) 867-3450
Pyramid Construction Inc.		(014) 427-4427
Dickenson plc	KS	(785) 241-6200
Express Logistics and Transport	OR	(503) 421-7800

Here, `<instance>` is the Salesforce instance specific to your organization, for example, `na6.salesforce.com`.

The `SetControllerProperty` custom component assigns the value attribute to the controller property attribute:

```
<apex:component >
    <apex:attribute name="from" type="String" assignTo="{!to}"
      description="The value to set"/>
    <apex:attribute name="to" type="String"
      description="The controller property to set the value into"/>
</apex:component>
```

The Visualforce pages set the type of account to be retrieved into the controller property via the custom component:

```
<c:SetControllerProperty from="Customer - Direct"
to="{!accType}" />
```

See also

- The *Updating attributes in component controllers* recipe in this chapter shows how a custom component can update an attribute that is a property of the enclosing page controller.
- The *Passing attributes to components* recipe in this chapter shows how an `sObject` may be passed as an attribute to a custom component.

Multiselecting related objects

One task that users often find unwieldy when implementing Salesforce is setting up the sObjects to represent many-to-many relationships. A junction object allows a single instance of one sObject type to be related to multiple instances of another sObject type and vice versa.

This requires the user to create a new instance of the junction object and populate master-detail fields to associate two sObjects with each other, resulting in a large number of clicks and page transitions.

In this recipe, we will create a custom object– account group – that acts as a container for multiple accounts. We will then create a page that allows a number of accounts to be associated with a single custom sObject. We will use junction objects for the relationship to allow a single account to be related to multiple account groups, and a single account group to be associated with multiple accounts. A custom Visualforce component will manage the action of presenting the available accounts and allowing the user to choose which to relate with the account group. The component will use the mechanism described in the *Updating attributes in component controllers* recipe to make the selected values available to the page controller via a custom string container class.

Getting ready

This recipe requires two custom sObjects: the account group, and the junction object between an account group and an account:

1. First, create the account group custom sObject by navigating to **Your Name | Setup | Develop | Objects**.
2. Click on the **New Custom Object** button.
3. Enter Account Group in the **Label** field.
4. Enter Account Groups in the **Plural Label** field.
5. Select the **Starts with vowel sound** box.
6. Leave all other input values at their defaults and click on the **Save** button.
7. Next, create the junction object to associate an account group with an account by navigating to **Your Name | Setup | Develop | Objects**.
8. Click on the **New Custom Object** button.

9. Enter `Account Group JO` in the **Label** field.

10. Enter `Account Group JOs` in the **Plural Label** field.

11. Select the **Starts with vowel sound** box.

12. Leave all other input values at their defaults and click on the **Save** button.

13. On the resulting page, create the master-detail relationship for the account group by scrolling down to the **Custom Fields and Relationships** section and clicking on the **New** button.

14. On the next page, **Step 1. Choose the field type**, select the **Master-Detail Relationship** from the **Data Type** radio buttons and click on the **Next** button.

15. On the next page, **Step 2. Choose the related object**, choose **Account Group** from the **Related To** picklist and click on the **Next** button.

16. On the next page, **Step 3. Enter the label and name for the lookup field**, leave all the fields at their default values and click on the **Next** button.

17. On the next page, **Step 4. Establish field-level security for reference field**, leave all the fields at their default values and click on the **Next** button.

18. On the next page, **Step 5. Add reference field to page layouts**, leave all the fields at their default values and click on the **Next** button.

19. On the final page, **Step 6. Add Custom Related Lists**, leave all the fields at their default values and click on the **Save** button.

20. Next, create the master-detail relationship for the account by scrolling down to the **Custom Fields and Relationships** section and click on the **New** button.

21. On the next page, **Step 1. Choose the field type**, select the **Master-Detail Relationship** from the **Data Type** radio buttons and click on the **Next** button.

22. On the next page, **Step 2. Choose the related object**, choose **Account** from the **Related To** picklist and click on the **Next** button.

23. On the next page, **Step 3. Enter the label and name for the lookup field**, leave all the fields at their default values and click on the **Next** button.

24. On the next page, **Step 4. Establish field-level security for reference field**, leave all the fields at their default values and click on the **Next** button.

25. On the next page, **Step 5. Add reference field to page layouts**, leave all the fields at their default values and click on the **Next** button.

26. On the final page, **Step 6. Add Custom Related Lists**, leave all the fields at their default values and click on the **Save** button.

How to do it...

1. Create the custom string container class by navigating to the **Apex Classes** setup page by clicking on **Your Name | Setup | Develop | Apex Classes**.

2. Click on the **New** button.

3. Paste the contents of the `StringContainer.cls` Apex class from the code downloaded into the **Apex Class** area.

4. Click on the **Save** button.

5. Next, create the custom controller for the Visualforce component by navigating to the **Apex Classes** setup page by clicking on **Your Name | Setup | Develop | Apex Classes**.

6. Click on the **New** button.

7. Paste the contents of the `MultiSelectRelatedController.cls` Apex class from the code downloaded into the **Apex Class** area.

8. Click on the **Save** button.

9. Next, navigate to the Visualforce Components setup page by clicking on **Your Name | Setup | Develop | Components**.

10. Click on the **New** button.

11. Enter `MultiSelectRelated` in the **Label** field.

12. Accept the default **MultiSelectRelated** that is automatically generated for the **Name** field.

13. Paste the contents of the `MultiSelectRelated.component` file from the code downloaded into the **Visualforce Markup** area and click on the **Save** button.

14. Next, create the custom controller for the Visualforce page by navigating to the **Apex Classes** setup page by clicking on **Your Name | Setup | Develop | Apex Classes**.

15. Click on the **New** button.

16. Paste the contents of the `AccountGroupController.cls` Apex class from the code downloaded into the **Apex Class** area.

17. Click on the **Save** button.

18. Finally, create the Visualforce page by navigating to the Visualforce setup page by clicking on **Your Name | Setup | Develop | Visualforce Pages**.

19. Click on the **New** button.

20. Enter `AccountGroup` in the **Label** field.

21. Accept the default **AccountGroup** that is automatically generated for the **Name** field.

22. Paste the contents of the `AccountGroup.page` file from the code downloaded into the **Visualforce Markup** area and click on the **Save** button.

23. Navigate to the Visualforce setup page by clicking on **Your Name | Setup | Develop | Visualforce Pages**.

24. Locate the entry for the **AccountGroup** page and click on the **Security** link.

25. On the resulting page, select which profiles should have access and click on the **Save** button.

How it works...

Opening the Visualforce page in your browser displays the account group create page: `https://<instance>/apex/AccountGroup`.

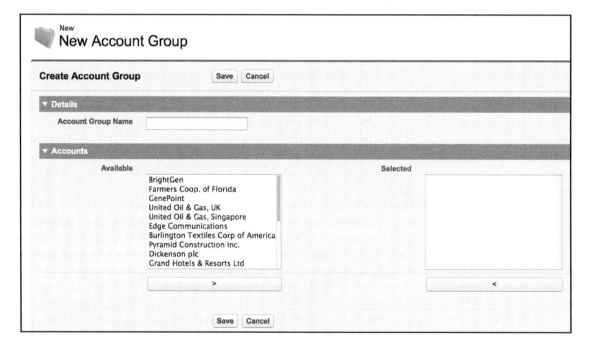

Here, `<instance>` is the Salesforce instance specific to your organization, for example, `na6.salesforce.com`.

The chosen account IDs are stored as semi-colon separated values in a property of the page controller. The page controller constructor extracts all accounts and creates a standard `SelectOption` class for each one:

```
accountOptions=new List<SelectOption>();
for (Account acc : [select id, Name from Account])
{
   accountOptions.add(new SelectOption(acc.id, acc.name));
}
```

The custom component controller contains two collections of options: **available** and **chosen**. The component iterates the full set of account options and adds the option to available or chosen depending on whether the account ID is present in the semi-colon separated string of chosen IDs:

```
availableItems=new List<SelectOption>();
chosenItems=new List<SelectOption>();
for (SelectOption sel : allOptions)
{
   String selId=sel.getValue();
   if (selected.value.contains(selId+';'))
   {
      chosenItems.add(sel);
   }
   else
   {
      availableItems.add(sel);
   }
}
```

Accounts can be moved between the **Available** and **Selected** lists by highlighting the options and clicking on the > or < buttons.. The following image shows the component content after a number of accounts have been selected to be added to the account group:

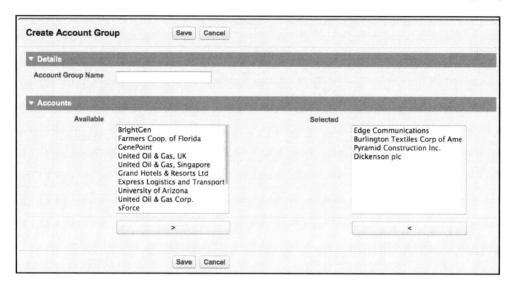

Each button invokes an `action` method in the component controller that adds or removes the account IDs from the semi-colon separated chosen string, and then rebuilds the available and chosen lists.

Clicking on the **Save** button creates the account group record and a junction object for each account ID in the chosen string:

```
public PageReference save()
{
  insert accountGroup;
  List<Account_Group_JO__c> agJOs=
       new List<Account_Group_JO__c>();

  for (String accId : chosenAccounts.value.split(';'))
  {
    Account_Group_JO__c agJO=
      new Account_Group_JO__c(
          Account_Group__c=accountGroup.id,
          Account__c=accId);
    agJOs.add(agJO);
  }
  insert agJOs;
  return new PageReference('/' + accountGroup.id);
}
```

Notifying the containing page controller

In the earlier recipes, we have seen how components can accept an attribute that is a property from the containing page controller and update the value of the property in response to a user action. If the containing page controller needs to determine if the property has changed, it must capture the previous value of the property and compare that with the current value. The same applies if the attribute passed to the component is a field from an sObject managed by the parent page controller.

In this recipe, we will create a custom component that can notify its containing page controller when an attribute value is changed. In order to avoid tying the component to a particular page controller class, we will create an interface that defines the method to be used to notify the page controller. This will allow the component controller to notify any page controller that implements the interface.

 Interfaces define a *contract* between the calling code and the implementing code. The calling code is able to rely on the method(s) defined in the interface being available without having to know the details of the underlying code that is implementing the interface. This allows the implementing code to be swapped in and out without affecting the calling code.

Getting ready

This recipe requires that you have already completed the *Multiselecting related objects* recipe, as it relies on the custom sObjects created in that recipe.

How to do it...

1. First, create the interface by navigating to the **Apex Classes** setup page by clicking on **Your Name** | **Setup** | **Develop** | **Apex Classes**.
2. Click on the **New** button.
3. Paste the contents of the Notifiable.cls Apex class from the code downloaded into the **Apex Class** area.
4. Click on the **Save** button.
5. Next, create the component controller by navigating to the **Apex Classes** setup page by clicking on **Your Name** | **Setup** | **Develop** | **Apex Classes**.
6. Click on the **New** button.

7. Paste the contents of the `NotifyingMultiSelectRelatedController.cls` Apex class from the code downloaded into the **Apex Class** area.

8. Click on the **Save** button.

9. Next, create the custom component by navigating to the Visualforce Components setup page by clicking on **Your Name** | **Setup** | **Develop** | **Components**.

10. Click on the **New** button.

11. Enter `NotifyingMultiSelectRelated` in the **Label** field.

12. Accept the default **NotifyingMultiSelectRelated** that is automatically generated for the **Name** field.

13. Paste the contents of the `NotifyingMultiSelectRelated.component` file from the code downloaded into the **Visualforce Markup** area and click on the **Save** button.

14. Next, create the custom controller for the Visualforce page by navigating to the **Apex Classes** setup page by clicking on **Your Name** | **Setup** | **Develop** | **Apex Classes**.

15. Click on the **New** button.

16. Paste the contents of the `NotifiableAccountGroupController.cls` Apex class from the code downloaded into the **Apex Class** area.

17. Click on the **Save** button.

18. Next, create the Visualforce page by navigating to the Visualforce setup page by clicking on **Your Name** | **Setup** | **Develop** | **Visualforce Pages**.

19. Click on the **New** button.

20. Enter `NotifiableAccountGroup` in the **Label** field.

21. Accept the default **NotifiableAccountGroup** that is automatically generated for the **Name** field.

22. Paste the contents of the `NotifiableAccountGroup.page` file from the code downloaded into the **Visualforce Markup** area and click on the **Save** button.

23. Navigate to the Visualforce setup page by clicking on **Your Name** | **Setup** | **Develop** | **Visualforce Pages**.

24. Locate the entry for the **NotifiableAccountGroup** page and click on the **Security** link.

25. On the resulting page, select which profiles should have access and click on the **Save** button.

How it works…

Opening the following URL in your browser displays the **NotifiableAccountGroup** page: `https://<instance>/apex/NotifiableAccountGroup`.

Here, `<instance>` is the Salesforce instance specific to your organization, for example, `na6.salesforce.com`, and `<account_id>` is the ID of an account from your Salesforce instance.

When accounts are moved between the **Available** and **Selected** lists, the component controller notifies the parent page controller, which writes a message onto the page with the notification details:

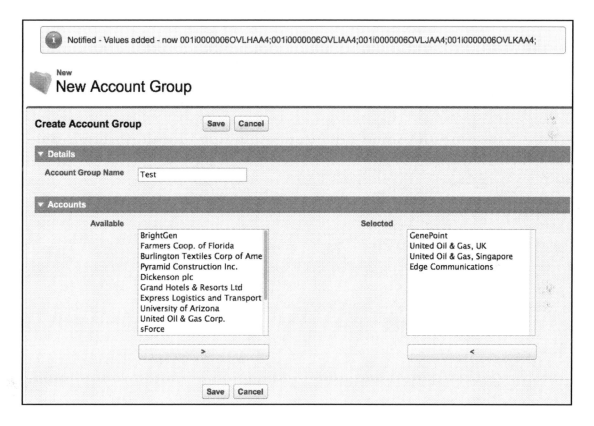

The parent page controller, `NotifiableAccountGroupController`, implements the `Notifiable` interface:

```
public with sharing class NotifiableAccountGroupController
            implements Notifiable
```

The implementation of the `notify` method wraps the notification text in an `ApexPages.Message` class and adds this to the messages for the page:

```
public void notify(String detail)
{
  ApexPages.addMessage(new ApexPages.Message(
    ApexPages.Severity.INFO, 'Notified - ' + detail));
}
```

The custom component takes a parameter of type `Notifiable`, which is assigned to a property in its controller:

```
<apex:attribute name="notify"
   description="The entity to notify when the selection changes"
   type="Notifiable" assignTo="{!notifiable}" />
```

The custom component also takes a `rerender` parameter, which is used to update part of the containing page, when the selection changes:

```
<apex:attribute name="rerender"
   description="The component to rerender when the selection changes"
   type="String" />
```

In this case, the page passes through the ID of its `<apex:pageMessages />` component to display the message added in the page controller's `notify` method, as described earlier.

When the `action` methods to move accounts between the **Available** and **Selected** lists are executed, these invoke the `notify` method with details of the change:

```
if (null!=notifiable)
{
  notifiable.notify('Values deleted - now ' + selected.value);
}
```

See also

- The *Updating attributes in component controllers* recipe in this chapter shows how a custom component can update an attribute that is a property of the enclosing page controller.
- The *Passing attributes to components* recipe in this chapter shows how an sObject may be passed as an attribute to a custom component.
- The *Multiselecting related objects* recipe in this chapter shows how to create a custom multiselect picklist style component.

3
Capturing Data Using Forms

In this chapter, we will cover the following recipes:

- Editing a record in Visualforce
- Adding error messages to field inputs
- Adding error messages to non-field inputs
- Using field sets
- Adding a custom lookup to a form
- Adding a custom datepicker to a form
- Retrieving fields when a lookup is populated
- Breaking up forms with action regions
- The Please wait spinner
- Action chaining

Introduction

Forms are a key feature of any application that makes use of Visualforce. They provide a mechanism to capture data entered by the user and send this to the page controller for processing, for example, to create, edit, or delete sObject records, or to send the user to a specific page.

Users enter data through input components. Visualforce provides a specific standard component, `<apex:inputField />`, for entering sObject field data. This component renders the appropriate device for entering data based on the field type, such as a JavaScript date picker for a field of type Date.

Input components are bound to `sObject` fields or controller properties via the merge syntax. Controller properties that are public and have a public getter and setter may be bound to input components without writing any further code.

Processing of the submitted form is carried out via action methods. These may be provided automatically by the platform in the case of standard controllers, or coded using Apex in the case of extension or custom controllers. Action methods can rely on all `sObject` fields and controller properties bound to input components containing the latest user input when they execute.

Editing a record in Visualforce

The standard record edit page does not allow customization outside the layout of fields. Editing records with Visualforce pages allows customization of all aspects of the page, including styling, content, and displayed buttons.

In this recipe, we will create a Visualforce page that provides contact edit capability, but does not allow a contact to be reparented to a different account. The account lookup field is editable until the record is saved with the lookup populated, after which it becomes read-only. This page will also render a different section heading depending on whether the contact is being created or edited.

Getting ready

This recipe makes use of a standard controller, so we only need to create the Visualforce page.

How to do it...

1. Navigate to the Visualforce setup page by clicking on **Your Name** | **Setup** | **Develop** | **Visualforce Pages**.
2. Click on the **New** button.
3. Enter `ContactCreateEdit` in the **Label** field.
4. Accept the default **ContactCreateEdit** that is automatically generated for the **Name** field.

5. Paste the contents of the `ContactCreateEdit.page` file from the code download into the **Visualforce Markup** area and click on the **Save** button.

6. Navigate to the Visualforce setup page by clicking on **Your Name** | **Setup** | **Develop** | **Visualforce Pages**.

7. Locate the entry for the **ContactCreateEdit** page and click on the **Security** link.

8. On the resulting page, select which profiles should have access and click on the **Save** button.

How it works…

Opening the following URL in your browser displays the **ContactCreateEdit** page to create a new record: `https://<instance>/apex/ContactCreateEdit`.

Here, `<instance>` is the Salesforce instance specific to your organization, for example, `na6.salesforce.com`.

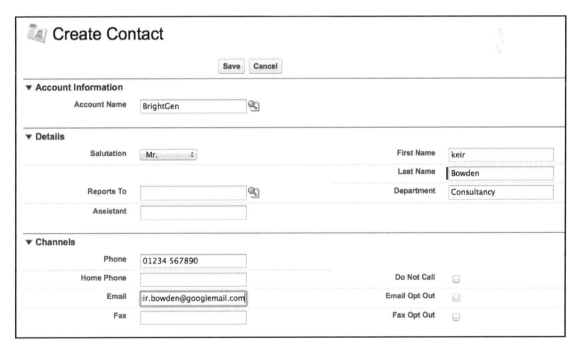

Note that the section heading for the page is **Create Contact**, and the **Account Name** field is editable. Save this record and edit it again via the same page using the following URL: `https://<instance>/apex/ContactCreateEdit?id=<contact_id>`.

Here, `<contact_id>` is the record ID of the newly created contact, and it displays the edit form of the page with a different section heading and the **Account Name** field is changed to read-only:

The Visualforce page utilizes a standard controller and conditionally renders the section heading, and input/output variants of the **Account Name** field based on the ID of the record:

```
<apex:sectionHeader
     />

<apex:inputField value="{!Contact.AccountId}"
       rendered="{!null==Contact.AccountId}" />
<apex:outputField value="{!Contact.AccountId}"
       rendered="{!null!=Contact.AccountId}" />
```

See also

- The *Using field sets* recipe in this chapter shows how an administrator can control the editable fields on a Visualforce page.

Adding error messages to field inputs

When users are editing or creating a record via a Visualforce page, they will often make mistakes or enter invalid data. The required fields will present an error message underneath the field itself, but validation rules or exceptions will simply send the user to a new page with a large error message, telling them that the insert or update failed.

In this recipe, we will create a Visualforce page to allow a user to create or edit a contact record. The contact standard controller and a controller extension manage the page. The extension controller checks whether the e-mail address or phone number field has been populated. If either of the fields is populated, the record will be saved, but if both are missing, an error message will be added to both fields asking the user to populate at least one of them.

Getting ready

This recipe makes use of a controller extension, so this will need to be created before the Visualforce page.

How to do it...

1. First, create the controller extension by navigating to the **Apex Classes** setup page by clicking on **Your Name** | **Setup** | **Develop** | **Apex Classes**.
2. Click on the **New** button.
3. Paste the contents of the InputFieldErrorExt.cls Apex class from the code download into the **Apex Class** area.
4. Click on the **Save** button.
5. Next, create the Visualforce page by navigating to the Visualforce setup page by clicking on **Your Name** | **Setup** | **Develop** | **Visualforce Pages**.
6. Click on the **New** button.
7. Enter InputFieldError in the **Label** field.
8. Accept the default **InputFieldError** that is automatically generated for the **Name** field.
9. Paste the contents of the InputFieldError.page file from the code download into the **Visualforce Markup** area and click on the **Save** button.
10. Navigate to the Visualforce setup page by clicking on **Your Name** | **Setup** | **Develop** | **Visualforce Pages**.
11. Locate the entry for the **InputFieldError** page and click on the **Security** link.
12. On the resulting page, select which profiles should have access and click on the **Save** button.

How it works...

Opening the following URL in your browser displays the **InputFieldError** page:
`https://<instance>/apex/InputFieldError`.

Here, `<instance>` is the Salesforce instance specific to your organization, for example, `na6.salesforce.com`.

Leaving both the **Phone** and **Email** fields blank causes a tailored error message to be displayed underneath the fields:

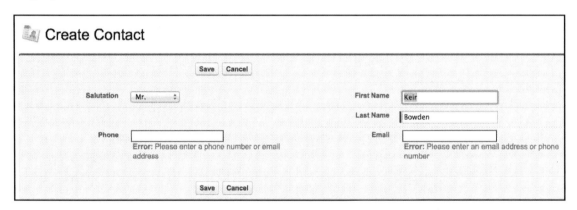

The Visualforce page controller extension declares a `Save` method, which overrides the standard controller's `Save` method. If the contact's **Phone** and **Email** fields are both empty, the controller uses the `addError` method of the `sObject` field to associate an error message with the field. When the page is rendered, Visualforce will automatically display the error message with the field. If either of the **Phone** or **Email** fields are populated, the controller extension delegates it to the standard controller `Save` method and returns the result:

```
public PageReference save()
{
  PageReference result=null;
  Contact cont=(Contact) stdCtrl.getRecord();
  if ( (String.IsBlank(cont.Email)) &&
       (String.IsBlank(cont.Phone)) )
{
    cont.email.addError
      ('Please enter an email address or phone number');
    cont.phone.addError
      ('Please enter a phone number or email address');
  }
  else
  {
```

```
      result=stdCtrl.save();
   }
   return result;
}
```

See also

- The *Adding error messages to non-field inputs* recipe in this chapter shows how error messages can be displayed against input elements associated with controller properties.

Adding error messages to non-field inputs

In the previous recipe, *Adding error messages to field inputs*, the platform took care of positioning the error message based on whether the field had any errors associated with it. Visualforce automatically provides this functionality for `<apex:inputField />` components, but if a different input component is used, such as `<apex:inputText />` or `<apex:selectList />`, there is no equivalent functionality.

In this recipe, we will create a Visualforce page to allow a user to create or edit a contact record. The contact standard controller and a controller extension manage the page. The ID of the account that the contact is associated with is entered via an `<apex:selectList />` component, which is bound to a controller property rather than an `sObject` field. If the user does not select an account to associate the contact with, an error message is displayed under the `<apex:selectList />` component.

Getting ready

This recipe makes use of a controller extension, so this will need to be created before the Visualforce page.

How to do it...

1. First, create the Visualforce page controller extension by navigating to the **Apex Classes** setup page by clicking on **Your Name** | **Setup** | **Develop** | **Apex Classes**.
2. Click on the **New** button.

3. Paste the contents of the `InputSelectErrorExt.cls` Apex class from the code download into the **Apex Class** area.

4. Click on the **Save** button.

5. Next, create the Visualforce page by navigating to the Visualforce setup page by clicking on **Your Name** | **Setup** | **Develop** | **Visualforce Pages**.

6. Click on the **New** button.

7. Enter `InputSelectError` in the **Label** field.

8. Accept the default **InputSelectError** that is automatically generated for the **Name** field.

9. Paste the contents of the `InputSelectError.page` file from the code download into the **Visualforce Markup** area and click on the **Save** button.

10. Navigate to the Visualforce setup page by clicking on **Your Name** | **Setup** | **Develop** | **Visualforce Pages**.

11. Locate the entry for the **InputSelectError** page and click on the **Security** link.

12. On the resulting page, select which profiles should have access and click on the **Save** button.

How it works...

Opening the following URL in your browser displays the **InputSelectError** page: `https://<instance>/apex/InputSelectError`.

Here, `<instance>` is the Salesforce instance specific to your organization, for example, `na6.salesforce.com`.

Leaving the selected account value as **— Choose —** causes the save to fail and an error message to be displayed under the selected component:

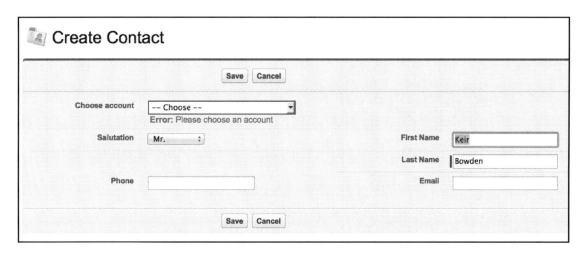

In order to display the error message in the correct place, it must be coupled with the property that the input component is bound to. The controller extension defines an inner class that contains two `String` properties; one to hold the input value and another to hold the error message. The class also exposes a method to determine if the input value is currently in error:

```
public class ValueAndError
{
  public String value {get; set;}
  public String error {get; set;}
  public Boolean getHasError()
  {
    return (!String.IsBlank(error));
  }
}
```

An instance of this class is used by the controller extension to contain the ID of the selected account:

```
public ValueAndError accountIdVal {get; set;}
```

The controller extension defines a `Save` method, which overrides the standard controller save method. If the `value` property of the `ValueAndError` instance remains at the default, an error message is added to the instance:

```
if (String.IsBlank(accountIdVal.value))
{
  accountIdVal.error='Please choose an account';
}
```

The Visualforce page conditionally adds the `error` style class to the input component if the `ValueAndError` instance indicates there is an error. Additionally, the actual error message is displayed using a style class of `errorMsg`:

```
<apex:selectList value="{!accountIdVal.value}" size="1"
  styleClass="{!IF(accountIdVal.hasError,'error','')}">
  <apex:selectOptions value="{!accountOptions}" />
</apex:selectList>
<div class="errorMsg"
  style="display:{!IF(accountIdVal.hasError,'block','none')}">
  <strong>Error:</strong> {!accountIdVal.error}
</div>
```

The `error` and `errorMsg` style classes are from the standard Salesforce stylesheets. Using these classes entails the risk that if Salesforce updates its styling, these classes may be changed or removed entirely, which would break the error message styling. In order to avoid this, clone the Salesforce styles into your own stylesheet.

See also

- The *Adding error messages to field inputs* recipe in this chapter shows how error messages can be displayed against input elements associated with `sObject` fields.

Using field sets

A **field set** defines a group of `sObject` fields. A Visualforce page can iterate the fields contained in the set and access the values and other information, such as label or type, through the merge syntax. This decouples maintenance of the page from the skill set required to author Visualforce pages, and allows administrators to add or remove fields through point and click.

In this recipe, we will create two field sets for the contact `sObject`: one to display the address information and another to display information about the contact. We will then create a Visualforce page that uses these field sets to render input components inside a page block section, which allows a contact record to be created or edited.

Getting ready

This recipe relies on two field sets, which must be created before the Visualforce page can be created:

1. First, create the contact detail field set. Navigate to the contact field sets setup page by clicking on **Your Name** | **Setup** | **Customize** | **Contacts** | **Field Sets**.
2. Click on the **New** button.
3. Enter Detail in the **Field Set Label** field.
4. Accept the default **Detail** that is automatically generated for the **Field Set Name** field.

> Ensure that the name is correctly set, as the Visualforce page uses this to retrieve the field set.

5. Enter In the cookbook field sets example page in the **Where is this used?** field and click on the **Save** button.
6. On the resulting page, drag the following fields onto the **In the Field Set** pane: **Name**, **Description**, **Phone**, and **Email**.

> If you wish to allow administrators to add additional fields to the field set, these must be dragged onto the **Available for the Field Set** pane.

7. Click on the **Save** button to commit the changes.
8. Next, create the contact address field set. Navigate to the contact field sets setup page by clicking on **Your Name** | **Setup** | **Customize** | **Contacts** | **Field Sets**.
9. Click on the **New** button.
10. Enter Address Information in the **Field Set Label** field.
11. Accept the default **Address_Information** that is automatically generated for the **Field Set Name** field.

> Ensure that the name is correctly set, as the Visualforce page uses this to retrieve the field set.

12. Enter `In the cookbook field sets example page` in the **Where is this used?** field and click on the **Save** button.
13. On the resulting page, drag all fields named **Mailing Address** and **Other Address** onto the **In the Field Set** pane.
14. Click on the **Save** button to commit the changes.

How to do it...

1. Create the Visualforce page by navigating to the Visualforce setup page by clicking on **Your Name** | **Setup** | **Develop** | **Visualforce Pages**.
2. Click on the **New** button.
3. Enter `FieldSets` in the **Label** field.
4. Accept the default **FieldSets** that is automatically generated for the **Name** field.
5. Paste the contents of the `FieldSets.page` file from the code downloaded into the **Visualforce Markup** area and click on the **Save** button.
6. Navigate to the Visualforce setup page by clicking on **Your Name** | **Setup** | **Develop** | **Visualforce Pages**.
7. Locate the entry for the **FieldSets** page and click on the **Security** link.
8. On the resulting page, select which profiles should have access and click on the **Save** button.

How it works...

Opening the following URL in your browser displays the **FieldSets** page:
`https://<instance>/apex/FieldSets`.

Here, `<instance>` is the Salesforce instance specific to your organization, for example,
`na6.salesforce.com`.

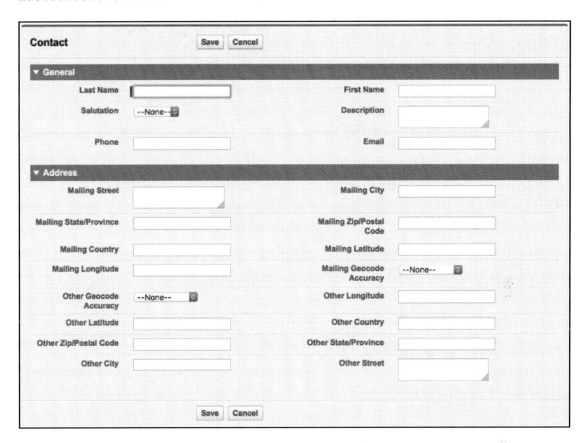

The Visualforce page uses the `$ObjectType` global variable to access a named field set and
iterate the contained fields, which are bound to input components:

```
<apex:pageBlockSection >
  <apex:repeat value="{!$ObjectType.Contact.FieldSets.Detail}"
        var="field">
    <apex:inputField value="{!Contact[field]}" />
  </apex:repeat>
</apex:pageBlockSection>
```

Adding a custom lookup to a form

The Salesforce standard lookup functionality renders a dialog that supports a small amount of customization. The fields displayed may be configured; if **Enhanced Lookups** has been enabled, the results can be filtered and ordered, and large result sets may be paged through. The lookup dialog's layout cannot be altered nor branded , nor can it contain additional help text.

In this recipe, we will create a Visualforce lookup page that replaces the lookup dialog and provides additional instructions to the user. An additional Visualforce page will demonstrate how this can be integrated into a custom opportunity create page.

Getting ready

This recipe makes use of a custom controller, so this will need to be created before the Visualforce page.

How to do it...

1. Navigate to the **Apex Classes** setup page by clicking on **Your Name** | **Setup** | **Develop** | **Apex Classes**.
2. Click on the **New** button.
3. Paste the contents of the `LookupController.cls` Apex class from the code downloaded into the **Apex Class** area.
4. Click on the **Save** button.
5. Next, create the custom lookup Visualforce page by navigating to the Visualforce setup page by clicking on **Your Name** | **Setup** | **Develop** | **Visualforce Pages**.
6. Click on the **New** button.
7. Enter `LookupPopup` in the **Label** field.
8. Accept the default **LookupPopup** that is automatically generated for the **Name** field.
9. Paste the contents of the `LookupPopup.page` file from the code downloaded into the **Visualforce Markup** area and click on the **Save** button.
10. Navigate to the Visualforce setup page by clicking on **Your Name** | **Setup** | **Develop** | **Visualforce Pages**.

11. Locate the entry for the **LookupPopup** page and click on the **Security** link.
12. On the resulting page, select which profiles should have access and click on the **Save** button.
13. Finally, create the custom create opportunity Visualforce page by navigating to the Visualforce setup page by clicking on **Your Name | Setup | Develop| Visualforce Pages**.
14. Click on the **New** button.
15. Enter Lookup in the **Label** field.
16. Accept the default **Lookup** that is automatically generated for the **Name** field.
17. Paste the contents of the Lookup.page file from the code downloaded into the **Visualforce Markup** area and click on the **Save** button.
18. Navigate to the Visualforce setup page by clicking on **Your Name | Setup | Develop | Visualforce Pages**.
19. Locate the entry for the **Lookup** page and click on the **Security** link.
20. On the resulting page, select which profiles should have access and click the **Save** button.

How it works...

Opening the following URL in your browser displays the custom opportunity create **Lookup** page: https://<instance>/apex/Lookup.

Here, <instance> is the Salesforce instance specific to your organization, for example, na6.salesforce.com.

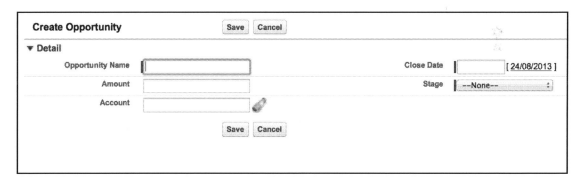

Clicking on the telescope icon to the right of the **Account** field opens the custom lookup dialog:

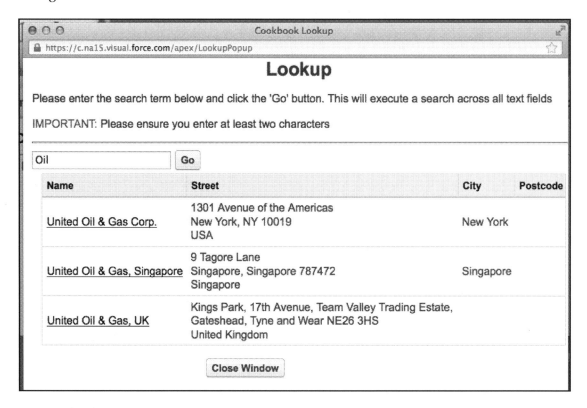

The **Lookup** page contains a hidden input component that is populated with the ID of the chosen account, while the text input component is used to display the name of the chosen account. JavaScript is used to execute the function to open the lookup dialog when the telescope icon is clicked:

```
<apex:inputHidden value="{!Opportunity.AccountId}"
    id="targetId" />
<apex:inputText size="20" id="targetName" onFocus="this.blur "/>
<a href="#" onclick="openLookupPopup('{!$Component.targetName}',
'{!$Component.targetId}'); return false">
<apex:image style="vertical-align:middle;width:21px; height:21px"
    value="/img/icon/telescope16.png" /></a>
```

Note that the input text component defines an `onFocus` handler that simply removes the focus from itself. This stops the user entering an account name directly, as there is no controller logic to retrieve the ID based on the name.

The ID of the input fields for the chosen account ID and name are passed to the dialog as URL parameters. This allows the dialog to populate the fields once the user has chosen an account.

In addition to opening the pop-up, the **Lookup** page also handles closing it. This is because many browsers do not allow a page to close a pop-up if it was not responsible for opening it:

```
var newWin=null;
function openLookupPopup(name, id)
{
  var url="/apex/LookupPopup?namefield=" + name +
    "&idfield=" + id;
  newWin=window.open(url, 'Popup',
    'height=500,width=600,left=100,top=100,resizable=no,
    scrollbars=yes,toolbar=no,status=no');
  if (window.focus)
  {
    newWin.focus();
  }
  return false;
}
function closeLookupPopup()
{
if (null!=newWin)
  {
    newWin.close();
  }
}
```

The **Lookup** pop-up attaches an `onclick` handler to each of the account names in the search results, to execute the JavaScript function that populates the name and ID of the chosen account:

```
<apex:column headerValue="Name">
  <apex:outputLink value="#"
    onclick="fillIn('{!account.Name}',
      '{!account.id}')">{!account.Name}
  </apex:outputLink>
</apex:column>
```

The `fillIn` function populates the fields in the parent window and then executes the JavaScript in the parent window to close the pop-up:

```
function fillIn(name, id)
{
var winMain=window.opener;
if (null==winMain)
{
    winMain=window.parent.opener;
}
var ele=winMain.document.getElementById
    ('{!$CurrentPage.parameters.namefield}');
ele.value=name;
ele=winMain.document.getElementById
    ('{!$CurrentPage.parameters.idfield}');
ele.value=id;
    winMain.closeLookupPopup();
}
```

See also

- The *Opening a pop-up window* recipe in `Chapter 1`, *General Utilities* shows how to create a pop-up window when a user clicks on a link in a Visualforce page.

Adding a custom datepicker to a form

The standard datepicker that is rendered when an `<apex:inputField />` component is bound to an `sObject` field of type `Date` or `DateTime` has a limited range of years available, as shown in the following screenshot:

The range of years presented is suitable for an opportunity close date, but it is unsuitable for capturing a contact's date of birth. One option to improve this is to add some JavaScript to the page that alters the datepicker year range, but this entails a risk as it relies on the standard datepicker code to remain the same.

In this recipe, we will integrate a third-party JavaScript datepicker with a Visualforce input field bound to a date. The datepicker used is from Design2Develop and can be downloaded from `http://www.design2develop.com/calendar/`. This has been chosen as the style class names do not conflict with any standard Salesforce style classes, as of the Summer 13 release of Salesforce.

Getting ready

This recipe requires the Design2Develop calendar ZIP file to be present as a static resource:

1. Download the custom datepicker ZIP file from `http://www.design2develop.com/calendar/#download`.
2. Navigate to the Static Resource setup page by clicking on **Your Name** | **Setup** | **Develop** | **Static Resources**.
3. Click on the **New** button.
4. Enter `D2DCalendar` in the **Name** field.
5. Enter `Design2Develop JavaScript Date Picker` in the **Description** field.
6. Click on the **Browse** button and select the `calendar.zip` file downloaded in step 1.
7. Accept the default **Private** value for the **Cache Control** field and click on the **Save** button.

How to do it…

1. First, create the Visualforce page that the datepicker will be used in by navigating to the Visualforce setup page by clicking on **Your Name** | **Setup** | **Develop** | **Visualforce Pages**.
2. Click on the **New** button.
3. Enter `DatePicker` in the **Label** field.
4. Accept the default **DatePicker** that is automatically generated for the **Name** field.
5. Paste the contents of the `DatePicker.page` file from the code downloaded into the **Visualforce Markup** area and click on the **Save** button.

6. Navigate to the Visualforce setup page by clicking on **Your Name** | **Setup** | **Develop** | **Visualforce Pages**.

7. Locate the entry for the **DatePicker** page and click on the **Security** link.

8. On the resulting page, select which profiles should have access and click on the **Save** button.

How it works...

Opening the following URL in your browser displays the **DatePicker** Visualforce page: `https://<instance>/apex/DatePicker`.

Here, `<instance>` is the Salesforce instance specific to your organization, for example, `na6.salesforce.com`.

Clicking on the **Date of Birth** input field renders the custom datepicker with a wider range of years, as shown in the following screenshot:

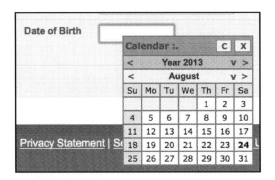

 Note that a side effect of this is that the styling of the datepicker may be customized. The sample code uses the `calendar_green.css` stylesheet supplied as part of the `calendar.zip` file to produce a datepicker that is colored green.

The **DatePicker** page provides an `onFocus` handler for the **Date of Birth** input field:

```
<apex:inputText id="birthdate" size="10"
  value="{!Contact.BirthDate}"
    onfocus="initialiseCalendar(this,
      '{!$Component.birthdate}')"/>
```

The `initialiseCalendar` JavaScript function extracts the existing date from the input component, if present, and passes this to the custom datepicker initialization code, which renders the datepicker with the existing date preselected, if defined:

```
function initialiseCalendar(obj, eleId)
{
  var element=document.getElementById(eleId);
  var params='close=true';
  if (null!=element)
  {
    if (element.value.length>0)
    {
      // date is formatted dd/mm/yyyy - pull out the month and year
      var month=element.value.substr(3,2);
      var year=element.value.substr(6,4);
      params+=',month='+month;
      params+=',year='+year;
    }
  }
  fnInitCalendar(obj, eleId, params);
}
```

See also

- The *Adding a custom lookup to a form* recipe in this chapter shows how to replace the standard lookup component with a custom version.

Retrieving fields when a lookup is populated

When viewing an `sObject` that has a lookup relationship to another `sObject`, additional fields from the related `sObject` can be displayed on the page using formula fields. When creating a new record, or editing an existing record and changing the lookup value, formula fields cannot be used, as the lookup field has only been populated with a record ID and the related record has not been retrieved.

In this recipe, we will create a Visualforce page that allows a user to create a case `sObject` record. The case standard controller and a controller extension manage the new case record. When the lookup to the account that the case is related to is populated, additional fields are retrieved from the account record and displayed.

Getting ready

This recipe makes use of a controller extension, so this will need to be present before the Visualforce page can be created.

How to do it...

1. First, create the controller extension for the Visualforce page by navigating to the **Apex Classes** setup page by clicking on **Your Name** | **Setup** | **Develop** | **Apex Classes**.
2. Click on the **New** button.
3. Paste the contents of the `PullLookupFieldsExt.cls` Apex class from the code downloaded into the **Apex Class** area.
4. Click on the **Save** button.
5. Next, create the Visualforce page by navigating to the Visualforce setup page by clicking on **Your Name** | **Setup** | **Develop** | **Visualforce Pages**.
6. Click on the **New** button.
7. Enter `PullLookupFields` in the **Label** field.
8. Accept the default **PullLookupFields** that is automatically generated for the **Name** field.
9. Paste the contents of the `PullLookupFields.page` file from the code downloaded into the **Visualforce Markup** area and click on the **Save** button.
10. Navigate to the Visualforce setup page, by clicking on **Your Name** | **Setup** | **Develop** | **Visualforce Pages**.
11. Locate the entry for the **PullLookupFields** page and click on the **Security** link.
12. On the resulting page, select which profiles should have access and click on the **Save** button.

How it works...

Opening the following page in your browser displays the **PullLookupFields** page:
`https://<instance>/apex/PullLookupFields`.

Here, `<instance>` is the Salesforce instance specific to your organization, for example, `na6.salesforce.com`.

Populating the account lookup automatically populates the **Website** and **Phone** output elements with the details from the account:

The **PullLookupFields** page executes an `action` method when the contents of the case account lookup field changes:

```
<apex:inputField value="{!Case.AccountId}">
  <apex:actionSupport event="onchange" action="{!accountSelected}"
    rerender="account, msgs" status="stat"/>
</apex:inputField>
```

When the `accountSelected` method is executed, it confirms that the field has not been cleared and retrieves the related account record, attaching this to the case record from the standard controller:

```
Case cs=(Case) stdCtrl.getRecord();

// handle the situation where the account field has been cleared
if (!String.isBlank(cs.AccountId))
{
    cs.Account=[select Website, Phone from Account
        where id=:cs.AccountId];
}
```

When the account section of the page is rerendered, the related fields are retrieved using the standard dot notation:

```
<apex:outputField value="{!Case.Account.Website}"/>
<apex:outputField value="{!Case.Account.Phone}"/>
```

Breaking up forms with action regions

The submission of a form in a Visualforce page causes the view state and all user inputs to be processed by the controller. In the event that the form is being submitted back, purely to introduce some additional information based on a single user input, this can be inefficient, especially if there are a large number of field inputs on the page. The `<apex:actionRegion />` component can be used to break the form up into discrete sections, reducing the amount of data processed by the controller and improving performance of the page.

In this recipe, we will create a Visualforce page that allows a user to create a case record. The case subject is automatically generated by a controller extension from a base subject entered by the user and the name of the account that the case is associated with. A change to either the base subject or the account lookup causes the form to be submitted in order to update the generated subject. Each of these fields is contained in an action region, ensuring that only the controller processes the updated value.

Getting ready

This recipe makes use of a controller extension, so this will need to be present before the Visualforce page can be created.

How to do it...

1. First, create the controller extension for the Visualforce page by navigating to the **Apex Classes** setup page by clicking on **Your Name** | **Setup** | **Develop** | **Apex Classes**.
2. Click on the **New** button.
3. Paste the contents of the `ActionRegionExt.cls` Apex class from the code downloaded into the **Apex Class** area.
4. Click on the **Save** button.
5. Next, create the Visualforce page by navigating to the Visualforce setup page by clicking on **Your Name** | **Setup** | **Develop** | **Visualforce Pages**.
6. Click on the **New** button.
7. Enter `ActionRegion` in the **Label** field.
8. Accept the default **ActionRegion** that is automatically generated for the **Name** field.

9. Paste the contents of the `ActionRegion.page` page from the code downloaded into the **Visualforce Markup** area and click on the **Save** button.

10. Navigate to the Visualforce setup page by clicking on **Your Name** | **Setup** | **Develop** | **Visualforce Pages**.

11. Locate the entry for the **ActionRegion** page and click on the **Security** link.

12. On the resulting page, select which profiles should have access and click on the **Save** button.

How it works...

Opening the following URL in your browser displays the **ActionRegion** page: `https://<instance>/apex/ActionRegion`.

Here, `<instance>` is the Salesforce instance specific to your organization, for example, `na6.salesforce.com`.

Entering a value in the **Base Subject** or **Account Name** field and losing focus on the field (by tabbing out or clicking into another field) updates the **Subject** field with the latest values from these fields:

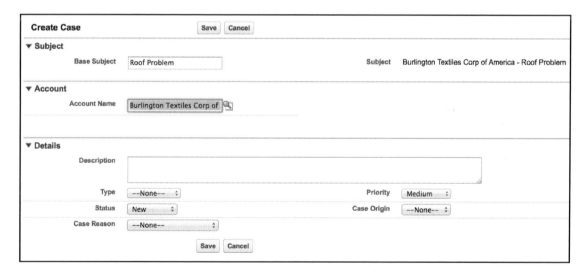

The **ActionRegion** page defines an action region for each of the fields that contribute to the **Subject** field value:

```
<apex:actionRegion>
  <apex:pageBlockSection  id="subject">
    <apex:pageBlockSectionItem >
      <apex:outputLabel value="Base Subject"/>
      <apex:inputText value="{!baseSubject}">
        <apex:actionSupport event="onchange"
          action="{!setupSubject}" rerender="subject, msgs"
          status="stat"/>
      </apex:inputText>
    </apex:pageBlockSectionItem>
    <apex:outputField value="{!Case.Subject}" />
  </apex:pageBlockSection>
</apex:actionRegion>
```

The `setupSubject` action method defined in the page controller extension concatenates the name of the selected account with the base subject and assigns this to the **Subject** field:

```
String subject='';
Case cs=(Case) stdCtrl.getRecord();

// handle the situation where the account field has been cleared
if (!String.isBlank(cs.AccountId))
{
  Account acc=[select Name from Account where id=:cs.AccountId];
  subject+=acc.Name + ' - ';
}

if (null!=baseSubject)
{
  subject+=baseSubject;
}
cs.Subject=subject;
```

See also

- The *Avoiding validation errors with action regions* recipe in `Chapter 10,` *Troubleshooting* shows how action regions may be used to submit part of a form for server-side processing that would otherwise be blocked, due to validation errors.

The Please wait spinner

When a user carries out an action that results in a Visualforce form submission, for example, clicking a button, it can be useful to render a visual indication that the submit is in progress. Without this, a user may click on the button again, or assume there is a problem and navigate away from the page. The standard Visualforce `<apex:actionStatus />` component can display messages when starting and stopping a request, but these messages are easily missed, especially if the user is looking at a different part of the page.

In this recipe, we will create a Visualforce page that allows a user to create a case `sObject` record utilizing the case standard controller. When the user clicks on the button to create the new record, a spinner GIF will be displayed. In order to ensure that we have the user's full attention, the page will be grayed out while the submit takes place.

How to do it...

This recipe makes use of a standard controller, so we only need to create the Visualforce page:

1. Navigate to the Visualforce setup page by clicking on **Your Name | Setup | Develop | Visualforce Pages**.
2. Click on the **New** button.
3. Enter `Working` in the **Label** field.
4. Accept the default **Working** that is automatically generated for the **Name** field.
5. Paste the contents of the `Working.page` file from the code downloaded into the **Visualforce Markup** area and click on the **Save** button.
6. Navigate to the Visualforce setup page by clicking on **Your Name | Setup | Develop | Visualforce Pages**.
7. Locate the entry for the **Working** page and click on the **Security** link.
8. On the resulting page, select which profiles should have access and click on the **Save** button.

How it works...

Opening the following URL in your browser displays the **Working** page:
`https://<instance>/apex/Working`.

Here, `<instance>` is the Salesforce instance specific to your organization, for example
`na6.salesforce.com`.

Populating the fields on the page and clicking on the Save button grays out the page
contents and displays a message with a spinning icon:

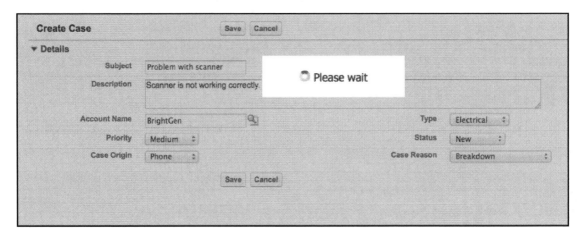

The **Working** page defines two `div` elements that are initially hidden, as follows:

```
<div id="opaque"/>
<div id="spinner">
  <p align="center"
    style='{font-family:"Arial", Helvetica, sans-serif; font-size:20px;}'>
    <apex:image value="/img/loading.gif"/> Please wait
</p>
</div>
```

The `opaque` div grays out the entire page when made visible. The style for this, and the
`spinner` div, is defined at the top of the Visualforce page.

The **Save** and **Cancel** buttons have `onclick` handlers that execute a JavaScript function that
makes the `opaque` and `spinner` div elements visible:

```
<script>
function showSpinner()
{
```

```
        document.getElementById('opaque').style.display='block';
        var popUp = document.getElementById('spinner');
        popUp.style.display = 'block';
    }
</script>

<apex:commandButton value="Save" action="{!save}"
        onclick="showSpinner()" />
<apex:commandButton value="Cancel" action="{!cancel}"
        onclick="showSpinner()" />
```

Action chaining

Action chaining allows multiple controller action methods to be executed in a series from a
Visualforce page, each in a separate transaction. This technique is rarely used, but does
solve the following problems:

- Working around governor limits; for example, repeatedly polling an external
  system to determine if processing triggered through a web service call has
  completed without breaching the limit for callouts per transaction. In this case,
  the same action would be chained to poll the external system and then update the
  Visualforce page to indicate to the user whether the action has been completed.

- Avoiding the MIXED_DML_OPERATION error when the controller must modify
  setup and nonsetup records; for example, changing a user and an opportunity
  record. In this case, the first action in the chain would modify the user record,
  while the second would modify the opportunity record.

In this recipe, we will create a Visualforce page to create an opportunity and move it
through a number of stages, with each stage transition taking place in a separate
transaction. This may be used to avoid governor limits in a situation where an opportunity
must progress through each stage individually, but the act of changing stage causes a
significant amount of processing to take place, or external systems must be updated as the
opportunity progresses.

Getting ready

This recipe makes use of a custom controller, so this will need to be created before the
Visualforce page.

How to do it...

1. First, create the custom controller for the Visualforce page by navigating to the **Apex Classes** setup page by clicking on **Your Name** | **Setup** | **Develop** | **Apex Classes**.
2. Click on the **New** button.
3. Paste the contents of the `ActionChainController.cls` Apex class from the code downloaded into the **Apex Class** area.
4. Click on the **Save** button.
5. Next, create the Visualforce page by navigating to the Visualforce setup page by clicking on **Your Name** | **Setup** | **Develop** | **Visualforce Pages**.
6. Click on the **New** button.
7. Enter `ActionChain` in the **Label** field.
8. Accept the default **ActionChain** that is automatically generated for the **Name** field.
9. Paste the contents of the `ActionChain.page` file from the code downloaded into the **Visualforce Markup** area and click on the **Save** button.
10. Navigate to the Visualforce setup page by clicking on **Your Name** | **Setup** | **Develop** | **Visualforce Pages**.
11. Locate the entry for the **ActionChain** page and click on the **Security** link.
12. On the resulting page, select which profiles should have access and click on the **Save** button.

How it works...

Opening the following URL in your browser displays the **ActionChain** page:
`https://<instance>/apex/ActionChain`.

Here, `<instance>` is the Salesforce instance specific to your organization, for example, `na6.salesforce.com`.

Filling in the opportunity record fields, setting the **Stage Name** field to **Prospecting**, and clicking on the **Save** button cause the chain of actions to execute, with each action displaying a message to indicate that the opportunity has progressed to a new stage:

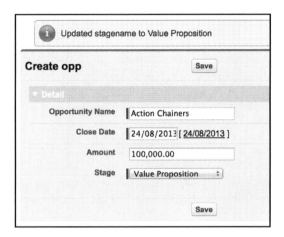

The **ActionChain** page conditionally renders one of a number of `actionfunction` components and JavaScript that executes the function based on the opportunity stage name:

```
<apex:outputPanel rendered="{!opp.StageName='Prospecting'}">
  <apex:actionFunction name="qualificationJS"
    action="{!qualification}" rerender="js,msgs,detail"
    status="stat"/>
  <script>
    qualificationJS();
  </script>
</apex:outputPanel>
<apex:outputPanel rendered="{!opp.StageName='Qualification'}">
  <apex:actionFunction name="needsAnalysisJS"
    action="{!needsAnalysis}" rerender="js,msgs,detail"
    status="stat"/>
  <script>
    needsAnalysisJS();
  </script>
</apex:outputPanel>
```

Each `actionfunction` executes a controller action method to progress the opportunity to the next stage, and rerenders the JavaScript section and any messages from the controller.

4
Managing Records

In this chapter, we will cover the following recipes:

- Styling fields as required
- Styling table columns as required
- Attaching an image to a record
- Managing attachments
- Maintaining custom settings
- Refreshing record details from embedded Visualforce
- Using wrapper classes
- Changing options based on the user input
- Changing page layout based on the user input
- Form-based searching

Introduction

One of the common use cases for Visualforce pages is to simplify, streamline, or enhance the management of sObject records. In earlier chapters, we covered how Visualforce can be used to provide a custom user interface to create and edit records.

In this chapter, we will use Visualforce to carry out some more advanced customization of the user interface-redrawing the form to change available picklist options, or capturing different information based on the user's selections. We will also see how Visualforce can be used to manage non-sObject information by providing custom user interfaces to maintain custom settings and attachments, and searching for records based on the values of specific fields.

Styling fields as required

Standard Visualforce input components, such as `<apex:inputText />`, can take an optional `required` attribute. If set to true, the component will be decorated with a red bar to indicate that it is required, and form submission will fail if a value has not been supplied, as shown in the following screenshot:

In the scenario where one or more inputs are required and there are additional validation rules, for example, when one of either the **Email** or **Phone** fields is defined for a contact, this can lead to a drip feed of error messages to the user. This is because the inputs make repeated unsuccessful attempts to submit the form, each time getting slightly further in the process.

In this recipe, we will create a Visualforce page that allows a user to create a contact record. The **Last Name** field is captured through a non-required input decorated with a red bar identical to that created for required inputs. When the user submits the form, the controller validates that the **Last Name** field is populated and that one of the **Email** or **Phone** fields is populated. If any of the validations fail, details of all errors are returned to the user.

Getting ready

This recipe makes use of a controller extension so this must be created before the Visualforce page.

How to do it...

1. Navigate to the **Apex Classes** setup page by clicking on **Your Name** | **Setup** | **Develop** | **Apex Classes**.
2. Click on the **New** button.
3. Paste the contents of the `RequiredStylingExt.cls` Apex class from the code downloaded into the **Apex Class** area.
4. Click on the **Save** button.
5. Navigate to the Visualforce setup page by clicking on **Your Name** | **Setup** | **Develop** | **Visualforce Pages**.

6. Click on the **New** button.
7. Enter `RequiredStyling` in the **Label** field.
8. Accept the default **RequiredStyling** that is automatically generated for the **Name** field.
9. Paste the contents of the `RequiredStyling.page` file from the code downloaded into the **Visualforce Markup** area and click on the **Save** button.
10. Navigate to the Visualforce setup page by clicking on **Your Name** | **Setup** | **Develop** | **Visualforce Pages**.
11. Locate the entry for the **RequiredStyling** page and click on the **Security** link.
12. On the resulting page, select which profiles should have access and click on the **Save** button.

How it works...

Opening the following URL in your browser displays the **RequiredStyling** page to create a new contact record: `https://<instance>/apex/RequiredStyling`.

Here, `<instance>` is the Salesforce instance specific to your organization, for example, `na6.salesforce.com`.

Clicking on the **Save** button without populating any of the fields results in the save failing with a number of errors:

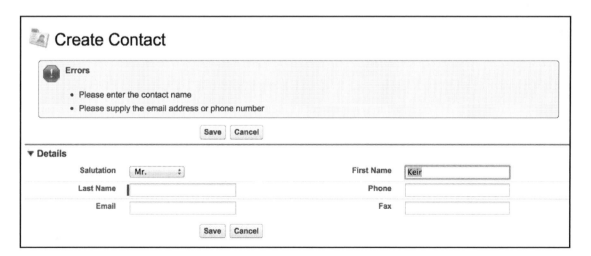

The **Last Name** field is constructed from a label and text input component rather than a standard input field, as an input field would enforce the required nature of the field and stop the submission of the form:

```
<apex:pageBlockSectionItem >
  <apex:outputLabel value="Last Name"/>
  <apex:outputPanel id="detailrequiredpanel" layout="block"
      styleClass="requiredInput">
    <apex:outputPanel layout="block" styleClass="requiredBlock" />
    <apex:inputText value="{!Contact.LastName}"/>
  </apex:outputPanel>
</apex:pageBlockSectionItem>
```

 The required styles are defined in the Visualforce page rather than relying on any existing Salesforce style classes to ensure that if Salesforce changes the names of its style classes, this does not break the page.

The controller extension `save` action method carries out validation of all fields and attaches error messages to the page for all validation failures:

```
if (String.IsBlank(cont.name))
{
  ApexPages.addMessage(new ApexPages.Message(
    ApexPages.Severity.ERROR,
    'Please enter the contact name'));
  error=true;
}

if ( (String.IsBlank(cont.Email)) &&
             (String.IsBlank(cont.Phone)) )
{
  ApexPages.addMessage(new ApexPages.Message(
    ApexPages.Severity.ERROR,
    'Please supply the email address or phone number'));
  error=true;
}
```

See also

- The *Styling table columns as required* recipe in this chapter explains how to style a column header to indicate that the contents of the column are required.

Styling table columns as required

When maintaining records that have required fields through a table, using regular input fields can end up with an unsightly collection of red bars striped across the table.

In this recipe, we will create a Visualforce page to allow a user to create a number of contact records via a table. The contact **Last Name** column header will be marked as required, rather than the individual inputs.

Getting ready

This recipe makes use of a custom controller, so this will need to be created before the Visualforce page.

How to do it...

1. First, create the custom controller by navigating to the **Apex Classes** setup page by clicking on **Your Name** | **Setup** | **Develop** | **Apex Classes**.
2. Click on the **New** button.
3. Paste the contents of the `RequiredColumnController.cls` Apex class from the code downloaded into the **Apex Class** area.
4. Click on the **Save** button.
5. Next, create a Visualforce page by navigating to the Visualforce setup page by clicking on **Your Name** | **Setup** | **Develop** | **Visualforce Pages**.
6. Click on the **New** button.
7. Enter `RequiredColumn` in the **Label** field.
8. Accept the default **RequiredColumn** that is automatically generated for the **Name** field.
9. Paste the contents of the `RequiredColumn.page` file from the code downloaded into the **Visualforce Markup** area and click on the **Save** button.
10. Navigate to the Visualforce setup page by clicking on **Your Name** | **Setup** | **Develop** | **Visualforce Pages**.
11. Locate the entry for the **RequiredColumn** page and click on the **Security** link.
12. On the resulting page, select which profiles should have access and click on the **Save** button.

How it works...

Opening the following URL in your browser displays the **RequiredColumn** page:
`https://<instance>/apex/RequiredColumn`.

Here, `<instance>` is the Salesforce instance specific to your organization, for example, `na6.salesforce.com`.

The **Last Name** column header is styled in red, indicating that this is a required field. Attempting to create a record where only **First Name** is specified results in an error message being displayed against the Last Name input for the particular row:

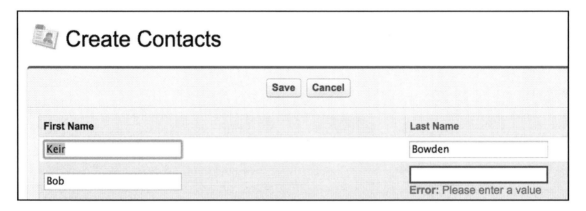

The Visualforce page sets the `required` attribute on the `inputField` components in the **Last Name** column to false, which removes the red bar from the component:

```
<apex:column >
  <apex:facet name="header">
    <apex:outputText styleclass="requiredHeader"
        value="{!$ObjectType.Contact.fields.LastName.label}" />
  </apex:facet>
  <apex:inputField value="{!contact.LastName}" required="false"/>
</apex:column>
```

The Visualforce page custom controller `Save` method checks if any of the fields in the row are populated, and if this is the case, it checks that the last name is present. If the last name is missing from any record, an error is added. If an error is added to any record, the save does not complete:

```
if ( (!String.IsBlank(cont.FirstName)) ||
   (!String.IsBlank(cont.LastName)) )
{
  // a field is defined - check for last name
```

```
if (String.IsBlank(cont.LastName))
{
   error=true;
   cont.LastName.addError('Please enter a value');
}
```

`String.IsBlank()` is used as this carries out three checks at once: to check that the supplied string is not null, it is not empty, and it does not only contain whitespace.

See also

- The *Styling fields as required* recipe in this chapter shows how to style an input field to indicate it is required without using the `required` attribute.

Attaching an image to a record

Associating an image with a record is a common requirement while implementing Salesforce, for example, adding a photo to a contact or a custom news story `sObject`. Using the standard attachments functionality creates a disconnect between the record and the image, requiring additional clicks to view the image, and often relying on the user following a naming convention when uploading the file.

In this recipe, we will create a Visualforce page to allow a user to attach an image to a contact record. The page also displays the image if one has been uploaded. This page will be embedded into the standard contact page layout.

While the size limit for record attachment in Salesforce is 5 MB, as the attachment in this recipe is rendered on a Visualforce page, it is important to keep the size of the file as small as possible to avoid lengthy download times and excessive bandwidth usage.

Getting ready

This recipe makes use of a controller extension, so this will need to be created before the Visualforce page.

How to do it...

1. Navigate to the **Apex Classes** setup page by clicking on **Your Name** | **Setup** | **Develop** | **Apex Classes**.
2. Click on the **New** button.
3. Paste the contents of the `AddImageExt.cls` Apex class from the code downloaded into the **Apex Class** area.
4. Click on the **Save** button.
5. Next, create the Visualforce page by navigating to the Visualforce setup page by clicking on **Your Name** | **Setup** | **Develop** | **Visualforce Pages**.
6. Click on the **New** button.
7. Enter `AddImage` in the **Label** field.
8. Accept the default **AddImage** that is automatically generated for the **Name** field.
9. Paste the contents of the `AddImage.page` file from the code downloaded into the **Visualforce Markup** area and click on the **Save** button.
10. Navigate to the Visualforce setup page by clicking on **Your Name** | **Setup** | **Develop** | **Visualforce Pages**.
11. Locate the entry for the **AddImage** page and click on the **Security** link.
12. On the resulting page, select which profiles should have access and click on the **Save** button.
13. Finally, add the page to the standard contact page layout. Navigate to the contact Page Layouts page by clicking on **Your Name** | **Setup** | **Customize** | **Contacts** | **Page Layouts**.
14. Locate the page layout you wish to add the Visualforce page to and click on the **Edit** link in the **Action** column.

 If there are multiple page layouts defined, choose the page layout assigned to your profile. You can view the assignments by clicking on the **Page Layout Assignment** button.

15. On the resulting page layout editor page, click on the **Visualforce Pages** link in the left-hand column of the palette, as shown in the following screenshot:

16. Drag the **+Section** option from the right-hand side of the palette and drop this beneath the **Address Information** section.

17. In the **Section Properties** pop-up, set **Section Name** to **Add Image**, select the **1-Column** radio button in the **Layout** section, and click on the **OK** button:

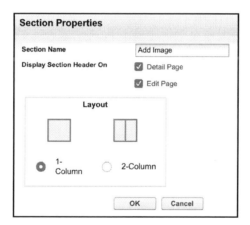

18. Drag the **AddImage** page from the right-hand side of the palette and drop this beneath the **Add Image** section.

19. Click on the **Save** button to commit the page layout changes.

20. Repeat steps 14 to 19 to add the page to any additional page layouts as required.

Only pages that make use of a standard controller may be embedded in a standard record view page.

How it works...

Navigating to the detail view of any contact record displays the new **Add Image** section. Only the **Upload** section is populated, as no image has been added to the record:

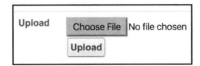

Once an image has been uploaded, this is displayed in the **Add Image** section:

The controller extension extracts the ID of the contact record from the standard controller and stores it in `parentId`:

```
parentId=std.getId();
```

When the file is uploaded, it is stored as an attachment on the record with the name of `image`:

```
public void uploadImage()
{
  att.parentId = parentId;
  att.Name='image';
  insert att;

  att=new Attachment();
}
```

The attached image is displayed using an `<apex:image />` standard component:

```
<apex:pageBlockSectionItem >
  <apex:image
       value="{!URLFOR($Action.Attachment.Download, ImageId)}"
       rendered="{!NOT(ISBLANK(ImageId))}" />
</apex:pageBlockSectionItem>
```

The controller retrieves the ID of the attached image by querying the record's attachments for one named `image`:

```
public Id getImageId()
{
  Id result=null;
  List<Attachment> images=[select id from Attachment
       where Name='image' and parentId=:parentId
       order by CreatedDate DESC LIMIT 1];
  if (images.size()>0)
{
    result=images[0].id;
}

  return result;
}
```

 Note that the resulting attachments are ordered by the `CreatedDate` field and the ID of the first result is used. This allows the user to upload a new image without having to remember to delete any existing images.

There's more...

As the controller extension deals with the ID of the record from the standard controller, rather than a specific `sObject` type, this can be used to extend any standard controller to provide this functionality.

See also

- The *Managing attachments* recipe in this chapter shows how to manage a record and its attachments from a single page.

Managing attachments

The standard mechanism of attaching files to Salesforce records navigates the user away from the record to a dedicated upload page. This leaves the user unable to see if they are duplicating an existing attachment, or see the exact details of any fields that may be required to name the attachment correctly.

In this recipe, we will create a Visualforce page to allow a user to attach files directly to a contact record, displaying fields from the record and details of any existing attachments.

Getting ready

This recipe makes use of a custom controller, so this must be present before the Visualforce page can be created.

How to do it...

1. Navigate to the **Apex Classes** setup page by clicking on **Your Name** | **Setup** | **Develop** | **Apex Classes**.
2. Click on the **New** button.
3. Paste the contents of the `AttachmentsExt.cls` Apex class from the code downloaded into the **Apex Class** area.
4. Click on the **Save** button.
5. Next, create a Visualforce page by navigating to the Visualforce setup page by clicking on **Your Name** | **Setup** | **Develop** | **Visualforce Pages**.
6. Click on the **New** button.
7. Enter `Attachments` in the **Label** field.
8. Accept the default **Attachments** that is automatically generated for the **Name** field.
9. Paste the contents of the `Attachments.page` file from the code downloaded into the **Visualforce Markup** area and click on the **Save** button.
10. Navigate to the Visualforce setup page by clicking on **Your Name** | **Setup** | **Develop** | **Visualforce Pages**.
11. Locate the entry for the **Attachments** page and click on the **Security** link.
12. On the resulting page, select which profiles should have access and click on the **Save** button.

How it works...

Opening the following URL in your browser displays the **Attachments** page:
`https://<instance>/apex/Attachments?id=<contact_id>`.

Here, `<instance>` is the Salesforce instance specific to your organization, for example, `na6.salesforce.com`, and `<contact_id>` is the ID of any contact record in your organization:

The Visualforce page retrieves the attachments associated with the contact record through the standard related list:

```
<apex:pageBlockTable value="{!Contact.attachments}"
          var="attachment" >
  <apex:column headerValue="Action">
    <apex:commandLink action="{!deleteAttachment}" value="Del">
      <apex:param name="deleteId"
        assignTo="{!selectedAttachmentId}"
        value="{!attachment.id}"/>
    </apex:commandLink>
     
```

```
<apex:outputLink
    value="{!URLFOR($Action.Attachment.Download,
attachment.id)}"
    target="_blank">View</apex:outputLink>
  </apex:column>
  <apex:column value="{!attachment.Name}" />
  <apex:column value="{!attachment.Description}" />
</apex:pageBlockTable>
```

Note that the **Del** link in the **Action** column passes the ID of the attachment to delete using the `<apex:param />` tag.

The controller extension sets `parentId` of the uploaded attachment to the ID of the contact record being managed by the standard controller, prior to inserting it into the database:

```
att.ParentId = recordId;
insert att;

att=new Attachment();

PageReference result=ApexPages.CurrentPage();
result.setRedirect(true);
return result;
```

Note that the `Redirect` attribute of the returned page reference is set to `true` to force a client-side redirect back to the same page. This causes the standard controller to be constructed from scratch, querying the latest attachments from the database.

There's more...

As the controller extension deals with the ID of the record from the standard controller rather than a specific `sObject` type, this can be used to extend any standard controller to provide this functionality.

See also

- The *Attaching an image to a record* recipe in this chapter shows how to upload an image as an attachment and display it in a record.

Maintaining custom settings

Custom settings are a natural fit for data that controls application behavior. They are similar to custom `sObjects` but are cached, and so do not have to be retrieved from the Salesforce database each time they are accessed. For more information, refer to the *Custom Settings Overview* page in the Salesforce online help. Unlike custom `sObjects`, custom settings do not have a configurable user interface provided by the platform, which can make maintenance a challenge for inexperienced administrators.

In this recipe, we will create a Visualforce frontend to an existing custom setting that allows an administrator to take an application in and out of maintenance, with an associated message to display to users.

Getting ready

This recipe makes use of a custom setting, so this will need to be created and populated before the Visualforce page can be created:

1. Navigate to the Custom Settings setup page by clicking on **Your Name** | **Setup** | **Develop** | **Custom Settings**.
2. Click on the **New** button.
3. Enter VF Cookbook Settings in the **Label** field.
4. Enter VF_Cookbook_Settings in the **Object Name** field.
5. Select the **List** option in the **Setting Type** picklist.
6. Select the **Protected** option in the **Visibility** picklist.
7. Enter Maintaining Custom Settings Recipe into the **Description** field and click on **Save**.
8. On the resulting page, click on the **New** button in the **Custom Fields** section.
9. Select the **Checkbox** radio button on the **Step 1. Choose the field type** page and click on the **Next** button.
10. Enter In Maintenance in the **Field Label** field on the **Step 2. Enter the Details** page.
11. Accept the default **In_Maintenance** that is automatically generated for the **Field Name** field.
12. Select **Unchecked** for the **Default Value** radio button and click on the **Next** button.
13. Click on the **Save & New button** on the **Step 3. Confirm information** page.

14. Select the **Text Area** radio button on the **Step 1. Choose the field type** page and click on the **Next** button.

15. Enter Message in the **Field Label** field on the **Step 2. Enter the Details** page.

16. Accept the default **Message** that is automatically generated for the **Field Name** field.

17. Click on the **Save** button on the **Step 3. Confirm information** page.

18. Next, create the instance of the custom setting that will be managed by the Visualforce page. Navigate to the **Custom Settings** setup page by clicking on **Your Name** | **Setup** | **Develop** | **Custom Settings**.

19. Locate the entry of the **VF Cookbook Settings** and click on the **Manage** link.

20. Click on the **New** button.

21. Enter VF Cookbook App in the **Name** field and leave the other fields empty.

 Ensure the **Name** field is set correctly as the Visualforce page custom controller relies on this to retrieve the custom setting.

How to do it...

1. Navigate to the **Apex Classes** setup page by clicking on **Your Name** | **Setup** | **Develop** | **Apex Classes**.

2. Click on the **New** button.

3. Paste the contents of the SettingsController.cls Apex class from the code downloaded into the **Apex Class** area.

4. Click on the **Save** button.

5. Navigate to the Visualforce setup page by clicking on **Your Name** | **Setup** | **Develop** | **Visualforce Pages**.

6. Click on the **New** button.

7. Enter Settings in the **Label** field.

8. Accept the default **Settings** that is automatically generated for the **Name** field.

9. Paste the contents of the Settings.page file from the code downloaded into the **Visualforce Markup** area and click on the **Save** button.

10. Navigate to the Visualforce setup page by clicking on **Your Name** | **Setup** | **Develop** | **Visualforce Pages**.

11. Locate the entry for the **Settings** page and click on the **Security** link.
12. On the resulting page, select which profiles should have access and click on the **Save** button.

How it works...

Opening the following URL in your browser displays the custom setting maintenance **Settings** page: `https://<instance>/apex/Settings`.

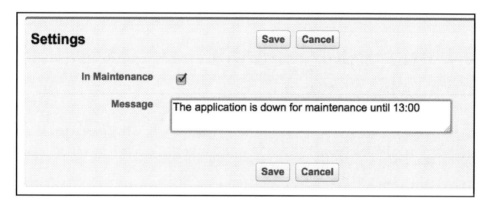

Here, `<instance>` is the Salesforce instance specific to your organization, for example, `na6.salesforce.com`.

Populating the fields and clicking on the **Save** button displays a message that the changes have been saved while clicking on the **Cancel** button takes the user back to their home page.

The custom controller defines the name of the custom setting as a `public final static` property (effectively a constant) to avoid hardcoding values in methods:

```
public final static String VF_COOKBOOK_APP='VF Cookbook App';
```

The custom controller retrieves the custom setting without consuming an SOQL query:

```
public VF_Cookbook_Settings__c settings {get; set;}

public SettingsController()
{
  settings=VF_Cookbook_Settings__c.
                       getInstance(VF_COOKBOOK_APP);
}
```

The action method executed by clicking on the **Save** button stores the custom setting through a DML `update` call:

```
public PageReference Save()
{
  update settings;
  ApexPages.addMessage(new ApexPages.Message(
    ApexPages.Severity.INFO, 'All changes saved'));

  return null;
}
```

Refreshing record details from embedded Visualforce

A Visualforce page can be embedded into a standard or custom `sObject` record view page, providing the standard controller for the `sObject` type manages it. This technique is often used to allow information to be added to a record or its related lists without leaving the view page. The Visualforce page is embedded in the record view page using an `iframe`. This means that returning a page reference to send the user to the record view page after an update results in the entire record view page being displayed inside the `iframe`, as shown in the following screenshot:

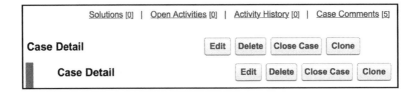

In this recipe, we will create a Visualforce page that is embedded inside the standard case `sObject` record view page and allows a case comment to be added directly from the page. Upon saving a case comment, the entire record view page will be refreshed to display the updated case comments related list.

Getting ready

This recipe makes use of a controller extension, so this must be present before the Visualforce page can be created.

How to do it...

1. Navigate to the **Apex Classes** setup page by clicking on **Your Name** | **Setup** | **Develop** | **Apex Classes**.
2. Click on the **New** button.
3. Paste the contents of the `RefreshEmbeddedExt.cls` Apex class from the code downloaded into the **Apex Class** area.
4. Click on the **Save** button.
5. Next, create the Visualforce page by navigating to the Visualforce setup page by clicking on **Your Name** | **Setup** | **Develop** | **Visualforce Pages**.
6. Click on the **New** button.
7. Enter `RefreshEmbedded` in the **Label** field.
8. Accept the default **RefreshEmbedded** that is automatically generated for the **Name** field.
9. Paste the contents of the `RefreshEmbedded.page` file from the code downloaded into the **Visualforce Markup** area and click on the **Save** button.
10. Navigate to the Visualforce setup page by clicking on **Your Name** | **Setup** | **Develop** | **Visualforce Pages**.
11. Locate the entry for the **RefreshEmbedded** page and click on the **Security** link.
12. On the resulting page, select which profiles should have access and click on the **Save** button.
13. Finally, add the page to the standard case page layout. Navigate to the case **Page Layouts** page by clicking on **Your Name** | **Setup** | **Customize** | **Case** | **Page Layouts**.
14. Locate the first page layout to add the page to and click on the **Edit** link in the **Action** column.

15. On the resulting page layout editor page, click on the **Visualforce Pages** link in the left-hand column of the palette:

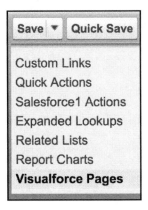

16. Drag the **+Section** option from the right-hand side of the palette and drop this beneath the standard and custom buttons.

17. In the **Section Properties** pop-up, set the **Section Name** to **RefreshEmbedded**, select the **1-Column** radio button in the **Layout** section, and click on the **OK** button:

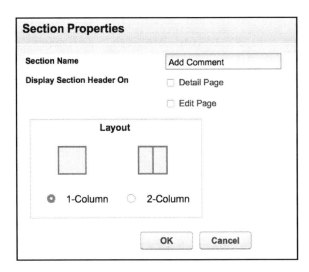

18. Drag the **RefreshEmbedded** page from the right-hand side of the palette and drop this beneath the **Add RefreshEmbedded** section.
19. Click on the **Save** button to commit the page layout changes.
20. Repeat steps 14 to 19 to add the page to additional page layouts.

How it works...

Navigating to the detail view of any case record displays the new **Add Comment** section:

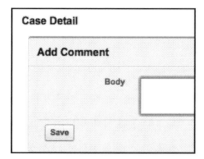

Entering a comment into the **Body input** field and clicking on the **Save** button refreshes the entire page and displays the new comment in the **Case Comments** related list:

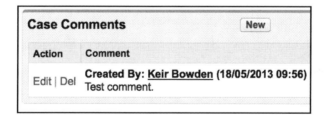

The action method invoked by the **Save** button sets a `Boolean` property to indicate that the page must be refreshed, and defines the target URL reference:

```
public PageReference save()
{
  cc.parentId=stdCtrl.getId();
  insert cc;
  refreshPage=true;
  pageRef=stdCtrl.view().getUrl();
  return null;
}
```

When the Visualforce page is refreshed, JavaScript is conditionally rendered based on the value of the `refreshPage` property to redirect the main page to the target URL:

```
<apex:outputPanel rendered="{!refreshPage}">
  <script>
    window.top.location='{!pageRef}';
  </script>
</apex:outputPanel>
```

 Note that this technique will not work when the record view is displayed in the Salesforce Service Cloud Console, as the record view is not the top-level page and thus cannot be accessed or refreshed through JavaScript.

Using wrapper classes

A common use case for Visualforce is to present a list of sObjects, allowing a user to select a number of these, and then choose an action to apply to the selected entries. Marking an sObject entry as selected presents a challenge, as it is associating transient information, the selected status, with a record persisted in the Salesforce database.

The solution is to use a **wrapper class** to encapsulate or wrap an sObject instance and some additional information associated with the sObject instance.

In this recipe, we will create a Visualforce page that presents a list of opportunity sObjects, and allows the user to select a number of records to remove from the displayed list.

Getting ready

This recipe makes use of a wrapper class which associates a checkbox with an opportunity sObject record:

1. Navigate to the **Apex Classes** setup page by clicking on **Your Name** | **Setup** | **Develop** | **Apex Classes**.
2. Click on the **New** button.
3. Paste the contents of the `SelectOpportunityWrapper.cls` Apex class from the code downloaded into the **Apex Class** area.
4. Click on the **Save** button.

How to do it...

1. First, create the custom controller for the Visualforce page by navigating to the **Apex Classes** setup page by clicking on **Your Name** | **Setup** | **Develop** | **Apex Classes**.

2. Click on the **New** button.

3. Paste the contents of the `SelectOpportunitiesController.cls` Apex class from the code downloaded into the **Apex Class** area.

4. Click on the **Save** button.

5. Next, create the Visualforce page by navigating to the Visualforce setup page by clicking on **Your Name** | **Setup** | **Develop** | **Visualforce Pages**.

6. Click on the **New** button.

7. Enter `SelectOpportunities` in the **Label** field.

8. Accept the default **SelectOpportunities** that is automatically generated for the **Name** field.

9. Paste the contents of the `SelectOpportunities.page` file from the code downloaded into the **Visualforce Markup** area and click on the **Save** button.

10. Navigate to the Visualforce setup page by clicking on **Your Name** | **Setup** | **Develop** | **Visualforce Pages**.

11. Locate the entry for the **SelectOpportunities** page and click on the **Security** link.

12. On the resulting page, select which profiles should have access and click on the **Save** button.

How it works...

Opening the following page in your browser displays the **SelectOpportunities** page: `https://<instance>/apex/SelectOpportunities`.

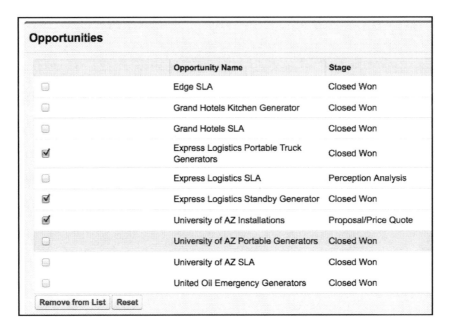

Here, `<instance>` is the Salesforce instance specific to your organization, for example, `na6.salesforce.com`.

Selecting a number of checkboxes and clicking on the **Remove from List** button removes the selected rows from the list:

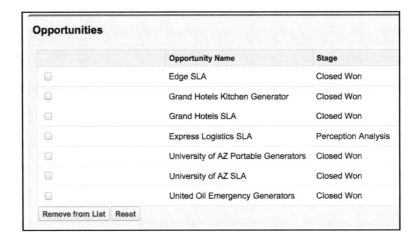

The custom controller extracts the opportunities for the page and encapsulates each of these in a `SelectOpportunityWrapper` class:

```
opps=new List<SelectOpportunityWrapper>();
for (Opportunity opp : [select id, Name, StageName
            from Opportunity order by CreatedDate limit 10])
{
    opps.add(new SelectOpportunityWrapper(opp));
}
```

The action method executed when the **Save** button is clicked iterates the list and removes any wrapper class instances where the selected checkbox property is set to `true`:

```
List<SelectOpportunityWrapper> keep=new
        List<SelectOpportunityWrapper>();
for (SelectOpportunityWrapper wrap : opps)
{
    if (!wrap.selected)
    {
        keep.add(wrap);
    }
}
opps=keep;
```

See also

- The *Changing options based on the user input* recipe in this chapter shows how a wrapper class can be used to choose options that will be displayed in a picklist.

Changing options based on the user input

In the earlier recipes, for example, *Retrieving fields when a lookup is populated* in Chapter 3, *Capturing Data Using Forms,* we have seen how to populate the contents of fields in response to user actions. This technique can also be used to change the characteristics of other input fields on the page in response to user selections.

In this recipe, we will create a Visualforce page that allows a user to create five task sObject records at once. Each task is associated with a contact selected from a picklist. The picklist options are configured through a series of checkboxes; clearing a checkbox removes the contact from the picklist.

Getting ready

This recipe makes use of a custom controller, so this will need to be present before the Visualforce page can be created.

How to do it...

1. First, create the custom controller for the Visualforce page by navigating to the **Apex Classes** setup page by clicking on **Your Name** | **Setup** | **Develop** | **Apex Classes**.

2. Click on the **New** button.

3. Paste the contents of the `SelectContactsController.cls` Apex class from the code downloaded into the **Apex Class** area.

4. Click on the **Save** button.

5. Next, create the Visualforce page by navigating to the Visualforce setup page by clicking on **Your Name** | **Setup** | **Develop** | **Visualforce Pages**.

6. Click on the **New** button.

7. Enter `SelectContacts` in the **Label** field.

8. Accept the default **SelectContacts** that is automatically generated for the **Name** field.

9. Paste the contents of the `SelectContacts.page` file from the code downloaded into the **Visualforce Markup** area and click on the **Save** button.

10. Navigate to the Visualforce setup page by clicking on **Your Name** | **Setup** | **Develop** | **Visualforce Pages**.

11. Locate the entry for the **SelectContacts** page and click on the **Security** link.

12. On the resulting page, select which profiles should have access and click on the **Save** button.

How it works...

Opening the following URL in your browser displays the **SelectContacts** page:
`https://<instance>/apex/SelectContacts`.

Here, `<instance>` is the Salesforce instance specific to your organization, for example, `na6.salesforce.com`.

The contact picklist for each task initially contains all 10 contact options:

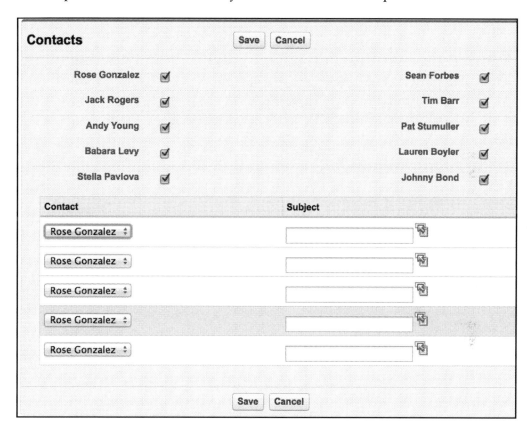

Clearing the checkboxes of a number of the contacts removes those contacts from the picklist:

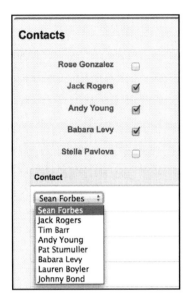

The displayed contacts are associated with their checkbox through an inner wrapper class in the custom controller:

```
public class ContactWrapper
{
  public Contact cont {get; set;}
  public Boolean available {get; set;}
  public ContactWrapper(Contact inContact)
  {
    cont=inContact;
    available=true;
  }
}
```

The custom controller creates the picklist options based on the value of each contact's checkbox:

```
available=new List<SelectOption>();
for (ContactWrapper cw : contacts)
{
  if (cw.available)
  {
    available.add(new SelectOption(cw.cont.id,
        cw.cont.FirstName + ' ' +
```

```
        cw.cont.LastName));
    }
  }
```

The **SelectContacts** page iterates the contact wrappers and renders a checkbox next to the contact name. An `<apex:actionsupport />` component is nested in each checkbox to automatically submit the form and rebuild the contact picklists when a contact checkbox is selected or cleared:

```
<apex:repeat value="{!contacts}" var="wrap">
  <apex:pageBlockSectionItem >
    <apex:outputLabel
          value="{!wrap.cont.FirstName} {!wrap.cont.LastName}" />
    <apex:inputCheckbox value="{!wrap.available}">
      <apex:actionSupport event="onchange"
          action="{!availableChanged}" />
    </apex:inputCheckbox>
  </apex:pageBlockSectionItem>
</apex:repeat>
```

See also

- The *Using wrapper classes* recipe in this chapter shows how to encapsulate an sObject record and a checkbox via a wrapper class.
- The *Changing page layout based on the user input* recipe in this chapter shows how the format of a page can change in response to user selections.

Changing page layout based on the user input

When a Visualforce form submission component specifies a rerender attribute, this causes a partial refresh of the page to take place, redrawing the specified components based on the result of the submission. This can be used to change the elements on the page based on the user input; for example, to guide the user through creating a record of a few fields at a time.

In this recipe, we will create a Visualforce page that allows the user to create an account record. If the user chooses an account type containing the word *customer*, additional fields will be rendered to capture additional customer-specific information.

Getting ready

This recipe makes use of a controller extension, so this needs to be present before the Visualforce page can be created.

How to do it...

1. First, create the custom controller for the Visualforce page by navigating to the **Apex Classes** setup page by clicking on **Your Name** | **Setup** | **Develop** | **Apex Classes**.
2. Click on the **New** button.
3. Paste the contents of the `ChangeContentExt.cls` Apex class from the code downloaded into the **Apex Class** area.
4. Click on the **Save** button.
5. Navigate to the Visualforce setup page by clicking on **Your Name** | **Setup** | **Develop** | **Visualforce Pages**.
6. Click on the **New** button.
7. Enter `ChangeContent` in the **Label** field.
8. Accept the default **ChangeContent** that is automatically generated for the **Name** field.
9. Paste the contents of the `ChangeContent.page` file from the code downloaded into the **Visualforce Markup** area and click on the **Save** button.
10. Navigate to the Visualforce setup page by clicking on **Your Name** | **Setup** | **Develop** | **Visualforce Pages**.
11. Locate the entry for the **ChangeContent** page and click on the **Security** link.
12. On the resulting page, select which profiles should have access and click on the **Save** button.

How it works...

Opening the following URL in your browser displays the **ChangeContent** page: `https://<instance>/apex/ChangeContent`.

Here, `<instance>` is the Salesforce instance specific to your organization, for example, `na6.salesforce.com`.

The page initially displays the **Detail** section for the user to fill in, as shown in the following screenshot:

Selecting any **Customer** option from the **Type** picklist causes the **Customer Information** section to be rendered to capture additional customer-specific information:

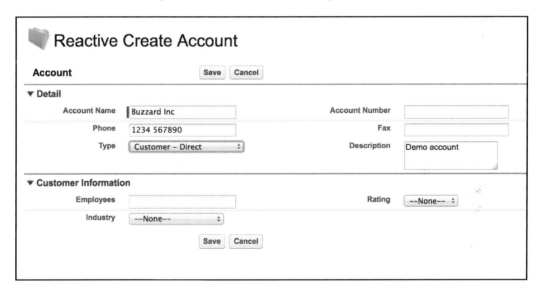

The **ChangeContent** page defines a conditionally rendered **Customer Information** section:

```
<apex:pageBlockSection
       rendered="{!showCustomerSection}">
  <apex:inputField value="{!Account.NumberOfEmployees}"/>
  <apex:inputField value="{!Account.Rating}"/>
  <apex:inputField value="{!Account.Industry}"/>
</apex:pageBlockSection>
```

The **Type** picklist contains a nested `<apex:actionSupport />` component to automatically submit the form when a value is selected:

```
<apex:actionRegion >
  <apex:pageBlockSection >
    <apex:inputField value="{!Account.Type}">
      <apex:actionSupport event="onchange" action="{!typeChanged}"
        rerender="customersection" />
    </apex:inputField>
    <apex:inputField value="{!Account.Description}"/>
  </apex:pageBlockSection>
</apex:actionRegion>
```

 Note that the **Type** field is nested inside an action region. This allows the form to be submitted even if the required **Account Name** field has not been populated.

The action method invoked when the `Type` value changes, sets the `showCustomerSection` property based on the selected value:

```
Account acc=(Account) stdCtrl.getRecord();
if (acc.Type.toLowerCase().contains('customer'))
{
  showCustomerSection=true;
}
else
{
  showCustomerSection=false;
}
```

See also

- The *Changing options based on the user input* recipe in this chapter shows how to alter picklist options based on user selections.

Form-based searching

Standard Salesforce searching looks for any occurrence of a supplied text value in all searchable fields of one or more `sObject` types. In the scenario where a user is interested in the occurrence of the text value in a particular field, this can lead to a number of unwanted results. For example, searching for an account whose name contains the text **United** will also retrieve all accounts with a mailing or billing address in the United Kingdom.

Form-based searching allows a user to specify the text that should be present in particular fields in order to be considered a match.

In this recipe, we will create a Visualforce page to allow a user to search for accounts that contain specified text in the **Account Name** or **Website** fields, or where the name entered in the **Industry** field matches one of a number of options.

Getting ready

This recipe makes use of a custom controller, so this will need to be created before the Visualforce page.

How to do it...

1. First, create the custom controller for the Visualforce page by navigating to the **Apex Classes** setup page by clicking on **Your Name** | **Setup** | **Develop** | **Apex Classes**.
2. Click on the **New** button.
3. Paste the contents of the `SearchAccountsController.cls` Apex class from the code downloaded into the **Apex Class** area.
4. Click on the **Save** button.
5. Next, create the Visualforce page by navigating to the Visualforce setup page by clicking on **Your Name** | **Setup** | **Develop** | **Visualforce Pages**.
6. Click on the **New** button.
7. Enter `SearchAccounts` in the **Label** field.
8. Accept the default **SearchAccounts** that is automatically generated for the **Name** field.

9. Paste the contents of the `SearchAccounts.page` file from the code downloaded into the **Visualforce Markup** area and click on the **Save** button.
10. Navigate to the Visualforce setup page by clicking on **Your Name** | **Setup** | **Develop** | **Visualforce Pages**.
11. Locate the entry for the **SearchAccounts** page and click on the **Security** link.
12. On the resulting page, select which profiles should have access and click on the **Save** button.

How it works...

Opening the following URL in your browser displays the **SearchAccounts** page: `https://<instance>/apex/SearchAccounts`.

Here, `<instance>` is the Salesforce instance specific to your organization, for example, `na6.salesforce.com`.

Filling in one or more of the search fields and clicking the **Go** button retrieves the **Account** records that match any of the search criteria:

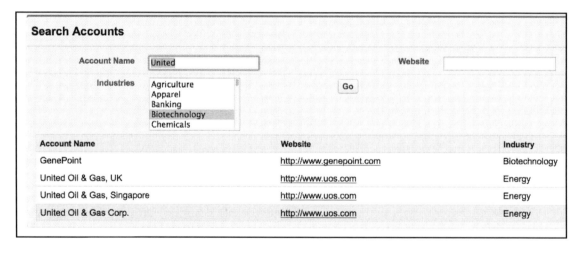

The **SearchAccountsController** page utilizes an account record to capture the **Account Name** and **Website** fields for searching. As the **Industries** picklist allows multiple values to be selected, the standard `Industry` field cannot be used to capture this. Instead, the controller interrogates the database schema to find the available options:

```
Schema.DescribeFieldResult fieldDesc =
    Account.Industry.getDescribe();
```

```
List<Schema.PicklistEntry> plEntries =
  fieldDesc.getPicklistValues();
for (Schema.PickListEntry plEntry : plEntries)
{
  SelectOption option=new
    SelectOption(plEntry.getValue(),
      plEntry.getLabel());
  industryOptions.add(option);
}
```

The action method executed by the **Go** button determines which of the search criteria fields have been populated and constructs a dynamic SOQL query to retrieve the matches:

```
if ( (null!=industries) && (industries.size()>0) )
{
  for (Integer idx=0; idx<industries.size(); idx++)
  {
    whereStr+=' OR Industry = '' + industries[idx] + ''';
  }
}
if (''!=whereStr)
{
  String queryStr='select Id, Name, Website, Industry from
    Account where ' + whereStr.substring(4);
  results=Database.query(queryStr);
}
```

 Note that a substring of the `whereStr` variable is used to generate the query, starting at position 4. This eliminates the initial `' OR '` added with the first selected industry.

See also

- The *Reacting to URL parameters* recipe in `Chapter 1`, *General Utilities* shows how to execute a text search based on a URL parameter.

5
Managing Multiple Records

In this chapter, we will cover the following recipes:

- Editing a record and its parent
- Managing a list of records
- Converting a lead
- Managing a hierarchy of records
- Inline editing a record from a list
- Creating a Visualforce report
- Displaying report data in Visualforce
- Loading records asynchronously

Introduction

When Visualforce pages utilize a controller extension or custom controller, they can retrieve additional records via SOQL queries. This allows pages to manage more than one record, regardless of the record sObject types or whether there is any relationship between the records.

 Salesforce Object Query Language (SOQL) allows information to be retrieved from the Salesforce database based on supplied criteria. It has an SQL-like syntax but does not support advanced operations such as wildcard field lists.

In this chapter, we will explore a number of scenarios to manage multiple records on a single page, ranging from a single record and its parent to a deep and wide hierarchy.

We will also see how Visualforce can be used to present details of a collection of records in response to user-specified criteria, in order to search for existing matches before creating a new record or to produce a custom report page.

Editing a record and its parent

A Visualforce page managed by a standard controller can provide the edit capability for a record and its parent. However, when the standard controller **Save** method is invoked, the object graph is not traversed and only the record being managed by the controller is saved.

In this recipe, we will create a Visualforce page to allow a user to edit fields from a contact and its parent account. Saving the record will also apply any changes made to the parent account record.

Getting ready

This recipe makes use of an extension controller, so this will need to be created before the Visualforce page.

How to do it...

1. First, create the custom controller by navigating to the **Apex Classes** setup page by clicking on **Your Name** | **Setup** | **Develop** | **Apex Classes**.
2. Click on the **New** button.
3. Paste the contents of the `ContactAndAccountEditExt.cls` Apex class from the code download into the **Apex Class** area.
4. Click on the **Save** button.
5. Next, create the Visualforce page by navigating to the Visualforce setup page by clicking on **Your Name** | **Setup** | **Develop** | **Visualforce Pages**.
6. Click on the **New** button.
7. Enter `ContactAndAccountEdit` in the **Label** field.
8. Accept the default **ContactAndAccountEdit** that is automatically generated for the **Name** field.

9. Paste the contents of the `ContactAndAccountEdit.page` file from the code download into the **Visualforce Markup** area and click on the **Save** button.

10. Navigate to the Visualforce setup page by clicking on **Your Name | Setup | Develop | Visualforce Pages**.

11. Locate the entry for the **ContactAndAccountEdit** page and click on the **Security** link.

12. On the resulting page, select which profiles should have access and click on the **Save** button.

How it works...

Opening the following URL in your browser displays the **ContactAndAccountEdit** page: `https://<instance>/apex/ContactAndAccountEdit?id=<contact_id>`.

Here, `<instance>` is the Salesforce instance specific to your organization, for example, `na6.salesforce.com`, and `<contact_id>` is the ID of any contact record in your organization:

The controller extension retrieves the related account record based on contact managed by the standard controller. If the contact does not have a parent account, a new account record is created:

```
cont=(Contact) stdCtrl.getRecord();
if ( (null!=cont.Id) && (null!=cont.AccountId) )
{
   acc=[select id, Name, Type, NumberOfEmployees, Industry
        from Account where id=:cont.AccountId];
}
else
{
   acc=new Account();
}
```

The action method invoked by clicking on the **Save** button upserts the account record, sets the parent account ID of the contact record if a new account record is created, and then delegates to the standard controller `save` action method to update the contact record:

```
upsert acc;
if (null==cont.AccountId)
{
   cont.AccountId=acc.id;
}
return stdCtrl.save();
```

See also

- The *Managing a list of records* recipe in this chapter shows how to maintain a list of sObject records of a single type.
- The *Managing a hierarchy of records* recipe in this chapter shows how to maintain a hierarchy of sObject records of different types.

Managing a list of records

Salesforce users often require the capability to work with a number of records at once. For example, a sales user may be communicating with a number of contacts, while they may also be creating or deleting contacts in response to information received through a number of channels. The Salesforce enhanced list view functionality allows a set of records that share a common record type to be inline edited but doesn't provide a way to add or remove records.

In this recipe, we will create a Visualforce page to allow a user to edit the details of a collection of existing contact records, and create or delete records dynamically. Upon saving the list, existing records will be updated, any new records will be inserted, and any records previously deleted from the collection will also be deleted from the database.

Getting ready

This recipe makes use of a wrapper class that needs to be created before the Visualforce page:

1. Navigate to the **Apex Classes** setup page by clicking on **Your Name** | **Setup** | **Develop** | **Apex Classes**.
2. Click on the **New** button.
3. Paste the contents of the `ContactKeyWrapper.cls` Apex class from the code download into the **Apex Class** area.
4. Click on the **Save** button.

How to do it...

1. Navigate to the **Apex Classes** setup page by clicking on **Your Name** | **Setup** | **Develop** | **Apex Classes**.
2. Click on the **New** button.
3. Paste the contents of the `ContactListEditController.cls` Apex class from the code download into the **Apex Class** area.
4. Click on the **Save** button.
5. Next, create the Visualforce page by navigating to the Visualforce setup page by clicking on **Your Name** | **Setup** | **Develop** | **Visualforce Pages**.
6. Click on the **New** button.
7. Enter `ContactListEdit` in the **Label** field.
8. Accept the default **ContactListEdit** that is automatically generated for the **Name** field.
9. Paste the contents of the `ContactListEdit.page` file from the code download into the **Visualforce Markup** area and click on the **Save** button.
10. Navigate to the Visualforce setup page by clicking on **Your Name** | **Setup** | **Develop** | **Visualforce Pages**.
11. Locate the entry for the **ContactListEdit** page and click on the **Security** link.

12. On the resulting page, select which profiles should have access and click on the **Save** button.

How it works...

Opening the following URL in your browser displays the **ContactListEdit** page:
`https://<instance>/apex/ContactListEdit`.

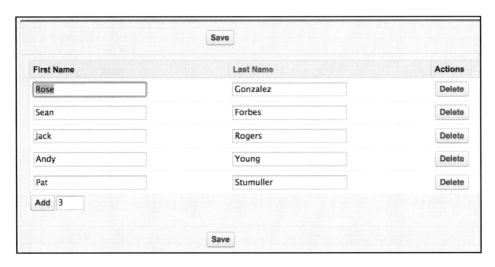

Here, `<instance>` is the Salesforce instance specific to your organization, for example,
`na6.salesforce.com`.

Each contact record managed by the custom controller is encapsulated in an instance of the
`ContactKeyWrapper` class. This ensures that both new and existing records have a unique
key, even if they have not been written to the database:

```
wrappers=new List<ContactKeyWrapper>();
List<Contact> contacts=[select id, FirstName, LastName from Contact order
by CreatedDate limit 5];
for (Contact cont : contacts)
{
   wrappers.add(new ContactKeyWrapper(mainKey++, cont));
}
```

The **Delete** button uses an `<apex:param />` component to send the key of the contact
wrapper record to be deleted:

```
<apex:commandButton value="Delete" action="{!removeItem}"
```

```
rerender="block">
  <apex:param name="keyToDelete" value="{!wrap.key}"
  assignTo="{!keyToDelete}" />
</apex:commandButton>
```

The action method invoked by clicking on the **Delete** button locates the record identified by the controller property the parameter is assigned to and inspects its id field. If this is null, the record can simply be removed from the list being managed, as it has not been written to the database yet. If it is not null, the record is not only removed from the list, but also added to a list of records to be deleted when the changes are saved:

```
for (ContactKeyWrapper wrap : wrappers)
{
  if (wrap.key==keyToDelete)
  {
    found=true;
    if (null!=wrap.cont.id)
    {
      toDelete.add(wrap.cont);
    }
    break;
  }
}
...
if (found)
{
  wrappers.remove(idx);
}
```

The user can add one to ten records to the list by entering the number of records and clicking on the **Add** button. This creates the appropriate number of instances of the ContactKeyWrapper class and appends these to the list. If the user enters a number outside this range, an error message is displayed.

Clicking on the **Save** button iterates the list of records and identifies those that have fields populated. These records are validated to ensure that all the required fields are populated. The method then executes a DML upsert for the populated records, updating existing records, and inserting new ones. The records in the toDelete list are then deleted from the database.

See also

- The *Editing a record and its parent* recipe in this chapter shows how to maintain an sObject record and its parent record from a single page.

- The *Managing a hierarchy of records* recipe in this chapter shows how to maintain a hierarchy of sObject records of different types.

Converting a lead

The standard Salesforce lead conversion page allows a user to create a new account and contact record or merge with existing records, and optionally create a new opportunity record. Information from the lead is copied to the existing or new records based on the lead field mapping configuration. If a user wishes to specify information after clicking on the **Convert** button, they must exit the conversion and edit the lead record.

In this recipe, we will create a Visualforce page to allow a user to convert a lead and in addition to creating or merging with existing records, populate additional fields on the opportunity that is created as part of the conversion.

Getting ready

This recipe makes use of a controller extension, so this must be present before the Visualforce page can be created.

How to do it...

1. Navigate to the **Apex Classes** setup page by clicking on **Your Name** | **Setup** | **Develop** | **Apex Classes**.
2. Click on the **New** button.
3. Paste the contents of the LeadConvertExt.cls Apex class from the code download into the **Apex Class** area.
4. Click on the **Save** button.
5. Next, create the Visualforce page by navigating to the Visualforce setup page by clicking on **Your Name** | **Setup** | **Develop** | **Visualforce Pages**.
6. Click on the **New** button.
7. Enter LeadConvert in the **Label** field.
8. Accept the default **LeadConvert** that is automatically generated for the **Name** field.
9. Paste the contents of the LeadConvert.page file from the code downloaded into the **Visualforce Markup** area and click on the **Save** button.

10. Navigate to the Visualforce setup page by clicking on **Your Name** | **Setup** | **Develop** | **Visualforce Pages**.
11. Locate the entry for the **LeadConvert** page and click on the **Security** link.
12. On the resulting page, select which profiles should have access and click on the **Save** button.

How it works...

Opening the following URL in your browser displays the **LeadConvert** page:
`https://<instance>/apex/LeadConvert?id=<lead_id>.`

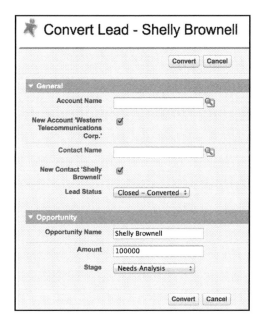

Here, <instance> is the Salesforce instance specific to your organization, for example, na6.salesforce.com, and <lead_id> is the ID of any unconverted lead record in your organization:

Populating the opportunity fields and clicking on the **Convert** button converts the lead to create new (or merge with existing) account and contact records, and redirects the user to the new opportunity record:

A case record is used as the carrier object for the account and contact information.

A **carrier object** is an sObject that is used to hold a set of fields for a page, rather than for its intended purpose. In this recipe, we need to hold references to account and contact records. While this could be achieved using Id properties, using a case sObject allows the standard <apex:inputField /> component to be used, which generates appropriate HTML markup for a record lookup:

```
<apex:pageBlockSection  columns="1">
  <apex:inputField value="{!carrier.AccountId}"/>
  <apex:pageBlockSectionItem>
    <apex:outputLabel value="New Account '{!Lead.Company}'" />
    <apex:inputCheckbox value="{!newAccount}" />
  </apex:pageBlockSectionItem>
  <apex:inputField value="{!carrier.ContactId}"/>
  <apex:pageBlockSectionItem>
    <apex:outputLabel value="New Contact '{!Lead.FirstName}
{!Lead.LastName}'" />
    <apex:inputCheckbox value="{!newContact}" />
  </apex:pageBlockSectionItem>
```

The list of available status field values for the converted lead is created by extracting all values from the `LeadStatus` database table where the `IsConverted` field is set to `true`, and creating `SelectOption` instances for each value:

```
List<LeadStatus> states=[select id, MasterLabel from
    LeadStatus where IsConverted=true];

for (LeadStatus state : states)
{
  if (null==convertedStatus)
  {
    convertedStatus=state.MasterLabel;
  }

  SelectOption option=new
  SelectOption(state.MasterLabel, state.MasterLabel);
  result.add(option);
}
```

If values are not populated for the account and contact lookup fields, the controller creates a new account and contact record. The checkboxes on the page are provided as a visual indicator to the user and the controller does not use the values:

```
if (null!=carrier.AccountId)
{
  leadConvert.setAccountId(carrier.AccountId);
}
```

If the **Opportunity Name** field is populated, a new opportunity is also created when the lead is converted:

```
if (String.IsBlank(opp.Name))
{
  leadConvert.setDoNotCreateOpportunity(true);
}
else
{
  leadConvert.setOpportunityName(opp.Name);
}
```

The additional opportunity fields are captured by an opportunity record instance in the controller, which is used to update the new opportunity after the lead conversion has taken place:

```
if (!String.IsBlank(opp.Name))
{
  Opportunity newOpp=[select id from Opportunity where
```

```
      id=:convertResult.getOpportunityId()];
      if (!String.IsBlank(opp.StageName))
      {
        newOpp.StageName=opp.StageName;
      }
```

Finally, the user is directed to one of the accounts or opportunity view pages depending on whether a new opportunity was created as part of the lead conversion or not:

```
if (!String.IsBlank(opp.Name))
{

    ...

    result=new PageReference('/' +
          convertResult.getOpportunityId());
}
else
{
    result=new PageReference('/' + convertResult.getAccountId());
}
```

There's more...

This Visualforce page can be configured as an override to the standard lead convert button:

1. Navigate to **Your Name** | **Setup** | **Customize** | **Leads** | **Buttons and Links**.
2. Locate the **Convert** entry on the resulting page and click on the **Edit** link.
3. On the following page, locate the **Override With** entry, check the **Visualforce Page** radio button, and choose **LeadConvert** from the list of available pages.
4. Click on the **Save** button.

Managing a hierarchy of records

Salesforce records often form part of a deep and wide hierarchy; for example, an account can contain a number of cases, each of which can have a number of comments associated with them. Creating and maintaining the elements of the hierarchy in isolation is a cumbersome and time-consuming task, as to add a comment a user must click through from the account record to the case record, and then click on the **New** button on the case comments related list to open the new comment page.

In this recipe, we will create a Visualforce page that allows a user to maintain an account, its associated cases, and the comments associated with those cases. The user can update or delete existing records, or create new records at any level of the hierarchy.

Getting ready

This recipe makes use of two wrapper classes that need to be created before the Visualforce page and controller:

1. Navigate to the **Apex Classes** setup page by clicking on **Your Name** | **Setup** | **Develop** | **Apex Classes**.
2. Click on the **New** button.
3. Paste the contents of the `CaseCommentKeyWrapper.cls` Apex class from the code download into the **Apex Class** area.
4. Click on the **Save** button.
5. Navigate to the **Apex Classes** setup page by clicking on **Your Name** | **Setup** | **Develop** | **Apex Classes**.
6. Click on the **New** button.
7. Paste the contents of the `CaseKeyWrapper.cls` Apex class from the code download into the **Apex Class** area.
8. Click on the **Save** button.

How to do it...

1. Navigate to the **Apex Classes** setup page by clicking on **Your Name** | **Setup** | **Develop** | **Apex Classes**.
2. Click on the **New** button.
3. Paste the contents of the `AccountCasesCommentsEditExt.cls` Apex class from the code download into the **Apex Class** area.
4. Click on the **Save** button.
5. Navigate to the Visualforce setup page by clicking on **Your Name** | **Setup** | **Develop** | **Visualforce Pages**.
6. Click on the **New** button.
7. Enter `AccountCasesCommentsEdit` in the **Label** field.
8. Accept the default **AccountCasesCommentsEdit** that is automatically generated for the **Name** field.

9. Paste the contents of the `AccountCasesCommentsEdit.page` file from the code download into the **Visualforce Markup** area and click on the **Save** button.

10. Navigate to the Visualforce setup page by clicking on **Your Name** | **Setup** | **Develop** | **Visualforce Pages**.

11. Locate the entry for the **AccountCasesCommentsEdit** page and click on the **Security** link.

12. On the resulting page, select which profiles should have access and click on the **Save** button.

How it works...

Opening the following URL in your browser displays the custom setting maintenance settings page:

`https://<instance>/apex/AccountCasesCommentsEdit?id=<account_id>.`

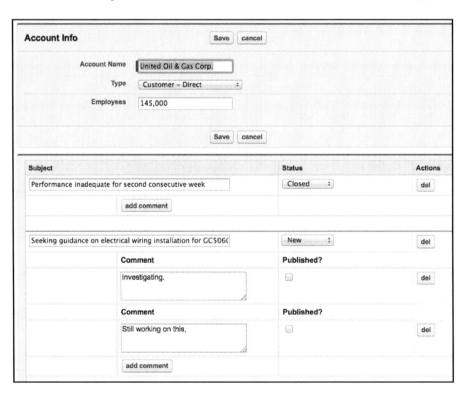

Here, `<instance>` is the Salesforce instance specific to your organization, for example, `na6.salesforce.com`, and `<account_id>` is the ID of any account record in your organization:

All case and child case comments managed by the controller are encapsulated in an instance of the `CaseKeyWrapper` and `CaseCommentKeyWrapper` classes respectively. This ensures that both new and existing records have a unique key even if they have not been written to the database. The cases are encapsulated in the controller extension constructor:

```
List<Case> cases=[select id, Status, Subject,
   (select id, CommentBody, IsPublished, ParentId from
      CaseComments)
   from Case
   whereAccountId=:stdCtrl.getId()];

caseWrappers=new list<CaseKeyWrapper>();
for (Case cs : cases)
{
  caseWrappers.add(new CaseKeyWrapper(key++, cs,
        cs.CaseComments));
}
```

While the comments are encapsulated in the `CaseKeyWrapper` constructor:

```
comments=new List<CaseCommentKeyWrapper>();
if (null!=inComments)
{
  for (CaseComment cc : inComments)
  {
    comments.add(new CaseCommentKeyWrapper(commentKey++,
                                     cc));
  }
}
```

The `commentKey` is an integer property of the `CaseKeyWrapper` class that starts at 1 and is incremented for each comment processed. This means that it must be concatenated with the key from its parent `CaseKeyWrapper` class in order to generate a unique value.

The **del** button to delete a case uses an `<apex:param />` component to send the key of the case wrapper record to be deleted:

```
<apex:commandButton value="del" action="{!deleteCase}"
rerender="list">
  <apex:param name="caseToDel" value="CS{!caseWrap.key}"
  assignTo="{!caseToDel}"/>
```

```
</apex:commandButton>
```

The **del** button to delete a case comment also uses an `<apex:param />` component, but requires the keys of both the comment wrapper and its parent case wrapper to be encoded in the parameter passed back by the controller in order to generate a unique value for the comment, as explained earlier:

```
<apex:commandButton value="del" action="{!deleteCaseComment}"
      rerender="list">
  <apex:param name="ccToDel"
      value="CS{!caseWrap.key}:CC{!commentWrap.key}"
      assignTo="{!ccToDel}"/>
</apex:commandButton>
```

The action method associated with each **del** button locates the record identified by the controller property the parameter is assigned to and inspects its id field. If this is null, the record can simply be removed from the list being managed, as it has not been written to the database yet. If it is not null, the record is not only removed from the list, but also added to a list of records to be deleted when the changes are saved.

Clicking on the **Save** button iterates the list of case wrappers, extracts the encapsulated cases, and executes a DML upsert. The case wrappers are then iterated again, and the child case comments are extracted from their wrapper class instances. The parentId field of any newly added comments will be null, so this will be set to id of the parent case:

```
List<CaseComment>caseComments=new List<CaseComment>();
for (CaseKeyWrapper wrapper : caseWrappers)
{
  for (CaseCommentKeywrapperccWrapper : wrapper.comments)
  {
    CaseComment comment=ccWrapper.comment;
    if (null==comment.ParentId)
    {
      comment.parentId=wrapper.cs.id;
    }
    caseComments.add(comment);
  }
}
```

A DML upsert operation is then carried out for the case comment records. Finally, DML operations are carried out to remove any deleted cases or comments from the database.

See also

- The *Managing a list of records* recipe in this chapter shows how to maintain a list of sObject records of a single type.
- The *Managing a record and its parent* recipe in this chapter shows how to maintain an sObject record and its parent record from a single page.

Inline editing a record from a list

In the previous recipes, all records in a list have been editable. This works well when the user is expecting to edit a number of records but is not a great experience for users that predominantly view records. In this situation, it is better to give the user a read-only view of the records and a rapid way to edit a record if required.

In this recipe, we will create a Visualforce page that presents a list of contacts in read-only mode. The user may double-click on any field in order to edit the record details. Any changes to the contact records are stored locally until the user chooses to save or discard them.

 Standard **Visualforce Markup** provides support for inline editing, but this requires each field to be double-clicked to edit individually.

Getting ready

This recipe makes use of a custom controller that must be present before the Visualforce page can be created.

How to do it...

1. Navigate to the **Apex Classes** setup page by clicking on **Your Name** | **Setup** | **Develop** | **Apex Classes**.
2. Click on the **New** button.
3. Paste the contents of the `ContactDblClickEditController.cls` Apex class from the code download into the **Apex Class** area.
4. Click on the **Save** button.
5. Next, create the Visualforce page by navigating to the Visualforce setup page by clicking on **Your Name** | **Setup** | **Develop** | **Visualforce Pages**.
6. Click on the **New** button.
7. Enter `ContactDblClickEdit` in the **Label** field.
8. Accept the default **ContactDblClickEdit** that is automatically generated for the **Name** field.
9. Paste the contents of the `ContactDblClickEdit.page` file from the code download into the **Visualforce Markup** area and click on the **Save** button.
10. Navigate to the Visualforce setup page by clicking on **Your Name** | **Setup** | **Develop** | **Visualforce Pages**.
11. Locate the entry for the **ContactDblClickEdit** page and click on the **Security** link.
12. On the resulting page, select which profiles should have access and click on the **Save** button.

How it works...

Opening the following URL in your browser displays the custom setting maintenance settings page: `https://<instance>/apex/ContactDblClickEdit`.

Here, `<instance>` is the Salesforce instance specific to your organization, for example, `na6.salesforce.com`.

Double-clicking on any of the fields changes the specific row into edit mode:

Clicking on the **Done** button applies any changes made to the record stored in the controller and reverts the row to read-only mode. Clicking on **Cancel** not only reverts the row to read-only mode but also discards any changes that the user has made.

The Visualforce page defines two sets of columns for the list of records: one set to render for records in read-only mode, and another to render input fields if the record is in edit mode:

```
<apex:pageBlockTable style="width:75%" value="{!contacts}"
var="contact" >
  <apex:column style="width:10%" headerValue="First Name"
    value="{!contact.FirstName}"
    rendered="{!contact.id!=chosenContactId}"
    ondblclick="editContact('{!contact.id}')" />

  . . .

  <apex:column style="width:10%" headerValue="First Name"
    rendered="{!contact.id==chosenContactId}">
    <apex:inputField style="width:80%"
    value="{!contact.FirstName}" />
  </apex:column>
</apex:pageBlockTable>
```

The `ondblclick` event handler for the read-only columns executes an action function that simply passes a parameter to the controller, identifying the record that the user would like to edit:

```
<apex:actionFunction name="editContact" rerender="contacts, msgs">
  <apex:param name="chosenContactId" value=""
    assignTo="{!chosenContactId}" />
</apex:actionFunction>
```

This causes the page to be refreshed and the edit-mode columns to be rendered for the record whose ID matches the `chosenContactId` controller property.

The buttons rendered in the action column for the record in edit mode are both associated with the same action method; this simply clears the value of the `chosenContactId` controller property. If the user is keeping their edits, the form submission will automatically update the details of the stored record. If the user chooses to cancel the edit, the `immediate="true"` attribute on the button will discard any data entered by the user and revert the page to display the last saved data from the controller:

```
<apex:commandButton action="{!done}" rerender="contacts, msgs"
    value="Done" />
<apex:commandButton action="{!done}" rerender="contacts, msgs"
    value="Cancel" immediate="true" />
```

Note that editing a record and then double-clicking a different row will save the outstanding edit as though the **Done** button had been clicked.

See also

- The *Managing a list of records* recipe in this chapter shows how to create an editable list of records.
- The *Managing a hierarchy of records* recipe in this chapter shows how to maintain a hierarchy of `sObject` records of different types.

Creating a Visualforce report

Salesforce provides powerful analytic capabilities through its report and dashboard builders, but there are times when reporting requirements cannot be satisfied through the standard functionality, for example, where data from a number of different sources is required to be presented in multiple formats. In this scenario, Visualforce can give fine-grained control over the layout of the results, while a custom controller allows retrieval of any accessible data in the system.

In this recipe, we will create a Visualforce report that retrieves all cases matching the criteria specified by the user and outputs these in a tabular format containing details of all cases, keeping a running total of the number of cases with the same status and origin. Two tables that provide the total count of cases for each status and origin value follow this.

Note that the replacement of the standard reporting functionality with Visualforce should only be carried out as a last resort. Coding complex reporting requirements can consume significant amounts of time and prevents users from customizing reports to their own requirements.

Getting ready

This recipe makes use of a wrapper class that needs to be created before the Visualforce page and controller:

1. Navigate to the **Apex Classes** setup page by clicking on **Your Name** | **Setup** | **Develop** | **Apex Classes**.

2. Click on the **New** button.

3. Paste the contents of the `CaseAndTotals.cls` Apex class from the code download into the **Apex Class** area.

4. Click on the **Save** button.

How to do it...

1. First, create the custom controller for the Visualforce page by navigating to the **Apex Classes** setup page by clicking on **Your Name** | **Setup** | **Develop** | **Apex Classes**.

2. Click on the **New** button.

3. Paste the contents of the `CaseReportController.cls` Apex class from the code download into the **Apex Class** area.

4. Click on the **Save** button.

5. Next, create the Visualforce page by navigating to the Visualforce setup page by clicking on **Your Name** | **Setup** | **Develop** | **Visualforce Pages**.

6. Click on the **New** button.

7. Enter `CasesReport` in the **Label** field.

8. Accept the default **CasesReport** that is automatically generated for the **Name** field.

9. Paste the contents of the `CasesReport.page` file from the code downloaded into the **Visualforce Markup** area and click on the **Save** button.

10. Navigate to the Visualforce setup page by clicking on **Your Name** | **Setup** | **Develop** | **Visualforce Pages**.

11. Locate the entry for the **CasesReport** page and click on the **Security** link.

12. On the resulting page, select which profiles should have access and click on the **Save** button.

How it works...

Opening the following page in your browser displays the **CasesReport** page:
`https://<instance>/apex/CasesReport`.

Here, `<instance>` is the Salesforce instance specific to your organization, for example, `na6.salesforce.com`.

Choosing either an option from the **Choose timeframe:** picklist or populating the **Enter custom criteria:** fields and clicking on the associated **Go** button retrieve cases that match the criteria for display in a tabular format, and also renders the case totals broken down by status and origin:

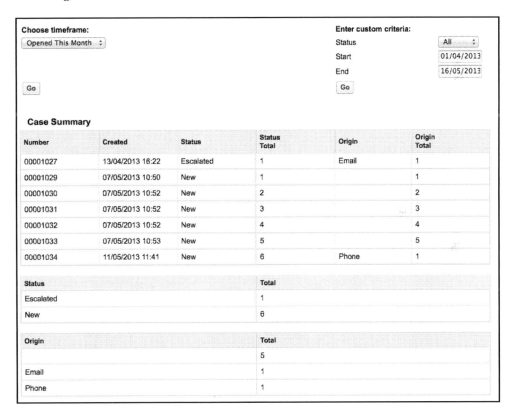

Each **Go** button has an associated action method to execute a query and retrieve the matching cases. The button associated with the **Choose timeframe:** picklist executes the `chooseTimeframe` method. As the value of each option in the picklist is an SOQL date literal, the chosen value can be bound directly into the query:

```
String queryStr='select id, CaseNumber, CreatedDate, Status,
                Origin from Case where CreatedDate=' + timeFrame +
                ' order by CreatedDate asc';
processCases(Database.query(queryStr));
```

 More information on SOQL date literals can be found in the Salesforce help at `https://login.salesforce.com/help/doc/en/custom_dates.ht m`.

The **Go** button associated with the **Enter custom criteria:** section executes the `runCustomQuery` action method; this constructs the query based on the user's inputs:

```
Date startDate=carrier1.ActivityDate;
Date endDate=carrier2.ActivityDate;
String queryStr='select id, CaseNumber, CreatedDate, Status,
                Origin from Case where CreatedDate>=:startDate ' +
                ' andCreatedDate<=:endDate ';
if (statusCriteria!='All')
{
  if ('Open'==statusCriteria)
  {
    queryStr+='and Status!='Closed'';
  }
  else if ('Closed'==StatusCriteria)
  {
    queryStr+='and Status='Closed'';
  }
}
queryStr+=' order by CreatedDateasc';
processCases(Database.query(queryStr));
```

 The custom criteria section uses task records as carriers for the **Start Date** and **End Date** inputs. A carrier object is an `sObject` that is used to hold a set of fields for a page, rather than for its intended purpose. While this could be achieved using `String` properties, using a task `sObject` allows the `<apex:inputField />` standard component to be used, which generates appropriate HTML markup for a datepicker.

Each method executes the appropriate query and delegates the results to the `processCases` method. This method updates the total number of cases for the case status and origin, encapsulates the record in a wrapper class, and adds it to the list of records to be displayed on the page.

The totals for case origin and status are stored in maps that are keyed by the status and origin values:

```
public Map<String, Integer>statusTotals {get; set;}
```

The page uses dynamic Visualforce bindings to iterate the keys from the map and output the associated values:

```
<apex:repeat value="{!statusTotals}" var="status">
  <tr>
    <td style="width:30%">
      <apex:outputText value="{!status}" />
    </td>
    <td style="width:30%">
      <apex:outputText value="{!statusTotals[status]}" />
    </td>
  </tr>
</apex:repeat>
```

 More information on using dynamic Visualforce bindings to reference Apex maps and lists can be found at http://www.salesforce.com/us/de veloper/docs/pages/Content/pages_dynamic_vf_maps_lists.htm.

Displaying report data in Visualforce

The Salesforce analytics API allows reports to be executed and the contents retrieved from Apex code. Using this technique in a Visualforce controller decouples the dataset, allowing an administrator to change the report filter criteria, altering the data that will be displayed in the Visualforce page, without having to change any controller code.

In this recipe, we will create a Salesforce report that displays account names and their associated contact names. We will then execute this report from a Visualforce controller, parse the results, and display these in a Visualforce page.

Getting ready

This recipe makes use of a custom Salesforce report that must be created before the Visualforce page and its controller:

1. Click on the **Reports** tab.
2. Click on the **New Report..** button.
3. Click on the plus icon to expand the **Accounts and Contacts** folder.
4. Click on **Contacts and Accounts** in the expanded report type list.
5. Click the **Create** button, at the bottom right of the page.
6. On the resulting page, click the **Tabular Format** entry in the preview panel and choose **Summary Format** from the menu.
7. Drag **Account Name** from the left-hand palette into the **Drop a field here to create a grouping** area.
8. Save the report into the **Unfiled Public Reports** folder with the name **VF Cookbook Accounts Contacts**.

 Ensure that the name of the report is correctly set, as the Visualforce controller uses this to execute the report.

9. Run the report and adjust the filters to display all contacts in your Salesforce instance.

How to do it...

1. First, create the custom controller for the Visualforce page by navigating to the **Apex Classes** setup page by clicking on **Your Name** | **Setup** | **Develop** | **Apex Classes**.
2. Click on the **New** button.
3. Paste the contents of the `AccountsAndContactsReportController.cls` Apex class from the code download into the **Apex Class** area.
4. Click on the **Save** button.
5. Next, create the Visualforce page by navigating to the Visualforce setup page by clicking on **Your Name** | **Setup** | **Develop** | **Visualforce Pages**.
6. Click on the **New** button.
7. Enter `AccountsAndContactsReport` in the **Label** field.

8. Accept the default **AccountsAndContactsReport** that is automatically generated for the **Name** field.

9. Paste the contents of the `AccountsAndContactsReport.page` file from the code download into the **Visualforce Markup** area and click on the **Save** button.

10. Navigate to the Visualforce setup page by clicking on **Your Name | Setup | Develop | Visualforce Pages**.

11. Locate the entry for the **AccountsAndContactsReport** page and click on the **Security** link.

12. On the resulting page, select which profiles should have access and click on the **Save** button.

How it works...

Opening the following page in your browser displays all contacts in your Salesforce instance: `https://<instance>/apex/AccountsAndContactsReport`.

Accounts and Contacts

Account BrightGen contacts:

  • Kathy Snyder

Account Burlington Textiles Corp of America contacts:

  • Jack Rogers

Account Dickenson plc contacts:

  • Andy Young

Account Edge Communications contacts:

  • Sean Forbes
  • Rose Gonzalez

Account Express Logistics and Transport contacts:

  • Josh Davis
  • Babara Levy

Here, `<instance>` is the Salesforce instance specific to your organization, for example, `na6.salesforce.com`.

Adjusting the report filters to change the retrieved contacts, for example, adding a filter that the account name must contain the text edge, and refreshing the page show that the data available to the page has been changed without updating the controller:

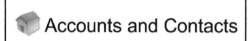

Accounts and Contacts

Account Edge Communications contacts:

- Rose Gonzalez
- Sean Forbes

The Salesforce report is executed by the controller based on its id:

```
Reports.reportResults results = Reports.ReportManager.runReport(repId,
true);
```

Each down-group grouping in the report represents an account and its related contacts:

```
Reports.Dimension dim = results.getGroupingsDown();
  List<Reports.GroupingValue> groupVals=dim.getGroupings();
  for (Reports.GroupingValue groupVal : groupVals)
  {
    String accountName=groupVal.getLabel();
```

The fact details from the grouping contain a row per contact, they are iterated to extract the first and last name fields:

```
Reports.ReportFactWithDetails factDetails =
    (Reports.ReportFactWithDetails) results.getFactMap().get(fmKey);
List<String> contactNames=new List<String>();
for (Reports.ReportDetailRow detailRow : factDetails.getRows())
{
  String contactName='';
  List<Reports.ReportDataCell> cells=detailRow.getDataCells();
  contactName=cells[fnameIdx].getLabel() + ' ' +
cells[lnameIdx].getLabel();
  contactNames.add(contactName);
}
```

The account and contact information are made available to the page in a Map, keyed by an account name containing the list of contact names:

```
public Map<String, List<String>> getReportDataMap()
```

The Visualforce page iterates the account names and outputs the associated collection of contact names as a bulleted list:

```
<apex:repeat value="{!accountNames}" var="accName">
  <p>Account {!accName} contacts:</p>
  <ul>
    <apex:repeat value="{!reportDataMap[accName]}" var="contName">
      <li>{!contName}</li>
    </apex:repeat>
  </ul>
</apex:repeat>
```

 More information on accessing Salesforce Reports and Dashboards via Apex can be found at: `https://developer.salesforce.com/docs/atlas`
`.en-us.apexcode.meta/apexcode/apex_analytics_intro.htm`.

Loading records asynchronously

In the previous recipes, all lists of records being managed by the page, or related to the record being managed, have been loaded synchronously; that is, the records have been retrieved by the controller and displayed when the page is initially loaded. In the event that the query retrieving the records is complex (and thus, time-consuming), or where the payload for the records is large due to the volume of records or the size of each individual record, this can result in a delay before the page is loaded. A delay of this nature is invariably a negative experience for the user, often leading them to conclude that the application has failed in some way.

In this recipe, we will create a Visualforce page that loads an account record prior to rendering the page for the first time, and then loads the opportunity records associated with the account asynchronously. A spinning GIF is displayed to the user indicating that the asynchronous load is taking place.

Getting ready

This recipe makes use of a controller extension, so this will need to be present before the Visualforce page can be created.

How to do it...

1. First, create the controller extension for the Visualforce page by navigating to the **Apex Classes** setup page by clicking on **Your Name** | **Setup** | **Develop** | **Apex Classes**.

2. Click on the **New** button.

3. Paste the contents of the `AsynchLoadExt.cls` Apex class from the code download into the **Apex Class** area.

4. Click on the **Save** button.

5. Next, create the Visualforce page by navigating to the Visualforce setup page by clicking on **Your Name** | **Setup** | **Develop** | **Visualforce Pages**.

6. Click on the **New** button.

7. Enter `AsynchLoad` in the **Label** field.

8. Accept the default **AsynchLoad** that is automatically generated for the **Name** field.

9. Paste the contents of the `AsynchLoad.page file` from the code download into the **Visualforce Markup** area and click on the **Save** button.

10. Navigate to the Visualforce setup page by clicking on **Your Name** | **Setup** | **Develop** | **Visualforce Pages**.

11. Locate the entry for the **AsynchLoad** page and click on the **Security** link.

12. On the resulting page, select which profiles should have access and click on the **Save** button.

How it works...

Opening the following URL in your browser displays the **AsynchLoad** page:
`https://<instance>/apex/AsynchLoad?id=<account_id>`.

Here, `<instance>` is the Salesforce instance specific to your organization, for example, `na6.salesforce.com`, and `<account_id>` is the ID of any account record in your organization.

This initially displays details of the account and the spinning GIF in the **Opportunities** section:

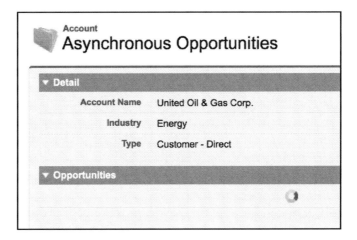

Once the asynchronous load completes, the opportunity details are rendered into the **Opportunities** section:

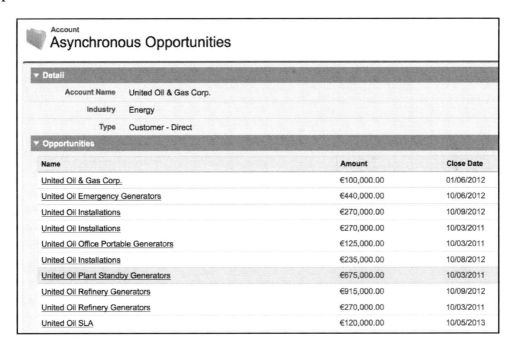

The controller extension defines a property, oppsNeeded, that indicates if the opportunities have been asynchronously loaded or not. When the page is initially loaded, an <apex:outputPanel /> component is rendered to execute an action function to load the opportunities and set the value of the oppsNeeded value to false:

```
<apex:outputPanel rendered="{!oppsNeeded}">
  <script>
    loadOppsJS();
  </script>
</apex:outputPanel>
```

> Note that in the code download the loadOppsJS() function call has been wrapped in a window.setTimeout call with a delay of five seconds to make it clear that the opportunities are being loaded asynchronously:
> window.setTimeout(function(){loadOppsJS()}, 5000);

Upon completion of the action function, the opportunities section is rerendered. This section displays a spinning GIF if the oppsNeeded property has a value of false, or the list of opportunities if the value is true:

```
<apex:outputPanel rendered="{!oppsNeeded}">
  <apex:pageBlockSection >
    <div id="spinner">
      <p align="center" style='{font-family:"Arial", Helvetica, sans-serif;
font-size:20px;}'>
        <apex:image value="/img/loading.gif"/>
      </p>
    </div>
  </apex:pageBlockSection>
</apex:outputPanel>

<apex:outputPanel rendered="{!NOT(oppsNeeded)}">
  <apex:pageBlockSection  columns="1">
    <apex:pageBlockTable value="{!opps}" var="opp"
rendered="{!oppsFound}">
      <apex:column
        headerValue="{!$ObjectType.Opportunity.fields.Name.label}">
        <apex:outputLink value="/{!opp.id}">
          {!opp.Name}
        </apex:outputLink>
      </apex:column>
      . . .
    </apex:pageBlockTable>
  </apex:pageBlockSection>
</apex:outputPanel>
```

6
Visualforce Charts

In this chapter, we will cover the following recipes:

- Creating a bar chart
- Creating a line chart
- Customizing a chart
- Adding multiple series
- Creating a stacked bar chart
- Adding a third axis
- Embedding a chart in a record view page
- Multiple charts per page

Introduction

Visualforce charting allows custom charts to be embedded into any Visualforce page using standard components; only server-side code is required. A key difference from the standard charting functionality available in reports and dashboards is that the data is provided by the Visualforce page controller and can be derived from any number of sObjects, regardless of whether any relationships between the sObjects exist.

 Visualforce charts became *generally available* in the Winter '13 release of Salesforce. Prior to this, custom charts required the use of a JavaScript framework, such as Dojo Charting or Google Charts.

In this chapter, we will create a number of Visualforce charts of increasing complexity, add a chart to a standard Salesforce record view page, and generate a number of charts on a single page, much like a standard Salesforce dashboard.

Creating a bar chart

Bar charts allow easy comparison of groups of data. A typical use in Salesforce is to view performance on a month-by-month basis; for example, to identify the effectiveness of a process improvement.

In this recipe, we will create a Visualforce page containing a bar chart that displays the total value of opportunities won per month for the previous 12 months. This allows a sales manager to view at a glance whether sales are increasing or decreasing and to identify any problem months that require further analysis.

Getting ready

This recipe makes use of a custom controller so this must be created before the Visualforce page.

How to do it...

1. Navigate to the **Apex Classes** setup page by clicking on **Your Name** | **Setup** | **Develop** | **Apex Classes**.
2. Click on the **New** button.
3. Paste the contents of the `BarChartController.cls` Apex class from the code download into the **Apex Class** area.
4. Click on the **Save** button.
5. Next, create the Visualforce page by navigating to the Visualforce setup page by clicking on **Your Name** | **Setup** | **Develop** | **Pages**.
6. Click on the **New** button.
7. Enter `BarChart` in the **Label** field.

8. Accept the default **BarChart** that is automatically generated for the **Name** field.

9. Paste the contents of the `BarChart.page` file from the code download into the **Visualforce Markup** area and click on the **Save** button.

10. Navigate to the Visualforce setup page by clicking on **Your Name** | **Setup** | **Develop** | **Pages**.

11. Locate the entry for the **BarChart** page and click on the **Security** link.

12. On the resulting page, select which profiles should have access and click on the **Save** button.

How it works...

Opening the following URL in your browser displays the **BarChart** page: `https://<instance>/apex/BarChart`.

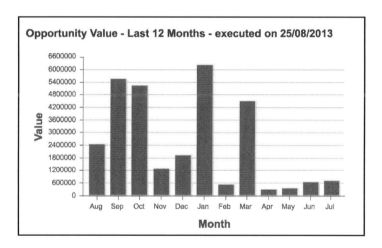

Here, `<instance>` is the Salesforce instance specific to your organization, for example, `na6.salesforce.com`.

The Visualforce chart is generated via an `<apex:chart/>` standard component, which defines the dimensions of the chart and the collection of data that will be plotted.

```
<apex:chart height="300" width="550" data="{!chartData}">
```

The bar series component defines the values from the chart data that will be used to plot the *x* and *y* values.

```
<apex:barSeries orientation="vertical" axis="bottom" xField="name"
    yField="oppTotal" />
```

 The *x* and *y* values *must* appear in every record of the chart data collection.

The axes for the chart are defined by `<apex:axis/>` components: one for the bottom axis displaying the month name and another for the left-hand axis displaying the total opportunity value.

```
<apex:axis type="Category" position="bottom" fields="name"
 />
<apex:axis type="Numeric" position="left" fields="oppTotal"
 grid="true"/>
```

The chart data is a collection of inner classes defined in the custom controller.

```
public class Data
{
  public String name { get; set; }
  public Decimal oppTotal { get; set; }
}
```

Here, the `name` property contains the month name, while the `oppTotal` property contains the total value of opportunities closed in that month.

The chart data collection is provided by the `getChartData()` controller method, which iterates all opportunities closed in the last year and adds the opportunity amount to the wrapper class instance for the month that the opportunity closed in.

```
DateTimestartDT=DateTime.newInstance(
    Date.today().addYears(-1).toStartOfMonth(),
    Time.newInstance(0, 0, 0, 0));
DateTimeendDT=DateTime.newInstance(Date.today(),
    Time.newInstance(23, 59, 59, 999));

    . . .
for (Opportunity opp : [select id, CloseDate, Amount
    from Opportunity
    where IsClosed = true
      and IsWon = true
      and CloseDate>=:startDT.date()
```

```
        and CloseDate<=:endDT.date()])
{
  Data cand=dataByMonth.get(opp.CloseDate.month()-1);
  cand.oppTotal+=opp.Amount;
}
```

In order to ensure that a bar is rendered for each month, the controller iterates the months and generates a random value for any month that has an opportunity total value of zero.

```
for (Integer idx=0; idx<12; idx++)
{
  Data cand=dataByMonth.get(idx);
  if (0.0==cand.oppTotal)
  {
    cand.oppTotal=Math.random()*750000;
  }
}
```

See also

- The *Creating a stacked bar chart* recipe in this chapter shows how to create a chart where each bar contains a breakdown of the data set.
- The *Adding multiple series* recipe in this chapter shows how to plot a bar and a line series on the same chart.

Creating a line chart

Line charts are useful to demonstrate changes in data over time. A typical use in Salesforce is to view the number of records with a particular characteristic over a period of time.

In this recipe, we will create a Visualforce page containing a line chart that displays the total number of closed cases per month for the previous 12 months.

Getting ready

This recipe makes use of a custom controller, so this will need to be created before the Visualforce page.

How to do it...

1. First, create the custom controller by navigating to the **Apex Classes** setup page by clicking on **Your Name** | **Setup** | **Develop** | **Apex Classes**.
2. Click on the **New** button.
3. Paste the contents of the `LineChartController.cls` Apex class from the code download into the **Apex Class** area.
4. Click on the **Save** button.
5. Next, create the Visualforce page by navigating to the Visualforce setup page by clicking on **Your Name** | **Setup** | **Develop** | **Pages**.
6. Click on the **New** button.
7. Enter `LineChart` in the **Label** field.
8. Accept the default **LineChart** that is automatically generated for the **Name** field.
9. Paste the contents of the `LineChart.page` file from the code download into the **Visualforce Markup** area and click on the **Save** button.
10. Navigate to the Visualforce setup page by clicking on **Your Name** | **Setup** | **Develop** | **Pages**.
11. Locate the entry for the **LineChart** page and click on the **Security** link.
12. On the resulting page, select which profiles should have access and click on the **Save** button.

How it works...

Opening the following URL in your browser displays the **LineChart** page:
`https://<instance>/apex/LineChart`.

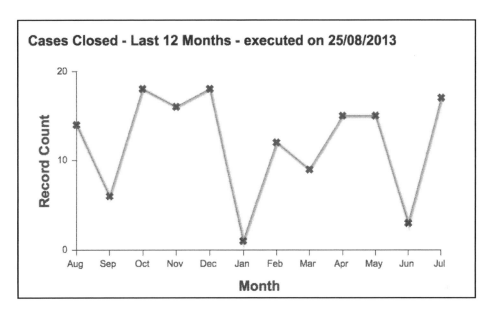

Here, `<instance>` is the Salesforce instance specific to your organization, for example, `na6.salesforce.com`.

The Visualforce chart is generated via an `<apex:chart/>` standard component, which defines the dimensions of the chart and the collection of data that will be plotted.

```
<apex:chart height="300" width="550" data="{!chartData}">
```

The line series component defines the values from the chart data that will be used to plot the *x* and *y* values, and how each point in the series should be decorated.

```
<apex:lineSeries axis="bottom" fill="false" xField="name"
    yField="recordCount"markerType="cross" markerSize="4"
    markerFill="#FF0000"/>
```

Unlike the majority of Visualforce components, no error will be generated at save time if `xField` or `yField` refers to properties that do not exist in the chart data collection. In this instance, no chart will be rendered and the browser will generate a JavaScript error.

The axes for the chart are defined by `<apex:axis/>` components: one for the bottom axis displaying the month name and another for the left-hand axis displaying the record count value.

```
<apex:axis type="Numeric" position="left" fields="recordCount"
  grid="false" steps="1"/>
<apex:axis type="Category" position="bottom" fields="name"
  />
```

The chart data is a collection of inner classes defined in the custom controller.

```
public class Data
{
   public String name { get; set; }
   publicDecimalrecordCount { get; set; }
}
```

Here, the `name` property contains the month name, while the `recordCount` property contains the total number of cases closed in that month.

The chart data collection is provided by the `getChartData()` controller method, which iterates all opportunities closed in the last year and increments the record count in the wrapper class instance for the month that the opportunity closed in.

```
DateTimestartDT=DateTime.newInstance(
    Date.today().addYears(-1).toStartOfMonth(),
    Time.newInstance(0, 0, 0, 0));
DateTimeendDT=DateTime.newInstance(Date.today(),
    Time.newInstance(23, 59, 59, 999));


    ...
for (Case cs : [select id, ClosedDate
    from Case
      where IsClosed = true
    and ClosedDate>=:startDT
    and ClosedDate<=:endDT])
{
   Data cand=dataByMonth.get(cs.ClosedDate.date().month()-1);
   cand.recordCount++;
}
```

In order to ensure that a point is plotted for each month, the controller iterates the months and generates a random value for any month that has a record count of zero.

```
for (Integer idx=0; idx<12; idx++)
{
  Data cand=dataByMonth.get(idx);
  if (0.0==cand.recordCount)
  {
    cand.recordCount=(Math.random()*20).intValue();
  }
}
```

See also

- The *Adding multiple series* recipe in this chapter shows how to plot a bar and a line series on the same chart.

Customizing a chart

Visualforce charts are highly customizable; colors, markers, line widths, highlighting, legends, labels, and more are under the control of the developer.

In this recipe, we will create a Visualforce page containing a bar chart displaying the total value of won opportunities per month for the last year.

The chart will be customized to display horizontal bars in a custom dark blue color that do not highlight when the user hovers over a bar. Finally, a legend will be displayed to show the user what the bars represent.

Getting ready

This recipe relies on the custom controller from the *Creating a bar chart* recipe in this chapter. If you have already completed that recipe, you can skip this section.

1. Navigate to the **Apex Classes** setup page by clicking on **Your Name** | **Setup** | **Develop** | **Apex Classes**.
2. Click on the **New** button.

3. Paste the contents of the `BarChartController.cls` Apex class from the code download into the **Apex Class** area.
4. Click on the **Save** button.

How to do it...

1. Navigate to the Visualforce setup page by clicking on **Your Name** | **Setup** | **Develop** | **Pages**.
2. Click on the **New** button.
3. Enter `CustomBarChart` in the **Label** field.
4. Accept the default **CustomBarChart** that is automatically generated for the **Name** field.
5. Paste the contents of the `CustomBarChart.page` file from the code download into the **Visualforce Markup** area and click on the **Save** button.
6. Navigate to the Visualforce setup page by clicking on **Your Name** | **Setup** | **Develop** | **Pages**.
7. Locate the entry for the **CustomBarChart** page and click on the **Security** link.
8. On the resulting page, select which profiles should have access and click on the **Save** button.

How it works...

Opening the following URL in your browser displays the **CustomBarChart** page:
`https://<instance>/apex/CustomBarChart`.

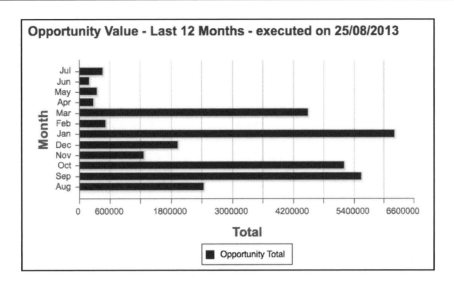

Here, `<instance>` is the Salesforce instance specific to your organization, for example, `na6.salesforce.com`.

The Visualforce chart is generated via an `<apex:chart/>` standard component, which defines the dimensions of the chart and the collection of data that will be plotted.

```
<apex:chart height="400" width="550" data="{!chartData}">
```

The bar series component defines the values from the chart data that will be used to plot the *x* and *y* values.

```
<apex:barSeries axis="bottom" xField="oppTotal" yField="name"
  colorSet="#00A" highlight="false"
  orientation="horizontal"/>
```

The following attributes override the default functionality of the bar series:

- `colorSet`: This defines the custom color for the bars
- `highlight`: This specifies whether the bar should be highlighted when the user hovers their mouse over it
- `orientation`: This specifies whether the bars should be drawn vertically (the default) or horizontally

The chart legend is created by an `<apex:legend/>` component nested inside the chart component.

```
<apex:legend position="bottom"/>
```

The axes for the chart are defined by `<apex:axis/>` components: one for the left-hand axis displaying the month name and another for the bottom axis displaying the opportunity total value.

```
<apex:axis type="Category" position="left" fields="name"
 />
<apex:axis type="Numeric" position="bottom" fields="oppTotal"
 grid="true"/>
```

The chart data is a collection of inner classes defined in the custom controller.

```
public class Data
{
  public String name { get; set; }
  public Decimal oppTotal { get; set; }
}
```

Here, the `name` property contains the month name, while the `oppTotal` property contains the total value of opportunities closed in that month.

The chart data collection is provided by the `getChartData()` controller method, which iterates all opportunities closed in the last year and adds the opportunity amount to the wrapper class instance for the month that the opportunity closed in.

```
DateTimestartDT=DateTime.newInstance(
    Date.today().addYears(-1).toStartOfMonth(),
    Time.newInstance(0, 0, 0, 0));
DateTimeendDT=DateTime.newInstance(Date.today(),
    Time.newInstance(23, 59, 59, 999));

    ...
for (Opportunity opp : [select id, CloseDate, Amount
    from Opportunity
    where IsClosed = true
      and IsWon = true
    and CloseDate>=:startDT.date()
    and CloseDate<=:endDT.date()])
{
  Data cand=dataByMonth.get(opp.CloseDate.month()-1);
  cand.oppTotal+=opp.Amount;
}
```

Adding multiple series

In the previous recipes in this chapter, each chart contained a single series. Visualforce charts are not limited to this and can plot multiple sets of data, regardless of whether there is a relationship between the data sets.

In this recipe, we will create a Visualforce page containing a chart that plots two series against the month for the last year. The first is a bar series of the number of opportunities lost in the month, while the second is a line series of the number of opportunities won in the month. This allows a sales director to see if the won/lost ratio is improving over time.

Getting ready

This recipe makes use of a custom controller, so this must be present before the Visualforce page can be created.

How to do it...

1. Navigate to the **Apex Classes** setup page by clicking on **Your Name** | **Setup** | **Develop** | **Apex Classes**.
2. Click on the **New** button.
3. Paste the contents of the `MultiSeriesChartController.cls` Apex class from the code download into the **Apex Class** area.
4. Click on the **Save** button.
5. Next, create the Visualforce page by navigating to the Visualforce setup page by clicking on **Your Name** | **Setup** | **Develop** | **Pages**.
6. Click on the **New** button.
7. Enter `MultiSeriesChart` in the **Label** field.
8. Accept the default **MultiSeriesChart** that is automatically generated for the **Name** field.
9. Paste the contents of the `MultiSeriesChart.page` file from the code download into the **Visualforce Markup** area and click on the **Save** button.
10. Navigate to the Visualforce setup page by clicking on **Your Name** | **Setup** | **Develop** | **Pages**.
11. Locate the entry for the **MultiSeriesChart** page and click on the **Security** link.
12. On the resulting page, select which profiles should have access and click on the **Save** button.

How it works...

Opening the following URL in your browser displays the **MultiSeriesChart** page:
`https://<instance>/apex/MultiSeriesChart`.

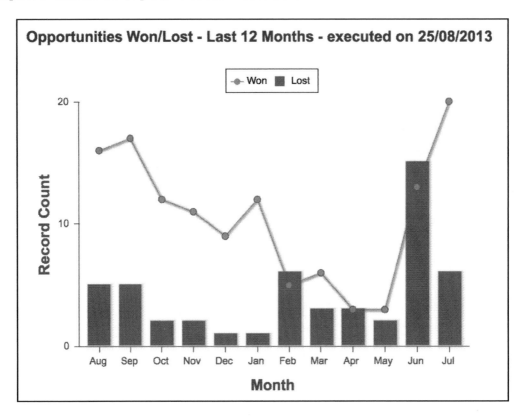

Here, `<instance>` is the Salesforce instance specific to your organization, for example, `na6.salesforce.com`.

The Visualforce chart is generated via an `<apex:chart/>` standard component, which defines the dimensions of the chart and the collection of data that will be plotted.

```
<apex:chart height="300" width="550" data="{!chartData}">
```

A bar series component defines the values from the chart data that will be used to plot the lost opportunity *x* and *y* values. The `title` attribute defines the title that will be used in the legend for the series.

```
<apex:barSeries orientation="vertical" axis="bottom" xField="name"
    yField="lostCount"  />
```

A line series component defines the values from the chart data that will be used to plot the *x* and *y* values, and how each point in the series should be decorated. Once again the `title` attribute defines the title that will be used in the legend for the series.

```
<apex:lineSeries axis="bottom" fill="false" xField="name"
    yField="wonCount" markerType="circle" markerSize="4"
    markerFill="#00FF00" />
```

The chart legend is created by an `<apex:legend/>` component nested inside the `chart` component. The `position` attribute defines the location of the legend; in this recipe, it will be displayed above the chart.

```
<apex:legend position="top"/>
```

The axes for the chart are defined by `<apex:axis/>` components: one for the bottom axis displaying the month name and another for the left-hand axis displaying the won and lost record count values. As there are multiple series being plotted against the left-hand axis, a comma-separated list of the chart data properties is specified as the value of the `fields` attribute.

```
<apex:axis type="Numeric" position="left"
fields="wonCount,lostCount" grid="true"
steps="1"/>
<apex:axis type="Category" position="bottom" fields="name"
 />
```

The chart data is a collection of inner classes defined in the custom controller.

```
public class Data
{
  public String name { get; set; }
  publicIntegerwonCount { get; set; }
  publicIntegerlostCount { get; set; }
}
```

Here, the `name` property contains the month name, the `wonCount` property contains the total number of opportunities won in that month, and the `lostCount` property contains the total number of opportunities lost in that month.

The chart data collection is provided by the `getChartData()` controller method, which iterates all opportunities closed in the last year and increments the won or lost count in the wrapper class instance for the month that the opportunity closed in.

```
DateTimestartDT=DateTime.newInstance(
    Date.today().addYears(-1).toStartOfMonth(),
    Time.newInstance(0, 0, 0, 0));
DateTimeendDT=DateTime.newInstance(Date.today(),
    Time.newInstance(23, 59, 59, 999));

    ...
for (Opportunity opp : [select id, CloseDate
        from Opportunity
        where IsClosed = true
          and CloseDate>=:startDT.date()
        and CloseDate<=:endDT.date()])
{
  Data cand=dataByMonth.get(opp.CloseDate.month()-1);
  if (opp.IsWon)
  {
    cand.wonCount++;
  }
  else
  {
    cand.lostCount++;
  }
}
```

In order to ensure that a bar and point are plotted for each month, the controller iterates the months and generates a random value for any month that has a won or lost record count of zero.

```
for (Integer idx=0; idx<12; idx++)
{
  Data cand=dataByMonth.get(idx);
  if (0.0==cand.wonCount)
  {
    cand.wonCount=(Math.random()*50).intValue();
  }
  if (0.0==cand.lostCount)
  {
    cand.lostCount=(Math.random()*50).intValue();
  }
}
```

See also

- The *Creating a bar chart* recipe in this chapter shows how to plot a data set as a series of bars.
- The *Creating a line chart* recipe in this chapter shows how to plot a data set as a line.

Creating a stacked bar chart

Stacked bar charts allow the contributing parts of data to be compared to the whole. An example of this is displaying a bar that represents the total number of opportunities that are currently open, with sections of the bar displaying the count of opportunity records that are in each stage of the sales process.

In this recipe, we will create a Visualforce page containing a stacked bar chart where each bar displays the total opportunity value that closed that month, both won and lost, for the last 12 months. Each bar is divided into two segments: the lower segment shows the total value of opportunities lost in a month, while the upper segment shows the total value won.

Getting ready

This recipe makes use of a custom controller, so this must be present before the Visualforce page can be created.

How to do it...

1. Navigate to the **Apex Classes** setup page by clicking on **Your Name** | **Setup** | **Develop** | **Apex Classes**.
2. Click on the **New** button.
3. Paste the contents of the `StackedBarChartController.cls` Apex class from the code download into the **Apex Class** area.
4. Click on the **Save** button.
5. Navigate to the Visualforce setup page by clicking on **Your Name** | **Setup** | **Develop** | **Pages**.
6. Click on the **New** button.
7. Enter **StackedBarChart** in the **Label** field.

8. Accept the default **StackedBarChart** that is automatically generated for the **Name** field.
9. Paste the contents of the `StackedBarChart.page` file from the code download into the **Visualforce Markup** area and click on the **Save** button.
10. Navigate to the Visualforce setup page by clicking on **Your Name** | **Setup** | **Develop** | **Pages**.
11. Locate the entry for the **StackedBarChart** page and click on the **Security** link.
12. On the resulting page, select which profiles should have access and click on the **Save** button.

How it works...

Opening the following URL in your browser displays the custom maintenance settings page: `https://<instance>/apex/StackedBarChart`.

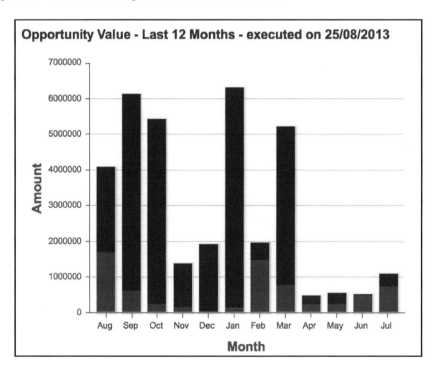

Here, `<instance>` is the Salesforce instance specific to your organization, for example, `na6.salesforce.com`.

The Visualforce chart is generated via an `<apex:chart/>` standard component, which defines the dimensions of the chart and the collection of data that will be plotted.

```
<apex:chart height="450" width="550" data="{!chartData}">
```

A bar series component defines the values from the chart data that will be used to plot the won/lost opportunity *x* and *y* values. Setting the `stacked` attribute to `true` specifies that the values should be stacked on top of each other in a single bar. Setting the `stacked` attribute to `false` causes the bars to be rendered side by side as shown in the following screenshot:

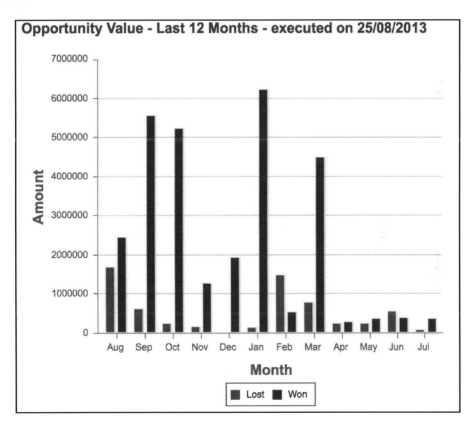

As this component is generating a stacked bar chart, the `yField` attribute contains comma-separated values for all segments of the bar, in this case, the lost and won opportunity totals.

```
<apex:barSeriescolorSet="#A00,#00A" orientation="vertical"
    axis="bottom" xField="name"
    yField="lostTotal,wonTotal"
     stacked="true"/>
```

The `colorSet` and `title` attributes also contain comma-separated values for each bar segment. The `colorSet` attribute defines the color to apply to each segment, while the `title` attribute defines the text to be displayed in the legend for each segment.

The colors in the `colorSet` attribute are specified as **RGB (Red, Green, Blue)** values, where `#A00` equates to a dark red color and `#00A` equates to a dark blue color.

The chart legend is created by an `<apex:legend/>` component nested inside the chart component. The `position` attribute defines the location of the legend; in this recipe, it will be displayed below the chart.

```
<apex:legend position="bottom"/>
```

The axes for the chart are defined by `<apex:axis/>` components: one for the bottom axis displaying the month name and another for the left-hand axis displaying the won and lost total values. As a stacked bar series is being plotted against the left-hand axis, a comma-separated list of the chart data properties is specified as the value of the `fields` attribute.

```
<apex:axis type="Category" position="bottom" fields="name"
    />
<apex:axis type="Numeric" position="left"
fields="wonTotal,lostTotal"
grid="true"/>
```

The chart data is a collection of inner classes defined in the custom controller.

```
public class Data
{
  public String name { get; set; }
  publicDecimalwonTotal { get; set; }
  publicDecimallostTotal { get; set; }
}
```

Here, the name property contains the month name, the wonTotal property contains the total value of opportunities won in that month, and the lostTotal property contains the total value of opportunities lost in that month.

The chart data collection is provided by the getChartData() controller method, which iterates all opportunities closed in the last year and applies the opportunity value to the appropriate won or lost property in the wrapper class instance for the month that the opportunity closed in.

```
DateTimestartDT=DateTime.newInstance(
    Date.today().addYears(-1).toStartOfMonth(),
    Time.newInstance(0, 0, 0, 0));
DateTimeendDT=DateTime.newInstance(Date.today(),
    Time.newInstance(23, 59, 59, 999));


    ...
for (Opportunity opp : [select id, CloseDate, Amount
        from Opportunity
        where IsClosed = true
          and CloseDate>=:startDT.date()
        and CloseDate<=:endDT.date()])
{
  Data cand=dataByMonth.get(opp.CloseDate.month()-1);
  if (opp.IsWon)
  {
    cand.wonTotal+=opp.Amount;
  }
  else
  {
    cand.lostTotal+=opp.Amount;
  }
}
```

In order to ensure that a stacked bar is plotted for each month, the controller iterates the months and generates a random value for any month that has a won or lost total of zero.

```
for (Integer idx=0; idx<12; idx++)
{
  Data cand=dataByMonth.get(idx);
  if (0.0==cand.wonTotal)
  {
    cand.wonTotal=(Math.random()*750000).intValue();
  }
  if (0.0==cand.lostTotal)
  {
    cand.lostTotal=(Math.random()*750000).intValue();
  }
```

```
}
```

See also

- The *Creating a bar chart* recipe in this chapter shows how to plot a data set as a series of bars.
- The *Adding multiple series* recipe in this chapter shows how to plot a line and a bar series on the same chart.

Adding a third axis

Plotting multiple series on a single graph can be problematic if the values of the two series vary widely. For example, if the total value of won opportunities were plotted against the record count of won opportunities, the total value number would likely be several hundred thousand times the record count number. Plotting these on a single chart would result in the record count plot being so close to zero as to be indistinguishable from it.

The solution to this problem is to display the third axis. The axis is scaled appropriately to the data set that is plotted against it.

In this recipe, we will create a Visualforce page containing a chart that displays the total value of the won and lost opportunities per month for the last year. The won/lost information is displayed as a stacked bar chart. The chart also displays a line series chart where each point on the line series is the number of opportunities that were won/lost in that month. As the number of opportunities will be considerably lower than the total value, a third axis is added for the opportunity number values.

Getting ready

This recipe makes use of a custom controller that must be present before the Visualforce page can be created.

How to do it...

1. Navigate to the **Apex Classes** setup page by clicking on **Your Name** | **Setup** | **Develop** | **Apex Classes**.
2. Click on the **New** button.
3. Paste the contents of the `MultiAxisChartController.cls` Apex class from the code download into the **Apex Class** area.

4. Click on the **Save** button.
5. Next, create the Visualforce page by navigating to the Visualforce setup page by clicking on **Your Name** | **Setup** | **Develop** | **Pages**.
6. Click on the **New** button.
7. Enter `MultiAxisChart` in the **Label** field.
8. Accept the default **MultiAxisChart** that is automatically generated for the **Name** field.
9. Paste the contents of the `MultiAxisChart.page` file from the code download into the **Visualforce Markup** area and click on the **Save** button.
10. Navigate to the Visualforce setup page by clicking on **Your Name** | **Setup** | **Develop** | **Pages**.
11. Locate the entry for the **MultiAxisChart** page and click on the **Security** link.
12. On the resulting page, select which profiles should have access and click on the **Save** button.

How it works...

Opening the following URL in your browser displays the **MultiAxisChart** page: `https://<instance>/apex/MultiAxisChart`.

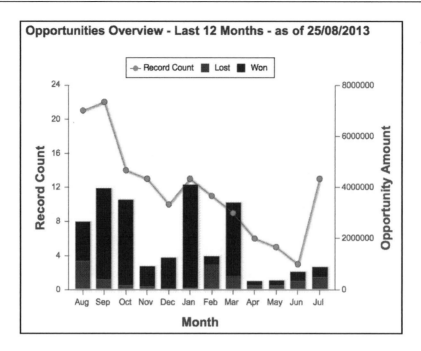

Here, `<instance>` is the Salesforce instance specific to your organization, for example, `na6.salesforce.com`.

The Visualforce chart is generated via an `<apex:chart/>` standard component, which defines the dimensions of the chart and the collection of data that will be plotted.

```
<apex:chart height="450" width="550" data="{!chartData}">
```

A bar series component defines the values from the chart data that will be used to plot the won/lost opportunity *x* and *y* values. Setting the `stacked` attribute to `true` specifies that the values should be stacked on top of each other in a single bar.

As this component is generating a stacked bar chart, the `yField` attribute contains comma-separated values for all segments of the bar, in this case, the lost and won opportunity totals.

```
<apex:barSeriescolorSet="#A00,#00A" orientation="vertical"
      axis="bottom" xField="name"
      yField="lostAmount,wonAmount"
       stacked="true"/>
```

The `colorSet` and `title` attributes also contain comma-separated values for each bar segment. The `colorSet` attribute defines the color to apply to each segment, while the `title` attribute defines the text to be displayed in the legend for each segment.

A line series component defines the values from the chart data that will be used to plot the *x* and *y* values, and how each point in the series should be decorated. Once again the `title` attribute defines the title that will be used in the legend for the series.

```
<apex:lineSeries axis="bottom" fill="false" xField="name"
    yField="recordCount"markerType="circle"
    markerSize="4" markerFill="#00FF00"
    />
```

The axes for the chart are defined by `<apex:axis/>` components: one for the bottom axis displaying the month name, one for the left-hand axis displaying the opportunity record count, and one for the right-hand axis displaying the won/lost total values. As a stacked bar series is being plotted against the right-hand axis, a comma-separated list of the chart data properties is specified as the value of the `fields` attribute.

```
<apex:axis type="Category" position="bottom" fields="name"
 />
<apex:axis type="Numeric" position="left" fields="recordCount"
 grid="false" steps="5"/>
<apex:axis type="Numeric" position="right"
fields="wonAmount,lostAmount"
 grid="false" steps="5"/>
```

The chart data is a collection of inner classes defined in the custom controller.

```
public class Data
{
   public String name { get; set; }
   publicDecimallostAmount { get; set; }
   publicDecimalwonAmount { get; set; }
   publicIntegerrecordCount { get; set; }
}
```

Here, the `name` property contains the month name, the `wonAmount` property contains the total value of opportunities won in that month, the `lostAmount` property contains the total value of opportunities lost in that month, and the `recordCount` property contains the number of opportunities won/lost in that month.

The chart data collection is provided by the getChartData() controller method, which iterates all opportunities closed in the last year, applies the opportunity value to the appropriate won or lost property in the wrapper class instance for the month that the opportunity closed in, and increments the opportunity record count:

```
DateTimestartDT=DateTime.newInstance(
    Date.today().addYears(-1).toStartOfMonth(),
    Time.newInstance(0, 0, 0, 0));
DateTimeendDT=DateTime.newInstance(Date.today(),
    Time.newInstance(23, 59, 59, 999));


    ...
for (Opportunity opp : [select id, CloseDate, Amount
        from Opportunity
        where IsClosed = true
        and CloseDate>=:startDT.date()
        and CloseDate<=:endDT.date()])
{
  Data cand=dataByMonth.get(opp.CloseDate.month()-1);
  if (opp.IsWon)
  {
    cand.wonAmount+=opp.Amount;
  }
  else
  {
    cand.lostAmount+=opp.Amount;
  }
  cand.recordCount+=opp.Amount;
}
```

In order to ensure that a stacked bar and point are plotted for each month, the controller iterates the months and generates a random value for any month that has a won total, lost total, or record count of zero.

```
for (Integer idx=0; idx<12; idx++)
{
  Data cand=dataByMonth.get(idx);
  if (0.0==cand.wonAmount)
  {
    cand.wonAmount=(Math.random()*750000).intValue();
  }
  if (0.0==cand.lostAmount)
  {
    cand.lostAmount=(Math.random()*750000).intValue();
  }
  if (0.0==cand.recordCount)
  {
```

```
        cand.recordCount=(Math.random()*20).intValue();
    }
}
```

See also

- The *Adding multiple series* recipe in this chapter shows how to plot a line and a bar series on the same chart.

Embedding a chart in a record view page

Visualforce charts can be generated wherever a Visualforce page can be displayed, including sidebar components, the homepage, and in standard record view pages.

In this recipe, we will create a Visualforce page containing a chart that displays a stacked bar chart that contains the total number of activities carried out with a contact per month for the last year. The stacked bars contain a segment for the events and tasks that make up the activity total. This Visualforce page is embedded into the standard contact record view page to allow a sales manager to see at a glance whether a contact is being neglected or receiving more than its fair share of attention.

Getting ready

This recipe makes use of a controller extension that must be present before the Visualforce page can be created.

How to do it...

1. First, create the controller extension for the Visualforce page by navigating to the **Apex Classes** setup page by clicking on **Your Name** | **Setup** | **Develop** | **Apex Classes**.
2. Click on the **New** button.
3. Paste the contents of the ContactActivitiesChartExt.cls Apex class from the code download into the **Apex Class** area.

1. Click on the **Save** button.
2. Next, create the Visualforce page by navigating to the Visualforce setup page by clicking on **Your Name** | **Setup** | **Develop** | **Pages**.
3. Click on the **New** button.
4. Enter ContactActivitiesChart in the **Label** field.
5. Accept the default **ContactActivitiesChart** that is automatically generated for the **Name** field.
6. Paste the contents of the ContactActivitiesChart.page file from the code download into the **Visualforce Markup** area and click on the **Save** button.
7. Navigate to the Visualforce setup page by clicking on **Your Name** | **Setup** | **Develop** | **Pages**.
8. Locate the entry for the **ContactActivitiesChart** page and click on the **Security** link.
9. On the resulting page, select which profiles should have access and click on the **Save** button.
10. Finally, add the page to the standard contact page layout. Navigate to the Contact Page Layouts page by clicking on **Your Name** | **Setup** | **Customize** | **Contact** | **Page Layouts**.
11. Locate the first page layout to add the page to and click on the **Edit** link in the **Action** column.
12. On the resulting page layout editor page, click on the **Visualforce Pages** link in the left-hand column of the palette, as shown in the following screenshot:

16. Drag the **+Section** option from the right-hand side of the palette and drop this beneath the standard and custom buttons.

17. In the **Section Properties** pop-up, set the **Section Name** to `Activities Last 12 Months`, select the **1-Column** radio button in the **Layout** section, and click on the **OK** button, as shown in the following screenshot:

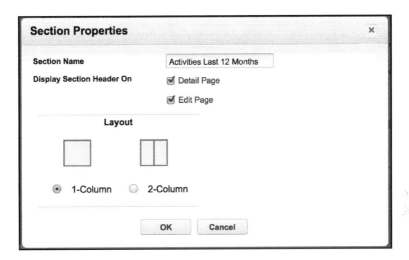

18. Drag the **ContactActivitiesChart** page from the right-hand side of the palette and drop this beneath the **Activities Last 12 Months** section.

19. Click on the **Save** button to commit the page layout changes.

20. Repeat steps 14 to 19 to add the Visualforce page to additional page layouts as required.

How it works...

Navigating to the record view page of any contact in your Salesforce instance displays the contact detail page with the new **Activities Last 12 Months** section as shown in the following screenshot:

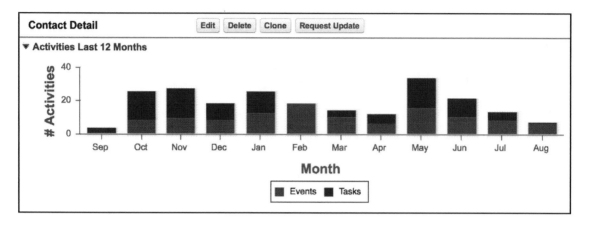

The Visualforce chart is generated via an `<apex:chart/>` standard component, which defines the dimensions of the chart and the collection of data that will be plotted.

```
<apex:chart height="200" width="100%" data="{!chartData}">
```

A bar series component defines the values from the chart data that will be used to plot the won/lost opportunity *x* and *y* values. Setting the `stacked` attribute to `true` specifies that the values should be stacked on top of each other in a single bar.

As this component is generating a stacked bar chart, the `yField` attribute contains comma-separated values for all segments of the bar, in this case, the event and task record counts.

```
<apex:barSeriescolorSet="#A00,#00A" orientation="vertical"
  axis="bottom" xField="name" yField="events,tasks"
    stacked="true"/>
```

The `colorSet` and `title` attributes also contain comma-separated values for each bar segment. The `colorSet` attribute defines the color to apply to each segment, while the `title` attribute defines the text to be displayed in the legend for each segment.

The axes for the chart are defined by `<apex:axis/>` components: one for the bottom axis displaying the month name and another for the left-hand axis displaying the activity record count. As a stacked bar series is being plotted against the right-hand axis, a comma-separated list of the chart data properties is specified as the value of the `fields` attribute.

```
<apex:axis type="Category" position="bottom" fields="name"
/>
<apex:axis type="Numeric" position="left" fields="events,tasks"
 grid="false" steps="1"/>
```

The chart data is a collection of inner classes defined in the custom controller.

```
public class Data
{
  public String name { get; set; }
  public Integer events { get; set; }
  public Integer tasks { get; set; }
}
```

Here, the `name` property contains the month name, the `events` property contains the event record count for the month, and the `tasks` property contains the task record count for the month.

The chart data collection is provided by the `getChartData()` controller method, which iterates all events and tasks associated with the contact in the last year, and increments the appropriate record count property in the wrapper class instance for the month that the activity took place in.

```
DateTimestartDT=DateTime.newInstance(
    Date.today().addYears(-1).toStartOfMonth(),
    Time.newInstance(0, 0, 0, 0));
DateTimeendDT=DateTime.newInstance(Date.today(),
    Time.newInstance(23, 59, 59, 999));

    ...
for (Event ev : [select id , EndDateTime
    from Event where WhoId=:cont.id
    and EndDateTime>=:startDT
    and EndDateTime<=:endDT])
{
  Data cand=dataByMonth.get(ev.EndDateTime.date().month()-1);
  cand.events++;
```

```
    }
    for (Task ts : [select id, ActivityDate
          from Task where WhoId=:cont.id
          and ActivityDate>=:startDT.date()
          and ActivityDate<=:endDT.date()])
    {
      Data cand=dataByMonth.get(ts.ActivityDate.month()-1);
      cand.tasks++;
    }
```

In order to ensure that a stacked bar is plotted for each month, the controller iterates the months and generates a random value for any month that has a task or activity count of zero.

```
    for (Integer idx=0; idx<12; idx++)
    {
      Data cand=dataByMonth.get(idx);
      if (0==cand.events)
      {
        cand.events=(Math.random()*20).intValue();
      }
      if (0==cand.tasks)
      {
        cand.tasks=(Math.random()*20).intValue();
      }
    }
```

Multiple charts per page

A common use case for Visualforce charting is producing a number of custom charts arranged into rows and columns, much like a standard dashboard. Simply adding chart components to HTML table cells results in all the charts being displayed in the top-left cell of the table, as shown in the following screenshot:

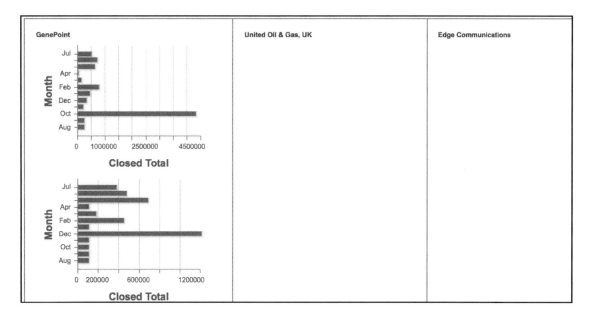

The solution to this is to use the chart `renderTo` attribute to specify the DOM component that the chart should be rendered inside.

In this recipe, we will create a Visualforce page that displays a table of bar charts. Each bar chart displays the total won opportunity value per month for the last year for a specific account.

Getting ready

This recipe makes use of a custom controller, so this will need to be present before the Visualforce page can be created.

How to do it...

1. First, create the custom controller for the Visualforce page by navigating to the **Apex Classes** setup page by clicking on **Your Name** I **Setup** I **Develop** I **Apex Classes**.
2. Click on the **New** button.
3. Paste the contents of the `ChartTableController.cls` Apex class from the code download into the **Apex Class** area.
4. Click on the **Save** button.
5. Next, create the Visualforce page by navigating to the Visualforce setup page by clicking on **Your Name** I **Setup** I **Develop** I **Pages**.
6. Click on the **New** button.
7. Enter `ChartTable` in the **Label** field.
8. Accept the default **ChartTable** that is automatically generated for the **Name** field.
9. Paste the contents of the `ChartTable.page` file from the code download into the **Visualforce Markup** area and click on the **Save** button.
10. Navigate to the Visualforce setup page by clicking on **Your Name** I **Setup** I **Develop** I **Pages**.
11. Locate the entry for the **ChartTable** page and click on the **Security** link.
12. On the resulting page, select which profiles should have access and click on the **Save** button.

How it works...

Opening the following URL in your browser displays the **ChartTable** page:
`https://<instance>/apex/ChartTable`.

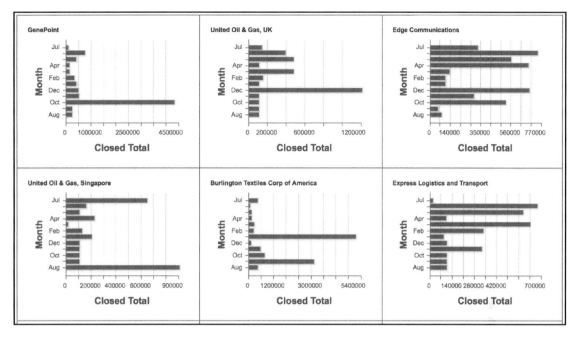

Here, `<instance>` is the Salesforce instance specific to your organization, for example, `na6.salesforce.com`.

The Visualforce charts are generated via a `<apex:chart/>` standard components in an HTML table. Each chart is nested in a `div` element that the chart is rendered to.

```
<div id="CHART{!chart.idx}">
  <apex:chart height="230" width="300" data="{!chart.months}"
      renderto="CHART{!chart.idx}">
```

A bar series component defines the values from the chart data that will be used to plot the won opportunity *x* and *y* values.

```
<apex:barSeries orientation="horizontal" axis="left"
      xField="oppTotal" yField="name" />
```

The axes for the chart are defined by `<apex:axis/>` components: one for the bottom axis displaying the month name and another for the left-hand axis displaying the won opportunity value.

```
<apex:axis type="Category" position="left" fields="name"
      />
<apex:axis type="Numeric" position="bottom" fields="oppTotal"
      grid="true"/>
```

The data is a collection of inner classes defined in the custom controller.

```
public class MonthData
{
  public String name { get; set; }
  public Decimal oppTotal { get; set; }
}
```

A second inner class associates a collection of the `MonthData` records with a unique index and the name of the account.

```
public class ChartData
{
  public Integer idx {get; set;}
  public String name {get; set;}
  public List<MonthData>months {get; set;}
}
```

A third and final inner class encapsulate a number of the `ChartData` instances in a collection. This class is used to generate a single row in the chart table.

```
public class Row
{
  public List<ChartData> charts {get; set;}
  public Row()
  {
    charts=new List<ChartData>();
  }
}
```

The chart data collection is provided by the `getRows()` controller method, which queries nine accounts and generates three rows of chart data, each containing chart data for three accounts.

```
for (Account acc : [select id, name from Account order by
                CreatedDate limit 9])
{
  if (0==Math.mod(idx,3))
```

```
    {
      row=new Row();
      result.add(row);
    }
    row.charts.add(getAccountChartData(idx++, acc));
}
```

The `getAccountChartData()` method iterates the opportunities won for the account over the last year and adds the opportunity amount to the wrapper class instance for the month that the opportunity was closed in.

```
DateTimestartDT=DateTime.newInstance(
    Date.today().addYears(-1).toStartOfMonth(),
    Time.newInstance(0, 0, 0, 0));
DateTimeendDT=DateTime.newInstance(Date.today(),
    Time.newInstance(23, 59, 59, 999));

    ...
for (Opportunity opp : [select id, CloseDate, Amount
        from Opportunity
        where AccountId=:acc.Id
        and IsClosed = true
        and IsWon = true
        and CloseDate>=:startDT.date()
        and CloseDate<=:endDT.date()])
{
   MonthDatacand=dataByMonth.get(opp.CloseDate.month()-1);
   cand.oppTotal+=opp.Amount;
}
```

In order to ensure that a bar is plotted for each month per account, the controller iterates the months and generates a random value for any month that has an opportunity total of zero.

```
for (Integer idx=0; idx<12; idx++)
{
   MonthDatacand=dataByMonth.get(idx);
   if (0.0==cand.oppTotal)
   {
     cand.oppTotal=(Math.random()*750000).intValue();
   }
}
```

7
Enhancing the Client with JavaScript

In this chapter, we will cover the following recipes:

- Using action functions
- Avoiding race conditions
- The confirmation dialog
- Pressing Enter to submit
- The onload handler
- Collapsible list elements
- Trapping navigation away
- Creating a record using JavaScript remoting

Introduction

JavaScript is used on a huge number of websites to add visual effects, validation, server interaction, and many more features. As JavaScript executes on the client side, it removes the latency involved with a round trip to the web server, resulting in more responsive applications and an improved user experience. JavaScript can also provide functionality that is not possible using HTML and server-side processing, for example, handling individual key clicks or mouse movements.

Visualforce has built-in capability to allow JavaScript interaction with the page controller. For example, the `<apex:actionSupport />` component allows controller action methods to be called in response to JavaScript events, while the `<apex:actionFunction />` component generates a JavaScript function that encapsulates a controller action method. Furthermore, many components provide the `on<event>` attributes, such as `onclick` and `onchange`, to allow custom JavaScript to be invoked in response to user actions.

JavaScript is not without its downsides however, browser compatibility is a common problem. Using a framework such as **jQuery** (`http://jquery.com/`), **Prototype** (`http://prototypejs.org/`), or **Dojo** (`http://dojotoolkit.org/`) simplifies the task of creating cross-browser compatible JavaScript, as well as providing a powerful set of utilities to traverse and manipulate the **Document Object Model (DOM)**.

In this chapter, we will use JavaScript to provide a variety of client-side enhancements, from ensuring that a user does not lose their work or commit it too early, through to providing a visual indicator of the number of remaining characters that an input can accommodate. We will also use JavaScript to create dynamic content, such as scrolling news and carousel messages.

 A number of the recipes in this chapter include JavaScript and CSS files from one or more **Content Delivery Networks (CDNs)**. This does introduce a dependency on the site hosting the CDN and in the event that this site was unavailable or access blocked, the recipe functionality would cease to work.

Using action functions

An **action function** allows an action method from a controller to be executed from JavaScript. The standard Visualforce `<apex:actionFunction />` component generates a named function that can be called from any JavaScript code.

In this recipe, we will create a Visualforce page that displays a list of cases and a countdown timer implemented in JavaScript. Once the timer expires, an action method from the page's controller is executed, which redirects the user's browser to the standard case tab.

Getting ready

This recipe makes use of a custom controller, so this must be created before the Visualforce page.

How to do it...

1. Navigate to the **Apex Classes** setup page by clicking on **Your Name** | **Setup** | **Develop** | **Apex Classes**.
2. Click on the **New** button.
3. Paste the contents of the `ActionFunctionController.cls` Apex class from the code download into the **Apex Class** area.
4. Click on the **Save** button.
5. Next, create the Visualforce page by navigating to the Visualforce setup page by clicking on **Your Name** | **Setup** | **Develop** | **Visualforce Pages**.
6. Click on the **New** button.
7. Enter `ActionFunction` in the **Label** field.
8. Accept the default **ActionFunction** that is automatically generated for the **Name** field.
9. Paste the contents of the `ActionFunction.page` file from the code download into the **Visualforce Markup** area and click on the **Save** button.
10. Navigate to the Visualforce setup page by clicking on **Your Name** | **Setup** | **Develop** | **Visualforce Pages**.
11. Locate the entry for the **ActionFunction** page and click on the **Security** link.
12. On the resulting page, select which profiles should have access and click on the **Save** button.

How it works...

Opening the following URL in your browser displays the **ActionFunction** page:
`https://<instance>/apex/ActionFunction`.

Cases		
Case Number	**Account Name**	**Status**
00001000	Edge Communications	Closed
00001001	United Oil & Gas Corp.	Closed
00001002	United Oil & Gas Corp.	New
00001004	Express Logistics and Transport	Closed
00001006	GenePoint	Closed
00001008	Grand Hotels & Resorts Ltd	Closed
00001009	United Oil & Gas, UK	Closed
00001007	Grand Hotels & Resorts Ltd	Closed
00001005	Express Logistics and Transport	Closed
00001003	Express Logistics and Transport	Closed

Going to tab in 4 seconds

Here, `<instance>` is the Salesforce instance specific to your organization, for example, `na6.salesforce.com`.

The countdown timer at the bottom-left is updated by a JavaScript function that executes every second:

```
countDownObj.count = function(i)
{
  countDownObj.innerHTML = 'Going to tab in ' + i + ' seconds';
  if (i == 0) {
    fn();
    return;
  }
  setTimeout(function()
      {
        countDownObj.count(i - 1);
      },
      pause);
}
```

The controller action method is exposed as a JavaScript function via an action function:

```
<apex:form >
  <apex:actionFunction name="goCasesTabJS"
                       action="{!goCasesTab}" />
</apex:form>
```

Note that as the action function executes an action method, a form submission takes place. For this reason, the `<apex:actionFunction />` component must always be nested inside the `<apex:form />` tags.

The action method invoked when the `goCasesTabJS` JavaScript function is executed simply returns the page reference for the case tab:

```
public PageReference goCasesTab()
{
   PageReference result=new PageReference('/500/o');
   return result;
}
```

Avoiding race conditions

An action function provides a way to submit a form programmatically via a JavaScript function call. When an action function is executed from a JavaScript event handler, the default browser behavior continues once the event handler has completed. If the event handler is attached to a Visualforce component that submits the form, an `onclick` handler for an `<apex:commandLink />` or `<apex:commandButton />` component, for example, the default browser behavior is to continue with the form submission. This results in a race condition as to which form submission request will be processed first by the server and will often produce unexpected results.

In this recipe, we will create a Visualforce page to execute a search for accounts matching a user-entered string of characters. When the user clicks on the button to start the search, a JavaScript function is invoked that checks the number of characters entered. If two or more characters have been entered, the search is executed via an action function. If fewer than two characters have been entered, any existing results are cleared and the search is not executed. In either case, the default form submission from the button is stopped.

Getting ready

This recipe makes use of a custom controller, so this will need to be created before the Visualforce page.

How to do it...

1. First, create the custom controller by navigating to the **Apex Classes** setup page by clicking on **Your Name** | **Setup** | **Develop** | **Apex Classes**.
2. Click on the **New** button.
3. Paste the contents of the `ActionFunctionSearchController.cls` Apex class from the code download into the **Apex Class** area.
4. Click on the **Save** button.
5. Next, create the Visualforce page by navigating to the Visualforce setup page by clicking on **Your Name** | **Setup** | **Develop** | **Visualforce Pages**.
6. Click on the **New** button.
7. Enter `ActionFunctionSearch` in the **Label** field.
8. Accept the default **ActionFunctionSearch** that is automatically generated for the **Name** field.
9. Paste the contents of the `ActionFunctionSearch.page` file from the code download into the **Visualforce Markup** area and click on the **Save** button.
10. Navigate to the Visualforce setup page by clicking on **Your Name** | **Setup** | **Develop** | **Visualforce Pages**.
11. Locate the entry for the **ActionFunctionSearch** page and click on the **Security** link.
12. On the resulting page, select which profiles should have access and click on the **Save** button.

How it works...

Opening the following URL in your browser displays the **ActionFunctionSearch** page: `https://<instance>/apex/ActionFunctionSearch`.

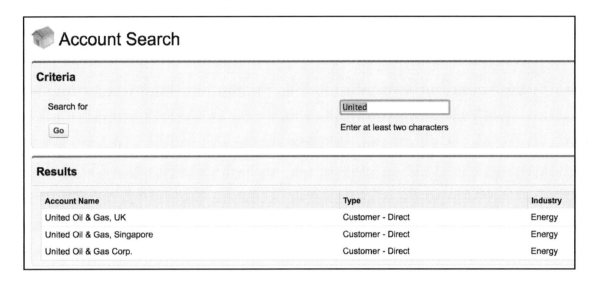

Here, `<instance>` is the Salesforce instance specific to your organization, for example, `na6.salesforce.com`.

The **Go** button defines an `onclick` handler that executes a JavaScript function to determine the number of characters entered and execute a search or clear the results:

```
function runSearch()
{
  // don't run the search unless there are enough characters
  var str = document.getElementById(
    '{!$Component.frm.crit_pb.crit_pbs.crit_str}').value;
  if (str.length>=2)
  {
    doSearchJS();
  }
  else
  {
    alert('Please enter at least two characters');
    clearResultsJS();
  }
}
```

Visualforce will automatically generate an ID for each HTML element based on the `id` attribute of the element and the `id` attribute of each ancestor element, which can make identification of an individual element challenging. To assist this, Visualforce provides a `$Component` global merge variable that uses a dot-notation based on the component hierarchy to identify an element.

For more information, visit: `http://www.salesforce.com/us/developer /docs/pages/Content/pages_best_practices_accessing_id.htm`.

The `onclick` handler returns `false` once the function has completed; this instructs the browser to stop handling the click event at that point, rather than continuing with the default behavior of submitting the form:

```
<apex:commandButton value="Go" onclick="runSearch();
    return false;" />
```

See also

- For more information on action functions, refer to the *Using action functions* recipe.

The confirmation dialog

A feature missing from the standard Salesforce record edit functionality is the ability for the user to confirm that they wish to execute an action. If a user inadvertently clicks on the **Cancel** button, their work will be discarded.

In this recipe, we will create a Visualforce page that allows a user to create an account record. If the user clicks on a button to save the record or cancel the creation, they will be requested to confirm that they wish to continue with the action.

Getting ready

This recipe makes use of a standard controller, so we only need to create the Visualforce page.

How to do it...

1. Navigate to the Visualforce setup page by clicking on **Your Name** | **Setup** | **Develop** | **Visualforce Pages**.
2. Click on the **New** button.
3. Enter `Confirmation` in the **Label** field.
4. Accept the default **Confirmation** that is automatically generated for the **Name** field.
5. Paste the contents of the `Confirmation.page` file from the code download into the **Visualforce Markup** area and click on the **Save** button.
6. Navigate to the Visualforce setup page by clicking on **Your Name** | **Setup** | **Develop** | **Visualforce Pages**.
7. Locate the entry for the **Confirmation** page and click on the **Security** link.
8. On the resulting page, select which profiles should have access and click on the **Save** button.

How it works...

Opening the following URL in your browser displays the **Confirmation** page: `https://<instance>/apex/Confirmation`.

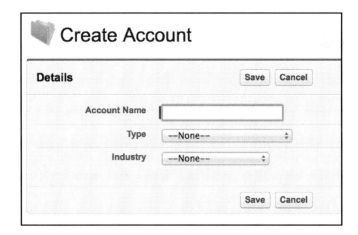

Here, `<instance>` is the Salesforce instance specific to your organization, for example, `na6.salesforce.com`.

If the user clicks on the **Save** or **Cancel** button, they are asked to confirm the action.

The **Save** and **Cancel** buttons each define an `onclick` handler that executes a JavaScript function. This function opens an appropriate confirmation dialog to ask the user to confirm the action:

```
function confirmCancel()
{
   return confirm("This will discard your changes\nAre you sure you wish to
continue?");
}
```

The `onclick` handlers return the result of the JavaScript function, ensuring that if the user chooses not to proceed, the default browser behavior of continuing with the form submission will not take place. Setting the `immediate` attribute to `true` discards any user input prior to invoking the action method.

```
<apex:commandButton value="Cancel" action="{!cancel}"
     onclick="return confirmCancel();" immediate="true" />
```

See also

- The *Trapping navigation away* recipe in this chapter shows how to ask the user to confirm they wish to navigate away from a page, even if they haven't clicked a button or link on the page.
- The *Pressing Enter to submit* recipe in this chapter intercepts the pressing of an *Enter* key in a form and asks the user to confirm they wish to save their changes.

Pressing Enter to submit

When the *Enter* key is pressed and a single-line HTML form element has focus, modern browsers will submit the form via the first submit button. If the user has pressed the Enter key expecting to move on to a new line and remain in the input element, this can lead to the submission of a partially filled in form, resulting in a low-quality record being created.

In this recipe, we will create a Visualforce page that allows a user to create an opportunity. If the user presses the *Enter* key while filling in any of the opportunity fields, they will be asked to confirm that they wish to submit the form.

Getting ready

This recipe makes use of a standard controller, so we only need to create the Visualforce page.

How to do it...

1. Create the Visualforce page by navigating to the Visualforce setup page by clicking on **Your Name** | **Setup** | **Develop** | **Visualforce Pages**.
2. Click on the **New** button.
3. Enter `PressEnter` in the **Label** field.
4. Accept the default **PressEnter** that is automatically generated for the **Name** field.
5. Paste the contents of the `PressEnter.page` file from the code download into the **Visualforce Markup** area and click on the **Save** button.
6. Navigate to the Visualforce setup page by clicking on **Your Name** | **Setup** | **Develop** | **Visualforce Pages**.
7. Locate the entry for the **PressEnter** page and click on the **Security** link.
8. On the resulting page, select which profiles should have access and click on the **Save** button.

How it works...

Opening the following URL in your browser displays the **PressEnter** page:
`https://<instance>/apex/PressEnter`.

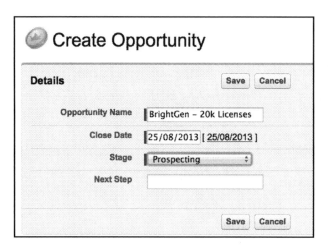

Here, `<instance>` is the Salesforce instance specific to your organization, for example, `na6.salesforce.com`.

If the user presses the *Enter* key while filling in one of the fields, they will be asked to confirm that they wish to submit the form.

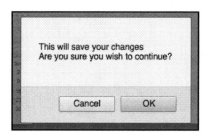

Each field in the form defines an `onkeypress` event that executes a JavaScript function:

```
<apex:inputField value="{!Opportunity.Name}"
        onkeypress="return keypress(event);" />
```

This function inspects the key pressed and if it is the *Enter* key, opens a confirmation dialog to ask the user to confirm the form submission. If the user confirms that they wish to continue, the **Save** button is located and programmatically clicked:

```
var result=true;
if (keyCode == 13)
{
  var ele=document.getElementById(
    '{!$Component.frm.pb.pb_btns.savebtn}');
  if (confirm("This will save your changes\nAre you sure you wish to
continue?"))
  {
    ele.click();
  }
  result=false;
}
return result;
```

The result of the function indicates whether the default browser behavior should continue; if the key pressed is not the *Enter* key, the result is `true` and the default behavior of adding the character to the field continues. If the key pressed is *Enter*, the result is `false` which stops the default form submission.

The key pressed is identified based on its code. For a list of JavaScript key codes, visit `http://www.cambiaresearch.com/articles/15/javascript-char-codes-key-codes`.

See also

- The *Trapping navigation away* recipe in this chapter shows how to ask the user to confirm they wish to navigate away from a page.
- The *The confirmation dialog* recipe in this chapter asks the user to confirm that they wish to execute the action associated with the button they have just clicked.

The onload handler

An `onload` handler allows JavaScript code to be executed when an HTML page has completed loading. When adding an `onload` handler to a Visualforce page, care must be taken not to interfere with any default `onload` handler added by the platform, to give focus to the first input field in the page, for example.

In this recipe, we will create a Visualforce page that allows a user to create an opportunity. An `onload` handler in the page executes a JavaScript function to set the default value for the opportunity `amount` field to `100000`. If the platform has specified an `onload` handler function, this is executed before the `amount` value is set.

How to do it...

This recipe makes use of a standard controller, so we only need to create the Visualforce page.

1. Create the Visualforce page by navigating to the Visualforce setup page by clicking on **Your Name** | **Setup** | **Develop** | **Visualforce Pages**.
2. Click on the **New** button.
3. Enter `Onload` in the **Label** field.
4. Accept the default **Onload** that is automatically generated for the **Name** field.
5. Paste the contents of the `Onload.page` file from the code download into the **Visualforce Markup** area and click on the **Save** button.
6. Navigate to the Visualforce setup page by clicking on **Your Name** | **Setup** | **Develop** | **Visualforce Pages**.
7. Locate the entry for the **Onload** page and click on the **Security** link.
8. On the resulting page, select which profiles should have access and click on the **Save** button.

How it works...

Opening the following URL in your browser displays the **Onload** page:
`https://<instance>/apex/Onload`.

Here, `<instance>` is the Salesforce instance specific to your organization, for example, `na6.salesforce.com`.

The opportunity **Amount** value is defaulted to **100000** by the JavaScript function executed by the `onload` handler:

```
function()
{
  document.getElementById(
    '{!$Component.frm.pb.pbs.amount}').value=
                                    '100000';
}
```

The `onload` handler is added by a JavaScript function that checks if there is an existing handler. If there is, a new function is created to execute the existing handler, followed by the new one. If there is not an existing handler, the function is applied as the `onload` handler:

```
function addLoadEvent(fn)
{
  var currentHandler = window.onload;
  if (typeof currentHandler != 'function')
  {
    window.onload = fn;
  }
  else
  {
    window.onload = function()
    {
        if (currentHandler)
```

```
      {
        currentHandler();
      }
      fn();
    }
  }
}
```

Note that the function to be executed when the page is loaded is passed as a parameter to the `addLoadEvent` function.

This mechanism allows any number of `onload` handlers to be chained together.

See also

- The *The confirmation dialog* and *Pressing Enter to submit* recipes in this chapter show how to handle other JavaScript events.
- The *The character counter* recipe in this chapter shows how to use jQuery to bind a JavaScript function to specified events.

Collapsible list elements

When a number of records and related information are rendered as a list, a user is often presented with a large amount of data that they must scroll through in order to access the items that they are interested in. One way to improve this is to allow items to be collapsed, showing enough headline information to allow the item to be identified, but taking up the minimum amount of screen real estate.

In this recipe, we will create a Visualforce page that displays a list of account records and their associated contact records. Each account record is collapsed when the page is initially rendered, and the user may click a record to expand it and see the associated contact information.

Visualforce provides collapsible behavior for the standard `<apex:pageBlockSection />` component. However, this forces the content that is to be expanded or collapsed to be nested inside this component, which styles the content in a similar fashion to a standard Salesforce section.

The solution presented in this recipe provides this behavior for a regular HTML table that may be used in a variety of situations with or without Salesforce styling.

Getting ready

This recipe uses the jQuery (`http://jquery.com/`), JavaScript framework, and jQuery User Interface (`http://jqueryui.com/`) library to produce, style, and transition the tooltip. The JavaScript and CSS files are included from the Google Hosted Libraries' content delivery network rather than being uploaded as Salesforce static resources, as this makes it straightforward to move to new versions simply by changing the URL of the included file.

This recipe also makes use of a custom controller, so this will need to be present before the Visualforce page can be created.

How to do it...

1. First, create the custom controller for the Visualforce page by navigating to the **Apex Classes** setup page by clicking on **Your Name** | **Setup** | **Develop** | **Apex Classes**.
2. Click on the **New** button.
3. Paste the contents of the `CollapsibleController.cls` Apex class from the code download into the **Apex Class** area.
4. Click on the **Save** button.
5. Next, create the Visualforce page by navigating to the Visualforce setup page by clicking on **Your Name** | **Setup** | **Develop** | **Visualforce Pages**.
6. Click on the **New** button.
7. Enter `Collapsible` in the **Label** field.
8. Accept the default **Collapsible** that is automatically generated for the **Name** field.
9. Paste the contents of the `Collapsible.page` file from the code download into the **Visualforce Markup** area and click on the **Save** button.
10. Navigate to the Visualforce setup page by clicking on **Your Name** | **Setup** | **Develop** | **Visualforce Pages**.
11. Locate the entry for the **Collapsible** page and click on the **Security** link.
12. On the resulting page, select which profiles should have access and click on the **Save** button.

How it works...

Opening the following URL in your browser displays the **Collapsible** page:
`https://<instance>/apex/Collapsible`.

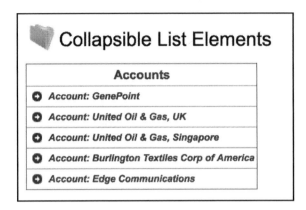

Here, `<instance>` is the Salesforce instance specific to your organization, for example, `na6.salesforce.com`.

Clicking on the right arrow icon next to the account name opens the account record to display the associated contact records.

The list of accounts is rendered as an HTML `<table>` element. Two `<tbody>` elements are rendered for each account, the first containing just the account name that is visible when the page is rendered:

```
<tbody id="{!acc.id}-collapsed}">
  <tr onclick="toggle('{!acc.id}');">
    <td colspan="2">
      <span style="float:left;" class="ui-accordion-header-icon ui-icon ui-
icon-circle-arrow-e"> </span>
       
      <span style="font-weight:bold; font-style:italic;">Account:
{!acc.Name}</span>
    </td>
  </tr>
</tbody>
```

The second `<tbody>` element contains the account name and the associated contact records, which is hidden when the page is initially rendered:

```
<tbody id="{!acc.id}-expanded" style="display:none">
  <tr onclick="toggle('{!acc.id}');">
    <td colspan="2">
      <span style="float:left;" class="ui-accordion-header-icon ui-icon ui-
icon-circle-arrow-s"> </span>
       
      <span style="font-weight:bold">Account: {!acc.Name}</span>
    </td>
  </tr>
  <apex:repeat value="{!acc.Contacts}" var="cont">
    <tr>
      <td style="border-right: none">
         
      </td>
      <td style="border-left: none">
        <span style="font-weight:bold">Contact:</span>
        <apex:outputLink
            value="/{!cont.id}">{!cont.Name}
        </apex:outputLink>
      </td>
    </tr>
  </apex:repeat>
</tbody>
```

Each `<tbody>` element defines an `onclick` handler:

```
onclick="toggle('{!acc.id}');"
```

The `toggle` function uses the jQuery `toggle` function (http://api.jquery.com/toggle/) to swap the visibility of both <tbody> elements associated with an account, hiding the currently visible element and showing the currently hidden element:

```
function toggle(baseId)
{
  $('tbody[id*="' + baseId + '"]').toggle();
}
```

Trapping navigation away

When a user is filling in a form and inadvertently clicks on a link to another page, or clicks the back button, it sends the browser to a new page and discards all user input. In the event that the form is large and complex, this can represent a significant lost effort.

In this recipe, we will create a Visualforce page that allows a user to create a contact record. If the user clicks on a button to save the record or cancel the creation, they will be requested to confirm that they wish to continue with the action. If the user clicks on the **Save** or **Cancel** button, this will submit the form without further confirmation.

Getting ready

This recipe uses the jQuery (http://jquery.com/) JavaScript framework to swap the buttons. The JavaScript file is included from the Google Hosted Libraries' content delivery network rather than being uploaded as a Salesforce static resource, as this makes it straightforward to move to new versions simply by changing the URL of the included file.

How to do it...

1. Navigate to the Visualforce setup page by clicking on **Your Name | Setup | Develop | Visualforce Pages**.
2. Click on the **New** button.
3. Enter `ConfirmLeavePage` in the **Label** field.
4. Accept the default **ConfirmLeavePage** that is automatically generated for the **Name** field.

5. Paste the contents of the `ConfirmLeavePage.page` file from the code download into the **Visualforce Markup** area and click on the **Save** button.

6. Navigate to the Visualforce setup page by clicking on **Your Name** | **Setup** | **Develop** | **Visualforce Pages**.

7. Locate the entry for the **ConfirmLeavePage** page and click on the **Security** link.

8. On the resulting page, select which profiles should have access and click on the **Save** button.

How it works...

Opening the following URL in your browser displays the **ConfirmLeavePage** page:
`https://<instance>/apex/ConfirmLeavePage`.

Here, `<instance>` is the Salesforce instance specific to your organization, for example, `na6.salesforce.com`.

If the user clicks any of the other tabs on the page, a confirmation dialog asks them to confirm that they wish to leave the page.

When the page is loaded, jQuery is used to add an `onbeforeunload` event handler:

```
window.onbeforeunload = function()
{
    return 'This will lose any unsaved changes you have made';
}
```

 The `onbeforeunload` Trapping navigation away its resources. Different browsers exhibit different behavior with regard to the message displayed to the user – some will use the message returned from the `window,beforeunload` method, while others will display their own standard message.

Each of the **Save** and **Cancel** buttons defines an `onclick` handler that removes the `onbeforeunload` handler, allowing the action to continue without requiring the user confirm they wish to continue:

```
<apex:commandButton value="Save" action="{!save}"
                    onclick="clearConfirm();"/>
        ...
function clearConfirm()
{
    window.onbeforeunload=null;
}
```

See also

- The *The confirmation dialog* recipe in this chapter shows how to ask the user to confirm they wish to continue when they click on a button to submit a form.
- The *Pressing Enter to submit* recipe in this chapter intercepts the pressing of an *Enter* key in a form and asks the user to confirm they wish to save their changes.

Creating a record using JavaScript remoting

Using Visualforce forms to capture user input and submit this back to the server requires use of the view state and round trip HTTP requests, both of which introduce an overhead to the processing. Additionally, when working in JavaScript, interacting with controller properties is not the most intuitive experience, as the properties are managed server side and made available to the page when it is rendered. This means that they must be treated as static text values by JavaScript before they can be inspected, and any changes must be manually inserted into standard input components in order to send them back to the server.

JavaScript remoting provides a mechanism to execute a controller Apex method directly from JavaScript in a stateless fashion and receive a callback with the results of the method call. The state of the page is managed in JavaScript and the server only receives the reduced set of information that it needs to execute the specific method.

While JavaScript remoting is a much more efficient mechanism of executing server-side code and thus provides a more responsive user experience, additional JavaScript code is required to maintain the state client-side and to update the page with the results of any server side methods that are executed.

In this recipe, we will create a Visualforce page that allows a user to create a lead record via JavaScript remoting and redirects them to the record home page for the lead. In the event that an error occurs server side when creating the lead, this will be surfaced to the user via a JavaScript alert.

Getting ready

This recipe makes use of a custom controller, so this will need to be present before the Visualforce page can be created.

How to do it...

1. First, create the custom controller for the Visualforce page by navigating to the **Apex Classes** setup page by clicking on **Your Name** | **Setup** | **Develop** | **Apex Classes**.
2. Click on the **New** button.
3. Paste the contents of the `RemotingController.cls` Apex class from the code download into the **Apex Class** area.
4. Click on the **Save** button.

5. Next, create the Visualforce page by navigating to the Visualforce setup page by clicking on **Your Name** | **Setup** | **Develop** | **Visualforce Pages**.

6. Click on the **New** button.

7. Enter `Remoting` in the **Label** field.

8. Accept the default **Remoting** that is automatically generated for the **Name** field.

9. Paste the contents of the `Remoting.page` file from the code download into the **Visualforce Markup** area and click on the **Save** button.

10. Navigate to the Visualforce setup page by clicking on **Your Name** | **Setup** | **Develop** | **Visualforce Pages**.

11. Locate the entry for the **Remoting** page and click on the **Security** link.

12. On the resulting page, select which profiles should have access and click on the **Save** button.

How it works...

Opening the following URL in your browser displays the **Remoting** page: `https://<instance>/apex/Remoting`.

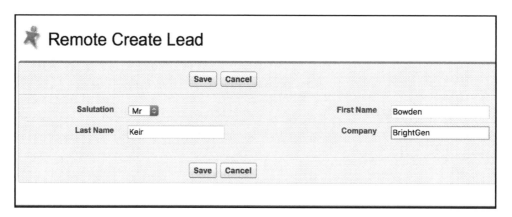

Here, `<instance>` is the Salesforce instance specific to your organization, for example, `na6.salesforce.com`.

When the user populates the form and clicks the **Save** button, a JavaScript function extracts the input values and invokes a server-side method to create the lead:

```
function remoteCreate() {
    var salutation=document.querySelector('#salutation').value;
    var firstname=document.querySelector('#firstname').value;
```

```
var lastname=document.querySelector('#lastname').value;
var company=document.querySelector('#company').value;
RemotingController.CreateLead(
             salutation, firstname, lastname, company,
             createLeadResponseHandler);
}
```

In order to be available as a remote method, the controller method must be annotated with `@RemoteAction`:

```
@RemoteAction
public static Lead CreateLead(String salutation, String firstName,
                              String lastName, String company)
{
    Lead ld=new Lead(Salutation=salutation ... );
    insert ld;
    return ld;
}
```

When the server-side method completes, the `createLeadResponse` handler is invoked with the ID of the newly created field or details of any errors that occurred. If there were no errors, the user is redirected to the record home page for the lead:

```
function createLeadResponseHandler(result, event)
{
    if (event.status) {
        alert('Lead created - id = ' + result.Id);
        window.location='/' + result.Id;
    }
    else if (event.type === 'exception') {
        alert('Exception in Remote Method:\n' + event.message);
    }
    else {
        alert('Something went wrong - that's all I know');
    }
}
```

See also

- A number of the recipes in Chapter 9, *Visualforce in Salesforce1*, use JavaScript remoting to communicate with the server.

8
Force.com Sites

In this chapter, we will cover the following recipes:

- Creating a site
- Record and field access
- Retrieving content from Salesforce
- Web to lead form
- Creating a website template
- Adding a header to a template
- Adding a sidebar to a template
- Conditional rendering in templates

Introduction

Force.com sites allow public websites to be created in, and hosted by, Salesforce, removing the requirement to configure, secure, and manage a web server. Visualforce pages that have direct access to Salesforce data via the page controller generate the site content.

In this chapter, we will create a Force.com site initially containing static content. We will then create a set of template pages to remove repetition of common markup. Finally, we will provide access to Salesforce data from a public website, allowing visitors to access records without logging in to Salesforce.

Unlike earlier chapters in this book, these recipes are best performed in order, as many recipes build on knowledge gained in earlier recipes and the first recipe, *Creating a site*, configures the Force.com site that is used to serve the content for all of the remaining recipes.

Salesforce supports an additional technology to host websites, Site.com, which does not use Visualforce to generate content. For more information on Site.com visit http://wiki.developerforce.com/page/Site.com.

Creating a site

In this recipe we will configure a Force.com site that displays a single page. The contents of the page are static, and the page will be publicly available to unauthenticated visitors.

Getting ready

This recipe uses the **Salesforce Lightning Design System** (SLDS) (https://www.lightning designsystem.com/) to style the page. The CSS, icons, and fonts must be uploaded to Salesforce as a static resource.

At the time of writing, the current version of the SLDS is 2.0.2 – if you download a later version and use a different name to that detailed in the following steps, you will need to update the Visualforce pages to use the name that you have chosen.

1. Set the **Cache Control** field to **Public** and click on the **Save** button.
2. Click on the **Browse** button and select the salesforce-lightning-design-system-2.0.2.zip file downloaded in step 1.
3. Enter Salesforce Lightning Design System v2.0.2 in the **Description** field.
4. Enter SLDS_2_0_2 in the **Name** field.
5. Click on the **New** button.
6. Navigate to the Static Resource setup page by clicking on **Your Name** | **Setup** | **Develop** | **Static Resources**.
7. Download the SLDS ZIP file from https://www.lightningdesignsystem.com/resources/downloads/.
8. Before the site can be configured, a subdomain prefix must be selected. This prefix will be used to generate the unique domain for the site.

9. Navigate to the Sites setup page by clicking on **Your Name** | **Setup** | **Develop** | **Sites**.

10. On the resulting page, choose your preferred subdomain, check the box to indicate you accept the terms of use, and click on the **Register My Force.com Domain** button.

Note that once you have chosen your domain name, it cannot be modified. As this domain will be used as the prefix for all Force.com sites created in your Salesforce instance, it should be a representative of your organization rather than a particular site.

How to do it...

1. First, create the Visualforce page that will be displayed by the site by navigating to the Visualforce setup page by clicking on **Your Name** | **Setup** | **Develop** | **Pages**.

2. Click on the **New** button.

3. Enter `SiteHome` in the **Label** field.

4. Accept the default **SiteHome** that is automatically generated for the **Name** field.

5. Paste the contents of the `SiteHome.page` file from the code download into the **Visualforce Markup** area and click on the **Save** button.

6. Next, create the site by navigating to the Sites setup page by clicking on **Your Name** | **Setup** | **Develop** | **Sites**.

7. Click on the **New** button.

8. Enter `Visualforce Cookbook` in the **Label** field.

9. Accept the default **Visualforce_Cookbook** that is automatically generated for the **Name** field.

10. Check the **Active** box to make the site active as soon as the configuration is saved.

11. Enter `SiteHome` in the **Active Site Home Page** field.

12. Leave all other fields with their default values and click on the **Save** button.

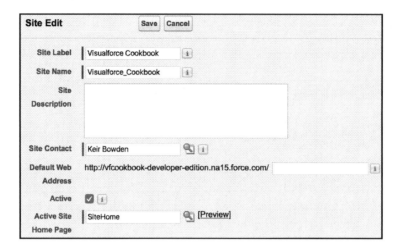

How it works...

Opening the following URL in your browser displays the **SiteHome** page: `http://<domain>/SiteHome`.

Here, `<domain>` is the Force.com domain name chosen when configuring the site, for example, `vfcookbook-developer-edition.na15.force.com`.

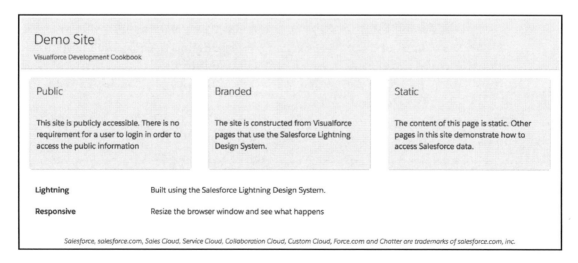

The standard header, sidebar, and stylesheets are hidden via attributes in the enclosing `<apex:page/>` standard component. As the page contains `<html>` and `<body>` tags, additional attributes specify that Visualforce should not insert its own version of these:

```
<apex:page applyHtmlTag="false" applyBodyTag="false" sidebar="false"
showHeader="false"
    standardStyleSheets="false">
```

The content is rendered inside an SLDS grid, with each grid column taking up 1/3 of the space in medium/large devices, but stacking taking up the entire row in extra small and small devices:

```
<div class="slds-col slds-size--1-of-1 slds-medium-size--1-of-3">
    <div class="slds-card slds-m-around--medium ">
        <div class="slds-card__header slds-grid grid--flex-spread">
            <h2 class="slds-text-heading--small slds-truncate">Public</h2>
        </div>
        <div class="slds-card__body slds-p-horizontal--small">
            <div class="slds-text-body--regular slds-p-top--large slds-p-
bottom--large">
                This site is publicly accessible. There is no requirement
for a user to login in order to access the public information
            </div>
        </div>
    </div>
</div>
```

See also

- The *Retrieving content from Salesforce* recipe in this chapter shows how to dynamically generate content for a Force.com site.
- The *Web to lead form* recipe in this chapter shows how to capture data for Salesforce from a Force.com site.

Record and field access

A common source of confusion for a Visualforce developer is configuring a Force.com site to allow unauthenticated access to Salesforce records and specific fields. This is usually configured via the Profiles menu located at **Your Name** | **Setup** | **Administration Setup** | **Profiles**. However, access to records and fields for a Force.com site is configured via the setup page for the site in question.

In this recipe, we will configure the Force.com site created in the first recipe to allow public access to contact records. We will then create a Visualforce page that allows a visitor to enter an e-mail address into a form on the Force.com site and extract the contact record matching the e-mail address, displaying the **First Name**, **Last Name**, and **Email** fields from the contact record.

Getting ready

This recipe requires that you have already completed the *Creating a Site* recipe, as it relies on the custom domain and Force.com site created in that recipe.

How to do it...

1. First, add access for the contact sObject to the Guest User Profile for the site. Navigate to the Sites setup page by clicking on **Your Name** | **Setup** | **Develop** | **Sites**.
2. Click on the **Visualforce Cookbook** link in the **Sites** section.
3. Click on the **Public Access Settings** button: this displays the Guest user profile for the site.
4. On the resulting page click the **Edit** button, select the **Read** checkbox for the **Contact** sObject in the **Custom Object Permissions** sections, and click on the **Save** button.
5. Next, add the required field access for the profile. Scroll down to the **Field Level Security** section and click on the **[View]** link for the **Contact** element.
6. On the resulting page, confirm that the **Visible** checkbox for the **Email** field is selected. If it is not, click on the **Edit** button and select the checkbox, and then click on the **Save** button.

 Note that the **Name** field is always visible to all profiles, so no action needs to be taken for that field.

7. Next, create the custom controller by navigating to the **Apex Classes** setup page by clicking on **Your Name** | **Setup** | **Develop** | **Apex Classes**.

8. Click on the **New** button.

9. Paste the contents of the `RetrieveContactController.cls` Apex class from the code download into the **Apex Class** area.

10. Click on the **Save** button.

11. Next, create the Visualforce page by navigating to the Visualforce setup page by clicking on **Your Name** | **Setup** | **Develop** | **Pages**.

12. Click on the **New** button.

13. Enter `RetrieveContact` in the **Label** field.

14. Accept the default **RetrieveContact** that is automatically generated for the **Name** field.

15. Paste the contents of the `RetrieveContact.page` file from the code download into the **Visualforce Markup** area and click on the **Save** button.

16. Navigate to the Sites setup page by clicking on **Your Name** | **Setup** | **Develop** | **Sites**.

17. Click on the **Visualforce Cookbook** link in the **Sites** section.

18. On the resulting page, scroll down to the **Site Visualforce Pages** list and click on the **Edit** button.

19. On the resulting page, **Enable Visualforce Page Access**, select **RetrieveContact** from the **Available Visualforce Pages** list, click on the Add icon to add it to the **Enabled Visualforce Pages** list, and click on the **Save** button.

How it works...

Opening the following URL in your browser displays the **RetrieveContact** page:
`http://<domain>/RetrieveContact`.

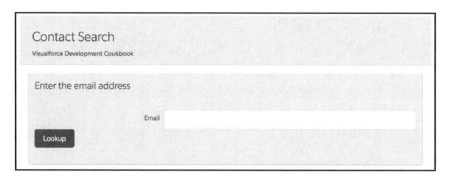

Here `<domain>` is the Force.com domain name chosen while configuring the site, for
example, `vfcookbook-developer-edition.na15.force.com`.

Filling in the **Email** field and clicking on the **Lookup** button displays the details of the first
contact with a matching e-mail address.

See also

- The *Creating a site* recipe in this chapter shows how to set up a Force.com site and make a static page publicly available.
- The *Retrieving content from Salesforce* recipe in this chapter shows how to extract records from Salesforce and use these to generate content on a Force.com site.

Retrieving content from Salesforce

Force.com sites allow unauthenticated visitors access to custom (and some standard) Salesforce sObjects. While providing public access to data stored in Salesforce might seem like a security risk, it is a perfect fit for dynamically-generated website content; content authors don't need to know to be able to edit Visualforce pages in order to update the content of the site.

In this recipe we will create a Visualforce page that renders content from the three most recently edited records of a custom sObject. We will then make this page publicly available via an unauthenticated Force.com site.

Getting ready

This recipe requires that you have already completed the *Creating a site* recipe, as it relies on the custom domain and Force.com site created in that recipe.

This recipe requires a custom sObject that encapsulates the items to display on the site.

1. First, create the site content custom sObject by navigating to **Your Name | Setup | Create | Objects**.
2. Click on the **New Custom Object** button.
3. Enter SiteItem in the **Label** field.
4. Enter SiteItems in the **Plural Label** field.
5. Leave all other input values at their defaults and click on the **Save** button.
6. On the resulting page, create the field that will contain the content detail, scroll down to the **Custom Fields and Relationships** section, and click on the **New** button.
7. On the next page, **Step 1. Choose the field type**, select **Text Area** from the **Data Type** radio buttons and click on the **Next** button.

8. On the next page, **Step 2. Enter the details**, enter `Detail` in the **Field Label** field, leave all other fields at their default values, and click on the **Next** button.

9. On the next page, **Step 3. Establish field-level security for reference field**, leave all the fields at their default values and click on the **Next** button.

10. On the final page, **Step 4. Add to page layouts**, leave all the fields at their default values and click on the **Save** button.

11. Next, create a tab for the `SiteItem` object to allow easy record creation by navigating to **Your Name** | **Setup** | **Create** | **Tabs**.

12. Click on the **New** button in the **Custom Object Tabs** section.

13. On the next page, **Step 1. Enter the details**, choose **SiteItem** from the **Object** picklist, click on the lookup icon in the **Tab Style** field, and choose a style from the resulting pop-up. Finally, click on the **Next** button.

14. On the next page, **Step 2. Add to profiles**, leave all fields at their default values and click on the **Next** button.

15. On the next page, **Step 3. Add to custom apps**, leave all fields at their default values and click on the **Save** button.

16. Next, add access to the custom sObject to **Guest User Profile** for the site. Navigate to the Sites setup page by clicking on **Your Name** | **Setup** | **Develop** | **Sites**.

17. Click on the **Visualforce Cookbook** link in the **Sites** section.

18. Click on the **Public Access Settings** button.

19. On the resulting page click on the **Edit** button, select the **Read** checkbox for the **SiteItem** sObject in the **Custom Object Permissions** sections, and click on the **Save** button.

20. Next, add access to the **Detail** field for the **Guest User Profile**. Scroll down to the **Field Level** Security section and click on the **[View]** link for the **SiteItem** element.

21. On the resulting page, click on the **Edit** button, select the **Visible** checkbox for the **Detail** field, and click on the **Save** button.

22. Finally, create at least three **SiteItem** records.

How to do it...

1. First, create the custom controller by navigating to the **Apex Classes** setup page by clicking on **Your Name** | **Setup** | **Develop** | **Apex Classes**.

2. Click on the **New** button.

3. Paste the contents of the `SiteItemController.cls` Apex class from the code download into the **Apex Class** area.

4. Click on the **Save** button.

5. Next, create the Visualforce page by navigating to the Visualforce setup page by clicking on **Your Name** | **Setup** | **Develop** | **Pages**.

6. Click on the **New** button.

7. Enter `SiteItem` in the **Label** field.

8. Accept the default **SiteItem** that is automatically generated for the **Name** field.

9. Paste the contents of the `SiteItem.page` file from the code download into the **Visualforce Markup** area and click on the **Save** button.

10. Navigate to the Sites setup page by clicking on **Your Name** | **Setup** | **Develop** | **Sites**.

11. Click on the **Visualforce Cookbook** link in the **Sites** section.

12. On the resulting page, scroll down to the **Site Visualforce Pages** list and click on the **Edit** button.

13. On the resulting page, **Enable Visualforce Page Access**, select **SiteItem** from the **Available Visualforce Pages** list, click on the Add icon to add it to the **Enabled Visualforce Pages** list, and click on the **Save** button.

How it works...

Opening the following URL in your browser displays the **SiteItem** page:
`http://<domain>/SiteItem`.

Demo Site

Visualforce Development Cookbook

No Developers

You don't need a developer to change the content. The layout of the site, on the other hand, requires Visualforce skills.

Dynamic Content

This content has been retrieved from the Salesforce database. Updating the content will update the site, subject to cache expiration.

Force.com Sites

Force.com Sites provide unauthenticated access to Salesforce data.

Lightning   Built using the Salesforce Lightning Design System.

Responsive   Resize the browser window and see what happens

Salesforce, salesforce.com, Sales Cloud, Service Cloud, Collaboration Cloud, Custom Cloud, Force.com and Chatter are trademarks of salesforce.com, inc.

Here, `<domain>` is the Force.com domain name chosen while configuring the site, for example, `vfcookbook-developer-edition.na15.force.com`.

The content is rendered inside an SLDS grid. The **SiteItem** records from the custom controller are iterated to generate a row of data. As the controller only returns three records, each column spans one-third of the row size:

```
<div class="slds-grid slds-wrap slds-m-around--large">
    <apex:repeat value="{!items}" var="item">
        <div class="slds-col slds-size--1-of-1 slds-medium-size--1-of-3">
            <div class="slds-m-left--medium slds-m-right--medium">
                <div class="slds-text-heading--small">{!item.Name}</div>
                <div class="slds-text-body--regular slds-m-bottom--medium
slds-m-top--medium">{!item.Detail__c}</div>
            </div>
        </div>
    </apex:repeat>
</div>
```

See also

- The *Creating a site* recipe in this chapter shows how to set up a Force.com site and make a static page publicly available.
- The *Web to lead form* recipe in this chapter shows how to capture data for Salesforce from a Force.com site.

Web to lead form

The standard Salesforce web to lead functionality allows a form to be embedded into a company's website to capture information that is then turned into a lead in the company's Salesforce instance. The form is submitted to a servlet that is common to all Salesforce instances and thus, may not be customized besides sending the user to a thank you page that is disconnected from the lead.

> For more information on web to lead, visit `http://login.salesforce.co m/help/doc/en/customize_leadcapture.htm`.

In this recipe, we will create a Visualforce page that captures a lead and redirects the user to a personalized thank you page that displays the ID of the lead for future reference. We will then make this page publicly available via an unauthenticated Force.com site.

Getting ready

This recipe requires that you have already completed the *Creating a site* recipe, as it relies on the custom domain and Force.com site created in that recipe.

How to do it...

1. First, create the thank you Visualforce page by navigating to the Visualforce setup page by clicking on **Your Name** | **Setup** | **Develop** | **Pages**.

2. Click on the **New** button.

3. Enter WebToLeadThanks in the **Label** field.

4. Accept the default **WebToLeadThanks** that is automatically generated for the **Name** field.

5. Paste the contents of the WebToLeadThanks.page file from the code download into the **Visualforce Markup** area and click on the **Save** button.

6. Next, create the web to lead page controller extension by navigating to the **Apex Classes** setup page by clicking on **Your Name** | **Setup** | **Develop** | **Apex Classes**.

7. Click on the **New** button.

8. Paste the contents of the WebToLeadExt.cls Apex class from the code download into the **Apex Class** area.

9. Click on the **Save** button.

10. Next, create the web to lead Visualforce page by navigating to the Visualforce setup page by clicking on **Your Name** | **Setup** | **Develop** | **Pages**.

11. Click on the **New** button.

12. Enter WebToLead in the **Label** field.

13. Accept the default **WebToLead** that is automatically generated for the **Name** field.

14. Paste the contents of the WebToLead.page file from the code download into the **Visualforce Markup** area and click on the **Save** button.

15. Navigate to the Sites setup page by clicking on **Your Name** | **Setup** | **Develop** | **Sites**.

16. Click on the **Visualforce Cookbook** link in the **Sites** section.

17. On the resulting page, scroll down to the **Site Visualforce Pages** list and click on the **Edit** button.
18. On the resulting page, **Enable Visualforce Page Access**, select **WebToLead** and **WebToLeadThanks** from the **Available Visualforce Pages** list, click on the Add icon to add it to the **Enabled Visualforce Pages** list, and click on the **Save** button.
19. Click on the **Public Access Settings** button.
20. On the resulting page click on the **Edit** button, select the **Read** and **Create** checkboxes for the **Lead** object in the **Standard Object Permissions** sections, and click on the **Save** button.

How it works...

Opening the following URL in your browser displays the **WebToLead** page: `http://<domain>/WebToLead`.

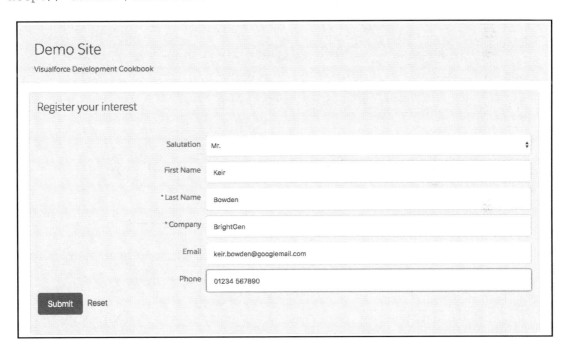

Here, `<domain>` is the Force.com domain name chosen when configuring the site, for example, `vfcookbook-developer-edition.na15.force.com`.

Filling out and submitting the form takes the visitor to the personalized thank you page.

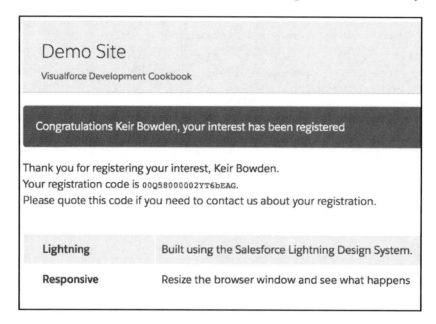

The form is laid out as a series of div elements using the SLDS style class `form-element`. Standard Visualforce components may be used with the SLDS as long as the appropriate SLDS class is supplied to the `styleClass` attribute of the standard component:

```
<div class="slds-form-element is-required">
    <label class="slds-form-element__label"><abbr class="slds-required"
>*</abbr>Last Name</label>
    <div class="slds-form-element__control">
        <apex:inputText styleClass="slds-input" value="{!Lead.LastName}" />
    </div>
</div>
```

 Note that the `<apex:inputText />` components are used to capture the user input rather than an `<apex:inputField />` component. This stops the required field classes being added to the input element, which would interfere with the SLDS styling.

See also

- The *Creating a site* recipe in this chapter shows how to set up a Force.com site and make a static page publicly available.
- The *Retrieving content from Salesforce* recipe in this chapter shows how to dynamically generate content for a Force.com site.

Creating a website template

In the previous recipes in this chapter, each page contained the entire Visualforce markup needed to display its content. This leads to repetition of common markup, to display headers and footers for example. In the event that the header or footer content needs to be changed, every page on a site needs to be updated with the new markup.

Visualforce provides a solution to this issue-templates. These allow the common elements of a site to be added to a template that is used as the starting point for rendering any page. The page then injects its specific content into the template at appropriate points.

In this recipe we will create a template version of the **SiteItem** Visualforce page from the *Retrieving content from Salesforce* recipe, where the template provides the header and footer markup. We will then make this page publicly available via an unauthenticated Force.com site.

Getting ready

This recipe requires that you have already completed the *Creating a site* and *Retrieving content from Salesforce* recipes, as it relies on the custom domain and Force.com site created in the first recipe, and the custom objects and controller from the second.

How to do it...

1. First, create the template; this is simply another Visualforce page. To do this, navigate to the Visualforce setup page by clicking on **Your Name** | **Setup** | **Develop** | **Pages**.
2. Click on the **New** button.

3. Enter `CookbookTemplate` in the **Label** field.
4. Accept the default **CookbookTemplate** that is automatically generated for the **Name** field.
5. Paste the contents of the `CookbookTemplate.page` file from the code download into the **Visualforce Markup** area and click on the **Save** button.
6. Next, create the Visualforce page by navigating to the Visualforce setup page by clicking on **Your Name** | **Setup** | **Develop** | **Pages**.
7. Click on the **New** button.
8. Enter `SiteItemTemplated` in the **Label** field.
9. Accept the default **SiteItemTemplated** that is automatically generated for the **Name** field.
10. Paste the contents of the `SiteItemTemplated.page` file from the code download into the **Visualforce Markup** area and click on the **Save** button.
11. Navigate to the Sites setup page by clicking on **Your Name** | **Setup** | **Develop** | **Sites**.
12. Click on the **Visualforce Cookbook** link in the **Sites** section.
13. On the resulting page, scroll down to the **Site Visualforce Pages** list and click on the **Edit** button.
14. On the resulting page, **Enable Visualforce Page Access**, select **CookbookTemplate** and **SiteItemTemplated** from the **Available Visualforce Pages** list, click on the Add icon to add it to the **Enabled Visualforce Pages** list and click on the **Save** button.

How it works...

Opening the following URL in your browser displays the **SiteItemTemplated** page: `http://<domain>/SiteItemTemplated`.

Demo Site
Visualforce Development Cookbook

No Developers

You don't need a developer to
change the content. The layout of
the site, on the other hand, requires
Visualforce skills.

Dynamic Content

This content has been retrieved
from the Salesforce database.
Updating the content will update
the site, subject to cache expiration.

Force.com Sites

Force.com Sites provide
unauthenticated access to
Salesforce data.

Lightning   Built using the Salesforce Lightning Design System.

Responsive   Resize the browser window and see what happens

Salesforce, salesforce.com, Sales Cloud, Service Cloud, Collaboration Cloud, Custom Cloud, Force.com and Chatter are trademarks of salesforce.com, inc.

Here, `<domain>` is the Force.com domain name chosen when configuring the site, for
example, `vfcookbook-developer-edition.na15.force.com`.

The template defines the common content and where pages utilizing the template can inject
their content. In the following code snippet, the `div` element with the style class of `slds`
generates the header and then inserts the body content provided by the page based on the
template:

```
<div class="slds">
    <div class="slds-page-header" role="banner">
        <div class="slds-media">
            <div class="slds-media__body">
                <p class="slds-page-header__title slds-truncate slds-align-
middle" >Demo Site</p>
                <p class="slds-text-body--small slds-page-
header__info">Visualforce Development Cookbook</p>
            </div>
        </div>
    </div>
    <apex:insert name="body" />
        ...
</div>
```

Note that there is no enclosing markup to indicate the page is a template.

The page making use of the template defines the content that will be inserted into the template when rendered, and encloses this in an `<apex:composition/>` component:

```
<apex:composition template="CookbookTemplate">
  <apex:define name="Title">
    Force.com Sites Recipe 5
  </apex:define>
        ...
</apex:composition>
```

See also

- The *Creating a site* recipe in this chapter shows how to set up a Force.com site and make a static page publicly available.
- The *Adding a header menu to a template* recipe in this chapter shows how to add a navigation menu to the header of a page template.

Adding a header menu to a template

A common requirement for a website is to display a navigation menu as part of the header. In the scenario where each page defines its own header and footer, it is straightforward to highlight a menu option to indicate the page that is currently being displayed. When a template provides the header and footer information, a mechanism is required to allow the page to identify itself to the template, which can then highlight the appropriate menu option.

In this recipe, we will create a Visualforce template that provides header and footer content to four other Visualforce pages: A **Home** page, an **About** page, a **Contact** page, and a **Links** page. We will then make these pages publicly available via an unauthenticated Force.com site.

Getting ready

This recipe requires that you have already completed the *Creating a site* recipe, as it relies on the custom domain and Force.com site created in that recipe.

How to do it...

1. First, create the template; this is simply another Visualforce page. Navigate to the Visualforce setup page by clicking on **Your Name** | **Setup** | **Develop** | **Pages**.

2. Click on the **New** button.

3. Enter CookbookTemplateV2 in the **Label** field.

4. Accept the default **CookbookTemplateV2** that is automatically generated for the **Name** field.

5. Paste the contents of the CookbookTemplateV2.page file from the code download into the **Visualforce Markup** area and click on the **Save** button.

6. Next, create the Home Visualforce page by navigating to the Visualforce setup page by clicking on **Your Name** | **Setup** | **Develop** | **Pages**.

7. Click on the **New** button.

8. Enter Home in the **Label** field.

9. Accept the default **Home** that is automatically generated for the **Name** field.

10. Paste the contents of the Home.page file from the code download into the **Visualforce Markup** area and click on the **Save** button.

11. Next, create the About Visualforce page by navigating to the Visualforce setup page by clicking on **Your Name** | **Setup** | **Develop** | **Pages**.

12. Click on the **New** button.

13. Enter About in the **Label** field.

14. Accept the default **About** that is automatically generated for the **Name** field.

15. Paste the contents of the About.page file from the code download into the **Visualforce Markup** area and click on the **Save** button.

16. Navigate to the Sites setup page by clicking on **Your Name** | **Setup** | **Develop** | **Sites**.

17. Next, create the Contact Visualforce page by navigating to the Visualforce setup page by clicking on **Your Name** | **Setup** | **Develop** | **Pages**.

18. Click on the **New** button.

19. Enter Contact in the **Label** field.

20. Accept the default **Contact** that is automatically generated for the **Name** field.
21. Paste the contents of the `Contact.page` file from the code download into the **Visualforce Markup** area and click on the **Save** button.
22. Next, create the Links Visualforce page by navigating to the Visualforce setup page by clicking on **Your Name** | **Setup** | **Develop** | **Pages**.
23. Click on the **New** button.
24. Enter `Links` in the **Label** field.
25. Accept the default **Links** that is automatically generated for the **Name** field.
26. Paste the contents of the `Links.page` file from the code download into the **Visualforce Markup** area and click on the **Save** button.
27. Navigate to the Sites setup page by clicking on **Your Name** | **Setup** | **Develop** | **Sites**.
28. Click on the **Visualforce Cookbook** link in the **Sites** section.
29. On the resulting page, scroll down to the **Site Visualforce Pages** list and click on the **Edit** button.
30. On the resulting page, **Enable Visualforce Page Access**, select **CookbookTemplateV2**, **Home**, **About**, **Contact**, and **Links** from the **Available Visualforce Pages** list, click on the Add icon to add it to the **Enabled Visualforce Pages** list, and click on the **Save** button.

How it works...

Opening the following URL in your browser displays the **Home** page:
`http://<domain>/Home.`

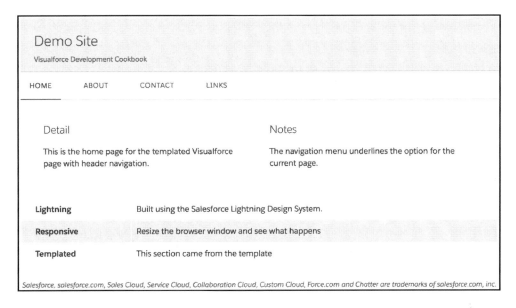

Here, `<domain>` is the Force.com domain name chosen when configuring the site, for example, `vfcookbook-developer-edition.na15.force.com`.

Clicking on any of the other pages in the header navigation bar updates the bar to indicate the current page.

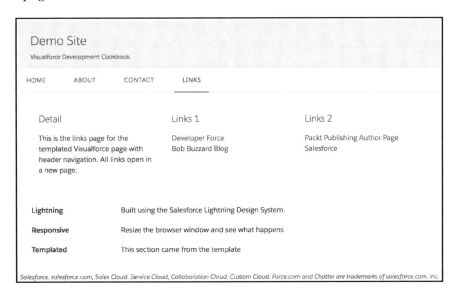

The template defines an empty value as the default:

```
<apex:variable var="page" value="" />
```

Each page defines markup to be injected into the template that overrides the page variable with its own value:

```
<apex:define name="page">
  <apex:variable var="page" value="home"/>
</apex:define>
```

The template inserts this markup:

```
<apex:insert name="page" />
```

For each tab, the template checks the value of the page variable and if it matches the tab content, adds the slds-active class to style it as the active tab:

```
<ul class="slds-tabs--default__nav" role="tablist">
    <li class="slds-tabs--default__item slds-text-heading--label
{!IF(page=='home','slds-active','')}"  role="presentation"><a class="slds-
tabs--default__link" href="/Home" role="tab" tabindex="0" aria-
selected="{!IF(page=='home','true','false')}" aria-controls="tab-
home">Home</a></li>
    ...
</ul>
```

See also

- The *Retrieving content from Salesforce* recipe in this chapter shows how to dynamically generate content for a Force.com site.
- The *Adding a sidebar to a template* recipe in this chapter shows how to add a sidebar component to a template.

Adding a sidebar to a template

Website content is not always suited to being broken up across a number of pages. A table of contents, while being potentially quite long, may be more usable when displayed on a single page. A sidebar can improve the user experience by providing links to allow the user to rapidly navigate around the lengthy content.

In this recipe, we will create a Visualforce template that provides header and footer content to two other Visualforce pages: A **TableOfContents** page (containing information about all chapters) and a **Chapter1** page (containing detailed information about the first chapter). Each page has a sidebar to assist with navigation through the page content. We will then make these pages publicly available via an unauthenticated Force.com site.

Getting ready

This recipe requires that you have already completed the *Creating a site* recipe, as it relies on the custom domain and Force.com site created in that recipe.

How to do it...

1. First, create the template; this is simply another Visualforce page. Navigate to the Visualforce setup page by clicking on **Your Name** | **Setup** | **Develop** | **Pages**.
2. Click on the **New** button.
3. Enter CookbookTemplateV3 in the **Label** field.
4. Accept the default **CookbookTemplateV3** that is automatically generated for the **Name** field.
5. Paste the contents of the CookbookTemplateV3.page file from the code download into the **Visualforce Markup** area and click on the **Save** button.
6. Next, create the TableOfContents Visualforce page by navigating to the Visualforce setup page by clicking on **Your Name** | **Setup** | **Develop** | **Pages**.
7. Click on the **New** button.
8. Enter TableOfContents in the **Label** field.
9. Accept the default **TableOfContents** that is automatically generated for the **Name** field.
10. Paste the contents of the TableOfContents.page file from the code download into the **Visualforce Markup** area and click on the **Save** button.
11. Next, create the Chapter1 Visualforce page by clicking on **Your Name** | **Setup** | **Develop** | **Pages** and navigating to the Visualforce setup page.
12. Click on the **New** button.
13. Enter Chapter1 in the **Label** field.
14. Accept the default **Chapter1** that is automatically generated for the **Name** field.
15. Paste the contents of the Chapter1.page file from the code download into the **Visualforce Markup** area and click on the **Save** button.

16. Navigate to the Sites setup page by clicking on **Your Name** | **Setup** | **Develop** | **Sites**.

17. Click on the **Visualforce Cookbook** link in the **Sites** section.

18. On the resulting page, scroll down to the **Site Visualforce Pages** list and click on the **Edit** button.

19. On the resulting page, **Enable Visualforce Page Access**, select **CookbookTemplateV3**, **TableOfContents**, and **Chapter1** from the **Available Visualforce Pages** list, click on the Add icon to add it to the **Enabled Visualforce Pages** list, and click on the **Save** button.

How it works...

Opening the following URL in your browser displays the **Home** page:
`http://<domain>/TableOfContents`.

Here, `<domain>` is the Force.com domain name chosen when configuring the site, for example, `vfcookbook-developer-edition.na15.force.com`.

Scrolling down or clicking on one of the navigation links in the sidebar allows quick navigation to the particular section.

```
Chapter 2 - Custom Components

  Passing Parameters to Components
  Updating Parameters in Components
  Passing Action Method Parameters to Components
  Data Driven Decimal Places
  Custom Iterator Components
  Set Value into Controller
  Multi-Select Related Object
  Notify Parent Page Controller

Chapter 3 - Capturing Data using Forms

  Editing a record in Visualforce
```

Clicking on the **Chapter 1 – General Utilities** link takes the user to the detail page for the first chapter, which also has a navigation sidebar.

Demo Site
Visualforce Development Cookbook

Table of Contents
  Recipe 1
  Recipe 2
  Recipe 3

1. Overriding Standard Buttons

How to Override a Standard record view to take the user to a Visualforce page

Lorem ipsum dolor sit amet, consectetur adipiscing elit. Fusce non pretium metus. In pulvinar vel lacus sed feugiat. Quisque a nunc tempus, dictum felis vel, ornare sapien. Mauris euismod iaculis imperdiet. Donec in nibh lectus. Aliquam erat volutpat. Curabitur laoreet felis est, eget aliquet est dignissim eget. Ut id elementum arcu. Nam lacinia commodo arcu ut sodales. Vestibulum tellus nunc, facilisis non mauris vitae, vulputate egestas augue. Aenean ipsum sapien, eleifend id mattis eu, placerat quis neque. Maecenas vel odio quam.

2. Data Driven Styling

Use an action poller to query the controller from the page until a condition is true, then disable the poller

The content is displayed in an SLDS grid, where the sidebar takes up one-quarter of the width of the page and the details take up three-quarters of the page on medium and large size devices. On small devices, the sidebar and details each stack and take up an entire row:

```
<div class="slds-grid slds-wrap slds-m-around--large">
    <div class="slds-col slds-size--1-of-1 slds-medium-size--1-of-4">
        <apex:insert name="sidebar" />
    </div>
    <div class="slds-col slds-size--1-of-1 slds-medium-size--3-of-4">
```

```
            <apex:insert name="body" />
        </div>
    </div>
```

Each page that utilizes the template provides the list of sidebar navigation elements and the content associated with each navigation element:

```
<apex:define name="sidebar">
    <ul class="slds-list--dotted">
        <li><a href="#chapter1"><i class="icon-arrow-right"></i> <span
class="lead">Chapter 1</span></a></li>
        <li><a href="#chapter2"><i class="icon-arrow-right"></i> <span
class="lead">Chapter 2</span></a></li>
        <li><a href="#chapter3"><i class="icon-arrow-right"></i> <span
class="lead">Chapter 3</span></a></li>
    </ul>
</apex:define>
<apex:define name="body">
    <ul class="slds-list--vertical">
        <li  id="chapter1" class="slds-list__item slds-has-divider--bottom-
space"><a href="/Chapter1">Chapter 1 - General Utilities</a></li>
        <li class="slds-list__item">
            <ul class="slds-list--vertical slds-is-nested">
                <li class="slds-list__item">Overriding Standard
Buttons</li>
                <li class="slds-list__item">Data Driven Styling</li>
                    ...
            </ul>
        </li>
    </ul
</apex:define>
```

It is important to make sure that every navigation item in the sidebar has associated content, or the user will experience viewing of content by clicking on links only in some instances.

See also

- The *Retrieving content from Salesforce* recipe in this chapter shows how to dynamically generate content for a Force.com site.
- The *Adding a header menu to a template* recipe in this chapter shows how to add a navigation menu to the header of a page template.

Conditional rendering in templates

Templating a website is an effective way to avoid repeated content and the associated maintenance overhead. There are occasions when this common content needs to be replaced for one or two exceptional pages; for example, a homepage may require slightly different header information than other pages in a site. This problem can be solved by the homepage not utilizing a template, but this then means that any common content that the homepage does require is repeated in the homepage and the template.

In this recipe we will create a Visualforce template that provides header and footer content. A page may override the header text provided by the template. We will then create two Visualforce pages that utilize this template: A StandardHeader page (that displays the standard header text) and a CustomHeader page (that provides its own custom text for use in the header). We will then make these pages publicly available via an unauthenticated Force.com site.

Getting ready...

This recipe requires that you have already completed the *Creating a site* recipe, as it relies on the custom domain and Force.com site created in that recipe.

How to do it...

1. First, create the template; this is simply another Visualforce page. Navigate to the Visualforce setup page by clicking on **Your Name** | **Setup** | **Develop** | **Pages**.
2. Click on the **New** button.
3. Enter `CookbookTemplateV4` in the **Label** field.
4. Accept the default **CookbookTemplateV4** that is automatically generated for the **Name** field.
5. Paste the contents of the `CookbookTemplateV4.page` file from the code download into the **Visualforce Markup** area and click on the **Save** button.
6. Next, create the StandardHeader Visualforce page by navigating to the Visualforce setup page by clicking on **Your Name** | **Setup** | **Develop** | **Pages**.
7. Click on the **New** button.
8. Enter `StandardHeader` in the **Label** field.
9. Accept the default **StandardHeader** that is automatically generated for the **Name** field.

10. Paste the contents of the `StandardHeader.page` file from the code download into the **Visualforce Markup** area and click on the **Save** button.

11. Next, create the CustomHeader Visualforce page by clicking on **Your Name** | **Setup** | **Develop** | **Pages** and navigating to the Visualforce setup page.

12. Click on the **New** button.

13. Enter `CustomHeader` in the **Label** field.

14. Accept the default **CustomHeader** that is automatically generated for the **Name** field.

15. Paste the contents of the `CustomHeader.page` file from the code download into the **Visualforce Markup** area and click on the **Save** button.

16. Navigate to the Sites setup page by clicking on **Your Name** | **Setup** | **Develop** | **Sites**.

17. Click on the **Visualforce Cookbook** link in the **Sites** section.

18. On the resulting page, scroll down to the **Site Visualforce Pages** list and click on the **Edit** button.

19. On the resulting page, **Enable Visualforce Page Access**, select **CookbookTemplateV4**, **StandardHeader**, and **CustomHeader** from the **Available Visualforce Pages** list, click on the Add icon to add it to the **Enabled Visualforce Pages** list, and click on the **Save** button.

How it works...

Opening the following URL in your browser displays the **StandardHeader** page: `http://<domain>/StandardHeader`.

Standard Header
Visualforce Development Cookbook

Detail

This is the first page for the Conditional Rendering in Templates recipe.

Notes

The 'Standard Header' text above is defaulted by the template, but may be overridden by a page.
For an example of this, click here.

Lightning   Built using the Salesforce Lightning Design System.

Responsive   Resize the browser window and see what happens

Templated   This section came from the template

Salesforce, salesforce.com, Sales Cloud, Service Cloud, Collaboration Cloud, Custom Cloud, Force.com and Chatter are trademarks of salesforce.com, inc.

Here, `<domain>` is the Force.com domain name chosen when configuring the site, for example, `vfcookbook-developer-edition.na15.force.com`.

Clicking on the **here** link in the **Notes** section displays the **CustomHeader** page with a different text in the header section.

Custom Header
Visualforce Development Cookbook

Detail

This is the second page for the Conditional Rendering in Templates recipe.

Notes

The 'Custom Header' text above is supplied by this page, and overrides the default value.
For an example of the default, click here.

Lightning   Built using the Salesforce Lightning Design System.

Responsive   Resize the browser window and see what happens

Templated   This section came from the template

Salesforce, salesforce.com, Sales Cloud, Service Cloud, Collaboration Cloud, Custom Cloud, Force.com and Chatter are trademarks of salesforce.com, inc.

The **CookbookTemplateV4** page defines a variable to indicate whether the standard header text should be used, and provides a mechanism for a page to inject Visualforce markup to override this:

```
<apex:variable var="header" value="standard" />
<apex:insert name="headerOverride" />
```

The standard header text is conditionally rendered based on the value of the header variable:

```
<apex:outputPanel rendered="{!header=='standard'}">
  Standard Header
</apex:outputPanel>
```

If the page has overridden the value of the header variable to `'custom'`, a mechanism is provided for the page-specific header text to be injected:

```
<apex:outputPanel rendered="{!header=='custom'}">
  <apex:insert name="customHeaderText" />
</apex:outputPanel>
```

A page may override the header text through the following markup:

```
<apex:define name="headerOverride">
  <apex:variable var="header" value="custom"/>
</apex:define>
<apex:define name="customHeaderText">
  Custom Header
</apex:define>
```

See also

- The *Retrieving content from Salesforce* recipe in this chapter shows how to dynamically generate content for a Force.com site.
- The *Adding a header menu to a template* recipe in this chapter shows how to add a navigation menu to the header of a page template.
- The *Adding a sidebar to a template* recipe in this chapter shows how to add a sidebar component to a template.

9

Visualforce in Salesforce1

In this chapter, we will cover the following topics and recipes:

- Navigating between pages
- Lightning forms
- Capturing the user's location
- Saving an image when creating a record
- Capturing a signature when creating a record
- Displaying a location in a map
- Scanning the QR code to access the record

Introduction

Salesforce1 was launched with Dreamforce 2013 and provides mobile access to Salesforce data and standard functionality including standard and custom objects, reports, dashboards, and chatter. In addition to this, Salesforce1 is a mobile application development platform that allows existing functionality to be extended and entirely new applications to be developed.

The Salesforce1 platform supports Visualforce in the following ways – note that in all cases the page must have the **Available for Salesforce mobile apps and Lightning Pages** checkbox selected:

- **Embedded in page layouts**: Using the same mechanism as the standard UI, the Visualforce page must extend the Standard Controller for the sObject type
- **Left Navigation Menu**: Visualforce tabs may be added directly to the menu

- **Publisher Actions**: Visualforce pages may be surfaced as publisher actions on record home pages as long as they extend the Standard Controller for the sObject type
- **Mobile Cards**: Displayed on the related information page for a record

In this chapter, we will create Visualforce pages to access and create Salesforce data, before moving on to more advanced techniques, including updating a record with the user's current location and saving an image when a record is created.

At the time of writing, only standard components in the apex namespace are supported in Salesforce1, so components such as <analytics:reportChart />, <chatter:feed /> and <flow:interview /> cannot be used in Visualforce for Salesforce1.

In addition, some standard components inside the apex namespace are not supported, typically those that render a significant amount of data or rely heavily on standard stylesheets, such as <apex:detail />, <apex:enhancedList /> and <apex:sectionHeader />

 For an up-to-date list of unsupported components, refer to the Visualforce Developer's Guide : https://developer.salesforce.com/docs/atlas.e n-us.salesforce1.meta/salesforce1/vf_dev_best_practices_compon ents_unsupported.htm.

Many standard components mimic the look and feel of the standard Salesforce UI, which generates markup that in turn relies on the standard Salesforce stylesheets. Standard stylesheets are suppressed when a Visualforce page is rendered in Salesforce1, which means that the markup will not render as expected. These components should therefore, be avoided in favor of either standard HTML markup, or a user interface framework such as Bootstrap or the Salesforce Lightning Design System.

Navigating between pages

Navigation in Salesforce1 is based on JavaScript events rather than URLs, which means a different approach needs to be taken to simply rendering HTML links. The navigation functionality is made available to Visualforce pages in Salesforce1 via the sforce.one JavaScript object.

This object provides a number of navigation functions, but the key ones are:

- `navigateToURL`: This navigates to the specified URL, which may be internal or external
- `navigateToSObject`: This navigates to the home page for a specific `sObject` record

 Full details of the sforce.one object can be found at: `https://developer.s alesforce.com/docs/atlas.en-us.salesforce1.meta/salesforce1/sa lesforce1_dev_jsapi_sforce_one.htm?search_text=navigate`.

The `sforce.one` object is not available when a Visualforce page is rendered in the standard Salesforce UI, so pages that rely on this navigation method will not work correctly in the standard UI. Visualforce pages intended for use in both the standard UI and Salesforce1 should check for the existence of the `sforce.one` JavaScript object and execute the appropriate navigation code based on the result. The page in this recipe includes an example of this.

In this recipe, we will create two Visualforce pages, the first displaying an account and its related contacts, and the second displaying the account and its related opportunities, and navigate between them. In the standard UI, the pages are accessed via a Visualforce button on the Account record view page. In Salesforce1, the button is automatically transformed to a publisher action on the record home page.

How to do it...

This recipe requires that you have already uploaded the Salesforce Lightning Design System version 2.0.2 as detailed in `Chapter 8`, *Force.com Sites*.

This recipe does not require any controllers, so we only need to create the Visualforce pages.

1. First, create the Visualforce page that displays the account and its related contacts by navigating to the Visualforce setup page by clicking on **Your Name | Setup | Develop | Visualforce Pages**.
2. Click on the **New** button.
3. Enter SF1AccountsContacts in the **Label** field.

4. Accept the default **SF1AccountsContacts** that is automatically generated for the **Name** field.

5. Check the box labeled **Available for Salesforce mobile apps and Lightning Pages**.

6. Paste the contents of the SF1AccountsContacts.page file from the code download into the **Visualforce Markup** area and click on the **Save** button.

7. Navigate to the Visualforce setup page by clicking on **Your Name | Setup | Develop | Visualforce Pages**.

8. Locate the entry for the **SF1AccountsContacts** page and click on the **Security** link.

9. On the resulting page, select which profiles should have access and click on the **Save** button.

10. Next, create the Visualforce page that that displays the account and its related opportunities. Navigate to the Visualforce setup page by clicking on **Your Name | Setup | Develop | Visualforce Pages**.

11. Click on the **New** button.

12. Enter SF1AccountsOpps in the **Label** field.

13. Accept the default **SF1AccountsOpps** that is automatically generated for the **Name** field.

14. Check the box labeled **Available for Salesforce mobile apps and Lightning Pages**.

15. Paste the contents of the SF1AccountsOpps.page file from the code download into the **Visualforce Markup** area and click on the **Save** button.

16. Navigate to the Visualforce setup page by clicking on **Your Name | Setup | Develop | Visualforce Pages**.

17. Locate the entry for the **SF1AccountsOpps** page and click on the **Security** link.

18. On the resulting page, select which profiles should have access and click on the **Save** button.

19. Next, create the custom button. Click **Your Name | Setup | Customize | Accounts | Buttons, Links, and Actions**.

20. Click on the **New Button or Link** button.

21. Enter ComboView in the **Label** field.

22. Accept the default **ComboView** that is automatically generated for the **Name** field.

23. Select **Detail Page Button** from the **Display Type** radio buttons.
24. Select **Visualforce Page** from the **Content Source** select list.
25. Select **SF1AccountsContacts** from the **Content** select list.
26. Click the **Save** button from the **Content** select list.
27. Finally, add the button to the Account page layout. Navigate to **Your Name** | **Setup** | **Customize** | **Accounts** | **Page Layouts**.
28. Click the **Edit** button to the right of the **Account Layout** entry on the resulting page.
29. Select the **Buttons** entry from the left-hand palette, drag the **ComboView** button to the **Custom Buttons** area in the **Account Detail** section and click the **Save** button.

How it works...

Open the Salesforce1 application and navigate to an account that has at least one opportunity and contact, and click the **Show More** icon in the publisher bar at the bottom of the screen:

From the resulting actions, scroll down and click the **ComboView** entry:

This displays the account and its contacts.

Clicking the **View Opps** button navigates to the page that displays the account and its opportunities.

In order to ensure that the most up-to-date browser functionality is available, Visualforce pages in Salesforce1 specify HTML5 as the document type.

```
<apex:page docType="html-5.0">
```

HTML5 is the fifth, and at the time of writing, current version of the HTML standard, with features designed specifically for low-powered devices such as smartphones and tablets.

The viewport `meta` tag is used to make the mobile device report its actual width with an initial scale multiplier of 1 – this ensures that the page is displayed at the actual resolution of the device. As `meta` tags must be placed inside the header tag, the attributes to disable automatic generation of the `HTML` and `BODY` tags are supplied to the page tag. When the `applyHtmlTag` attribute is set to false, the `showHeader` attribute must also be set to false in order for the Visualforce page to be saved.

```
<apex:page showHeader="false" applyHtmlTag="false" applyBodyTag="false"
docType="html-5.0">
    <head>
      <meta name="viewport" content="width=device-width, initial-
scale=1.0"></meta>
    </head>
```

 You will often see a recommendation to set the user-scalable property on the viewport `meta` tag to no, which stops the user from zooming the page in or out. Setting this can cause accessibility problems, for example partially sighted users may need to enlarge the text size in order to be able to read it.

The **View Opps** button is an `anchor` tag styled as a button that invokes a function to carry out the navigation.

```
<div class="slds-m-bottom-x--small slds-m-top --small slds-text-align--
center">
  <a href="javascript:navigateToOpps();" class="slds-button slds-button--
neutral">
     View Opps
  </a>
</div>
```

The `navigateToOpps` function generates a target URL, including the account ID, and determines if the `sforce.one` object is defined. If it is, this is used to navigate to the account and opportunities page. If it is not defined, the `window.location` value is set to the target, which will navigate to that URL in the standard UI.

```
function navigateToOpps() {
    var target='/apex/SF1AccountsOpps?id={!Account.id}';
    if (typeof sforce !== 'undefined' && sforce.one) {
        sforce.one.navigateToURL(target);
    }
    else {
        window.location=target;
    }
}
```

Each account, contact, or opportunity record is rendered as an SLDS tile – the fields appear in a grid, spanning a single row regardless of device size:

```
<div class="slds-tile__detail slds-text-body --small slds-m-top--small">
  <div class="slds-grid slds-wrap">
    <div class="slds-col slds-size--1-of-3">
      <strong>Industry:</strong>
    </div>
    <div class="slds-col slds-size--2-of-3">
      {!Account.Industry}
    </div>
  </div>
</div>
```

Lightning forms

Visualforce applications that maintain state across multiple requests to the server utilize the viewstate, which may be up to 135 Kb in size. The viewstate can be a significant resource for mobile devices to manage as they typically have a reduced memory footprint compared to desktop devices. The viewstate must also be sent with every HTTP request to the server, which over a 3G/4G network can be slow and expensive in terms of data plan usage.

Visualforce pages intended for Salesforce1 should make use of JavaScript remoting, as detailed in the JavaScript remoting recipe in `Chapter 7`, *Enhancing the Client with JavaScript*. These server calls are stateless (so the request only contains the data items that the server needs for the specific action), and take place via AJAX, which is a more performant protocol and doesn't require a full page reload for the server response.

Using Visualforce remoting is not without its downsides though – JavaScript code must be developed to extract and process any user inputs, create the request, and process the server response, including any DOM updates required, which would be handled by the browser when using `HTTP` requests and Visualforce forms.

In this recipe, we will create a Visualforce page for use in Salesforce1 that renders a form for the user to create an account and contact via a single form. The records will be created via a Visualforce remote method and the page updated to display the result. The page will be accessed from the Salesforce1 left-hand navigation menu, which requires to be available through a Visualforce tab.

Getting ready

This recipe requires that you have already uploaded the Salesforce Lightning Design System version 2.0.2 as detailed in `Chapter 8`, *Force.com Sites*.

How to do it...

This recipe requires a custom controller, so this will need to be present before the Visualforce page can be created

1. First, create the controller for the Visualforce page by navigating to the **Apex Classes** setup page by clicking on **Your Name** | **Setup** | **Develop** | **Apex Classes**.
2. Click on the **New** button.
3. Paste the contents of the `SF1LightningFormController.cls` Apex class from the code download into the **Apex Class** area.
4. Click on the **Save** button.
5. Next, create the Visualforce page, navigate to **Your Name** | **Setup** | **Develop** | **Visualforce Pages**.

6. Click on the **New** button.
7. Enter SF1LightningForm in the **Label** field.
8. Accept the default **SF1LightningForm** that is automatically generated for the **Name** field.
9. Check the box labeled **Available for Salesforce mobile apps and Lightning Pages**.
10. Paste the contents of the SF1LightningForm.page file from the code download into the **Visualforce Markup** area and click on the **Save** button.
11. Navigate to the Visualforce setup page by clicking on **Your Name** | **Setup** | **Develop** | **Visualforce Pages**.
12. Locate the entry for the **SF1LightningForm** page and click on the **Security** link.
13. On the resulting page, select which profiles should have access and click on the **Save** button.
14. Next, create the Visualforce tab for the page, navigate to **Your Name** | **Setup** | **Create** | **Tabs**.
15. Click on the **New** button in the **Visualforce Tabs** section.
16. On the resulting page, select **SF1LightningForm** button from the **Visualforce Page** select list.
17. Enter Form in the **Label** field.
18. Accept the default **Form** that is automatically generated for the **Name** field.
19. Click the lookup icon in the **Tab Style** field, choose any style in the resulting popup and click the **Next** button at the bottom right of the page.
20. On the resulting page, leave all fields at the default value and click the **Next** button at the bottom-right of the page.
21. On the resulting page, deselect the **Include Tab** checkbox and click the **Save** button at the bottom-right of the page.
22. Finally, add the tab to the Salesforce1 menu and navigate to **Your Name** | **Setup** | **Mobile Administration** | **Salesforce1 Navigation**.
23. Move the **Form** tab from the **Available** list to the top of the **Selected** list and click the **Save** button.

How it works...

Open the Salesforce1 application and select the **Form** entry from the left-hand menu.

Enter the account and contact information and click the Save button

An alert message is displayed indicating the records were successfully created.

The newly created account record home page is then opened.

The form is composed of regular HTML elements styled with the SLDS:

```
<div class="slds-form-element">
  <label class="slds-form-element__label">Industry</label>
  <div class="slds-form-element__control">
    <div class="slds-select_container">
      <select id="accIndustry" class="slds-select">
        <option>Agriculture</option>
        <option>Apparel</option>
        <option>Banking</option>
```

```
        </select>
      </div>
    </div>
  </div>
```

The HTML5 `type` attribute is used to define the type of data to be captured by an input.

```
<input id="accName" class="slds-input" type="text"
        placeholder="Name ..." />
```

 The `type` attribute causes the browser to render the appropriate control to capture the data. Specifying a type of `number` causes the browser to render a touch keyboard suitable for numeric input while specifying a type of `date` causes the browser to render a native date picker for the device.

 For a full list of the type options, see the Mozilla Developer Network input element documentation at: `https://developer.mozilla.org/en-US/doc s/Web/HTML/Element/input`.

When the user clicks the button to save the records, a JavaScript function is executed that extracts the field values and stores these in a JavaScript object that reflects the Salesforce `sObject`.

```
var name=document.querySelector('#accName').value;
var industry=document.querySelector('#accIndustry').value;
var website=document.querySelector('#accWebsite').value;
var account = {Name : name,
               Industry : industry,
               Website : website};
```

The account and contact JavaScript objects are converted to JSON strings for processing by the remote method.

```
SF1LightningFormController.CreateAccountAndContact(JSON.stringify(account),
JSON.stringify(contact), createAccountContactResponseHandler);
```

The Apex controller deserializes the JSON strings and inserts the records.

```
@RemoteAction
public static Id CreateAccountAndContact(String accountJSON, String
contactJSON)
{
  Account acc = (Account) JSON.deserialize(accountJSON, Account.class);
  insert acc;
```

The JavaScript remote method callback function either redirects the user to the account record home page, or displays details about any errors that occurred.

```
function createAccountContactResponseHandler(result, event) {
    if (event.status) {
        alert('Account and contact created');
        if (typeof sforce !== 'undefined' && sforce.one) {
            sforce.one.navigateToSObject(result);
        }
        else {
            window.location='/' + result;
        }
    }
    else if (event.type === 'exception') {
        alert('Exception in Remote Method:\n' + event.message);
    }
```

Capturing the user's location

Mobile devices, by their very nature, are used on the move and applications often need to capture the location of the user in order to provide the best user experience; for example, showing proximity to a business or services, or allowing users to check-in at a destination.

In this recipe, we will create a mobile Visualforce page to capture a lead and the location of the user at the point of lead creation. The location will be stored on the lead record in the Salesforce database in a custom geolocation field.

Getting ready

This recipe requires that you have already uploaded the Salesforce Lightning Design System version 2.0.2 as detailed in `Chapter 8`, *Force.com Sites*.

This recipe also requires a custom field on the lead `sObject` to capture the location.

1. Navigate to the lead fields setup page by clicking on **Your Name** | **Setup** | **App Setup** | **Customize** | **Lead** | **Fields**.
2. Scroll down to the **Lead Custom Fields and Relationships** section and click on the **New** button.
3. On the next page, **Step 1. Choose the field type**, select the **Geolocation** option from the **Data Type** radio buttons and click on the **Next** button.

4. On the next page, **Step 2. Enter the Details**, enter Location in the **Label** field, enter 10 in the **Decimal Places** field, accept the default name of **Location**, and click on the **Next** button.

5. On the next page, **Step 3. Establish field-level security for reference field**, leave all the fields at their default values and click on the **Next** button.

6. On the next page, **Step 4. Add to page layouts**, leave all the fields at their default values and click on the **Save** button.

How to do it...

This recipe requires a custom controller, so this needs to be present before the Visualforce page can be created.

1. First, create the controller for the Visualforce page by navigating to the **Apex Classes** setup page by clicking on **Your Name** | **Setup** | **Develop** | **Apex Classes**.

2. Click on the **New** button.

3. Paste the contents of the SF1CaptureLocationController.cls Apex class from the code download into the **Apex Class** area.

4. Click on the **Save** button.

5. Next, create the Visualforce page by navigating to the Visualforce setup page by clicking on **Your Name** | **Setup** | **Develop** | **Visualforce Pages**.

6. Click on the **New** button.

7. Enter SF1CaptureLocation in the **Label** field.

8. Accept the default **SF1CaptureLocation** that is automatically generated for the **Name** field.

9. Check the box labeled **Available for Salesforce mobile apps and Lightning Pages**.

10. Paste the contents of the SF1CaptureLocation.page file from the code download into the **Visualforce Markup** area and click on the **Save** button.

11. Navigate to the Visualforce setup page by clicking on **Your Name** | **Setup** | **Develop** | **Visualforce Pages**.

12. Locate the entry for the **SF1CaptureLocation** page and click on the **Security** link.

13. On the resulting page, select which profiles should have access and click on the **Save** button.

14. Next, create the Visualforce tab for the page and navigate to **Your Name** | **Setup** | **Create** | **Tabs**.

15. Click on the **New** button in the **Visualforce Tabs** section.

16. On the resulting page, select **SF1CaptureLocation** from the **Visualforce Page** select list.
17. Enter `Location` in the **Label** field.
18. Accept the default **Location** that is automatically generated for the **Name** field.
19. Click the lookup icon in the **Tab Style** field, choose any style in the resulting popup and click the **Next** button at the bottom-right of the page.
20. On the resulting page, leave all fields at the default value and click the **Next** button at the bottom-right of the page.
21. On the resulting page, deselect the **Include Tab** checkbox and click the **Save** button at the bottom-right of the page.
22. Finally, add the tab to the Salesforce1 menu and navigate to **Your Name | Setup | Mobile Administration | Salesforce1 Navigation**.
23. Move the **Location** tab from the **Available** list to the top of the **Selected** list and click the **Save** button.

How it works...

Open the Salesforce1 application and select the **Location** entry from the left-hand menu:

Fill out the form details and click on the **Save** button.

This executes JavaScript to retrieve the user's location, which may require that the user give explicit permission.

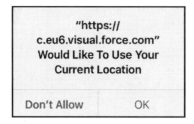

The lead is then saved to the Salesforce database, the form is cleared, and a confirmation message is displayed. In the event of an error or if retrieving the user's location fails, an error message is displayed in place of the confirmation message.

When the user clicks on the **Save** button, the page uses the built-in geolocation functionality, if available, to determine the current location.

```
if (navigator.geolocation) {
    navigator.geolocation.getCurrentPosition(
                geoSuccess,
                geoError,
                {
                    maximumAge: 0,
                    timeout:30000,
                    enableHighAccuracy: true
                }
    );
}
```

As the getCurrentPosition function is asynchronous, callback functions must be provided to handle error (geoError) and success (geoSuccess) results.

The geoSuccess function simply delegates to a common function process, the lead, passing the location as coordinate parameters.

```
function geoSuccess(position)
{
  uploadLead(position.coords.latitude,
            position.coords.longitude);
}
```

The `uploadLead` function executes the JavaScript remote controller method to store the lead record in the Salesforce database, which is also asynchronous and again requires a callback method to be specified.

```
function uploadLead(lat, long)
{
    var fname=document.querySelector('#firstname').value;
...
    SF1CaptureLocationController.CreateLead(fname, lname, company,
                        email, lat, long, leadCaptured, {escape:true});
}
```

The controller method is made available for execution in JavaScript via the `@RemoteAction` annotation.

```
@RemoteAction
public static String CreateLead(String fName, String lName,
                                String inCompany, String inEmail,
                                Double latitude, Double longitude)
{
    Lead newLead=new Lead(FirstName=fName
                ...);
    if (null!=latitude)
    {
        newLead.Location__Latitude__s=latitude;
        newLead.Location__Longitude__s=longitude;
    }

    ...
}
```

Saving an image when creating a record

When a user is creating a record in Salesforce, for example, a case that reports a problem with a piece of equipment, it can be useful to attach an image as proof of the problem or to make it clear exactly where the issue is.

In this recipe, we will create a Visualforce page that allows a user to raise a case and include an image as proof that there is a problem. The Visualforce page will be made available to the Salesforce1 application as a custom action on the account record home page.

Getting ready

This recipe requires that you have already uploaded the Salesforce Lightning Design System version 2.0.2 as detailed in `Chapter 8`, *Force.com Sites*.

This recipe also makes use of the Mega Pixel image rendering library created by Shinichi Tomita. Download `megapix-image.js` from `https://github.com/stomita/ios-imagefi le-megapixel/tree/master/src`.

Carry out the following steps to upload the library as a static resource.

1. Navigate to the Static Resource setup page by clicking on **Your Name | Setup | Develop | Static Resources**.
2. Click on the **New** button.
3. Enter `MegaPixelImg` in the **Name** field.
4. Enter Mega Pixel Image JavaScript in the **Description** field.
5. Click on the **Browse** button and select the `megapix-image.js` file downloaded in Step 1.
6. Accept the default **Private** value for the **Cache Control** field and click on the **Save** button.

How to do it...

This recipe requires a custom controller, so this will need to be present before the Visualforce page can be created

1. First, create the custom controller for the page by navigating to the **Apex Classes** setup page by clicking on **Your Name | Setup | Develop | Apex Classes**.
2. Click on the **New** button.
3. Paste the contents of the `SF1RecordAndImageController.cls` Apex class from the code download into the **Apex Class** area.
4. Click on the **Save** button.
5. Next, create the page that will capture the lead by navigating to the Visualforce setup page by clicking on **Your Name | Setup | Develop | Visualforce Pages**.
6. Click on the **New** button.
7. Enter `SF1RecordAndImage` in the **Label** field.
8. Accept the default **SF1RecordAndImage** that is automatically generated for the **Name** field.

9. Check the box labeled **Available for Salesforce mobile apps and Lightning Pages**.

10. Paste the contents of the `SF1RecordAndImage.page` file from the code download into the **Visualforce Markup** area and click on the **Save** button.

11. Navigate to the Visualforce setup page by clicking on **Your Name | Setup | Develop | Visualforce Pages**.

12. Locate the entry for the **SF1RecordAndImage** page and click on the **Security** link.

13. On the resulting page, select which profiles should have access and click on the **Save** button.

14. Next, create the Account custom action and navigate to **Your Name | Setup | Customize | Accounts | Buttons, Links, and Actions**.

15. On the resulting page, click the **New Action Button**.

16. Select **Custom Visualforce** from the **Action Type** options click the **New Action Button**.

17. Select **SF1RecordAndImage** from the **Visualforce Page** options and click the **New Action Button**.

18. Enter `500px` in the **Size** field.

19. Enter `Create Proof` in the **Size** field.

20. Accept the default **Create_Proof** that is automatically generated for the **Name** field.

21. Click the **Save** button.

22. Finally, add the custom action to the Account page layout. Navigate to **Your Name | Setup | Customize | Accounts | Page Layouts**.

23. Click the **Edit** button to the right of the **Account Layout** entry on the resulting page.

24. In the **Salesforce1 and Lightning Experience Actions** section click the **Override the predefined actions**.

25. Select the **Salesforce1 Actions** entry from the left-hand palette, drag the **Create Proof** action to the **Salesforce1 and Lightning Experience Actions** area and click the **Save** button.

How it works...

Open the Salesforce1 application and navigate to the record home page of any account.

Click the **Create Proof** entry in the action bar at the bottom of the screen.

Fill out the form details and click the **Choose File** button to capture an image. In the resulting dialog choose **Take Photo** and capture an image.

The canvas area is updated with the image. Portrait photos may appear sideways – if this happens click the **Rotate** button.

Click the **Save** button at the top-right to create the case and associated image in Salesforce (depending on your bandwidth, this may take a little while).

Once the `server` method has completed, the publisher closes and the record home page for the account is displayed again. Navigating to the **RELATED** tab shows the newly created case.

Clicking through to the case details **RELATED** tab and opening the **Attachments** related list shows the `CaseImage.png` file, which contains the captured image.

As the Visualforce page interacts with the Salesforce1 publisher, an additional JavaScript include is required.

```
<script type='text/javascript' src='/canvas/sdk/js/publisher.js'></script>
```

When the page is rendered, it subscribes to the event triggered when the user presses the **Save** button and enables the button for use.

```
Sfdc.canvas.publisher.subscribe({name: "publisher.post", onData:function(e)
{
  save();
}});
Sfdc.canvas.publisher.publish({name: "publisher.setValidForSubmit",
payload:"true"});
```

When an image is captured, the `onchange` handler for the file input fires, which makes the file the source of a hidden image element and creates a `MegaPixelImage` wrapper for it.

```
takePicture.onchange = function (event) {
    var files = event.target.files;
    if (files && files.length > 0) {
        file = files[0];
    try {
            var fileReader = new FileReader();
            fileReader.onload = function (event) {
                showPicture.src = event.target.result;
            };
          ....
        }
        catch (e) {
          ...
        }
        mpImg = new MegaPixImage(file);
    }
};
```

When the hidden image is populated, it is resized and the contents are rendered into the `canvas` element.

```
showPicture.onload = function(event)   {
    ...
  mpImg.render(mycanvas, { maxWidth: width, maxHeight: height });
};
```

The **Rotate** button allows pictures captured in portrait mode to be rotated once to landscape prior to uploading to Salesforce.

```
function rotateImage() {
  mpImg.render(mycanvas, { maxWidth: width, maxHeight: height, orientation:
6 });
}
```

When the **Save** button is clicked, the contents of the `canvas` element are extracted into a `dataURL` to be sent to the server.

 Data URLs use the Data URI Scheme to include data in-line in web pages as though they were external resources. For full details on the Data URI scheme see: `https://developer.mozilla.org/en-US/docs/Web/HTTP/data_URIs`.

```
var strDataURI;
if (gotPic) {
    strDataURI=mycanvas.toDataURL();
    if (null!=strDataURI) {
        strDataURI = strDataURI.split(',')[1];
    }
}
```

The Apex controller remote method creates the case record and inserts the image as a related attachment:

```
@RemoteAction
public static String SaveCase(String accountId, String subject, String
description, String pictureBody)
{
  Case cs = new Case(AccountId=accountId, Subject=subject ... );
  insert cs;
  ...

  Attachment a = new Attachment();
  a.ParentId = cs.id;
  a.ContentType = 'image/png';
  a.Name = 'CaseImage.png';
  a.Body = EncodingUtil.base64Decode(pictureBody);
  insert a;


  ...
  return cs.id;
}
```

The `remote` method JavaScript callback closes the publisher and refreshes the record detail page if the method completed successfully.

```
function caseCaptured(result, event) {
    if (event.status) {
        Sfdc.canvas.publisher.publish({name: "publisher.close",
                    payload:{ refresh:"true"}});
        ...
    }
}
```

See also

- The *Capturing a signature when creating a record* recipe in this chapter explains how a Visualforce page containing a `canvas` element may be used to capture the user's signature.

Capturing a signature when creating a record

With the advent of the HTML5 canvas API, it is now possible for a user to write their signature directly onto the screen of a mobile device, which can then be turned into an image and stored against a record in Salesforce.

In this recipe, we will create a Visualforce page for use in Salesforce1 that captures the details of a lead and their signature agreeing to receive marketing e-mails.

Getting ready

This recipe requires that you have already uploaded the Salesforce Lightning Design System version 2.0.2 as detailed in `Chapter 8`, *Force.com Sites*.

This recipe also makes use of the `signature_pad` JavaScript library created by Szymon Nowak. At the time of writing, the latest version of the `signature_pad` library is 1.5.3 – if you download a later version and use a different name from that detailed in the following steps, you will need to update the Visualforce pages to use the name that you have chosen.

Download `signature_pad.min.js` from `https://github.com/szimek/signature_pad/tree/v1.5.3`.

1. Navigate to the Static Resource setup page by clicking on **Your Name** | **Setup** | **Develop** | **Static Resources**.
2. Click on the **New** button.
3. Enter `SignaturePad_1_5_3` in the **Name** field.
4. Enter `SignaturePad version 1.5.3` in the **Description** field.
5. Click on the **Browse** button and select the `signature_pad.min.js` file downloaded in Step 1.
6. Accept the default **Private** value for the **Cache Control** field and click on the **Save** button.

How to do it...

This recipe requires a custom controller, so this will need to be present before the Visualforce page can be created

1. First, create the custom controller for the page by navigating to the **Apex Classes** setup page by clicking on **Your Name** | **Setup** | **Develop** | **Apex Classes**.
2. Click on the **New** button.
3. Paste the contents of the `SF1SignHereController.cls` Apex class from the code download into the **Apex Class** area.
4. Click on the **Save** button.
5. Next, create the page that will capture the lead by navigating to the Visualforce setup page by clicking on **Your Name** | **Setup** | **Develop** | **Visualforce Pages**.
6. Click on the **New** button.
7. Enter `SF1SignHere` in the **Label** field.
8. Accept the default **SF1SignHere** that is automatically generated for the **Name** field.
9. Check the box labeled **Available for Salesforce mobile apps and Lightning Pages**.
10. Paste the contents of the `SF1SignHere.page` file from the code download into the **Visualforce Markup** area and click on the **Save** button.

11. Navigate to the Visualforce setup page by clicking on **Your Name** | **Setup** | **Develop** | **Visualforce Pages**.

12. Locate the entry for the **SF1SignHere** page and click on the **Security** link.

13. On the resulting page, select which profiles should have access and click on the **Save** button.

14. Next, create the Visualforce tab for the page and navigate to **Your Name** | **Setup** | **Create** | **Tabs**.

15. Click on the **New** button in the **Visualforce Tabs** section.

16. On the resulting page, select **SF1SignHere** from the **Visualforce Page** select list.

17. Enter Sign in the **Label** field.

18. Accept the default **Sign** that is automatically generated for the **Name** field.

19. Click the lookup icon in the **Tab Style** field, choose any style in the resulting popup and click the **Next** button at the bottom-right of the page.

20. On the resulting page, leave all fields at the default value and click the **Next** button at the bottom-right of the page.

21. On the resulting page, deselect the **Include Tab** checkbox and click the **Save** button at the bottom-right of the page.

22. Finally, add the tab to the Salesforce1 menu and navigate to **Your Name** | **Setup** | **Mobile Administration** | **Salesforce1 Navigation**.

23. Move the **Sign** tab from the **Available** list to the top of the **Selected** list and click the **Save** button.

How it works...

Open the Salesforce1 application and select the **Sign** entry from the left-hand menu.

Fill out the form details, write your signature in the area under the **I agree to receiving marketing emails** label.

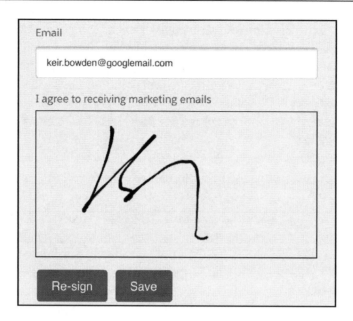

Clicking on the **Save** button executes JavaScript to convert the canvas content to an image URI and extract the fields from the form. The lead and image are then saved to the Salesforce database, the form is cleared, and a confirmation message is displayed.

In the event that an error occurs, an error message is displayed in place of the confirmation message.

Navigating to the newly created lead, accessing the Notes and Attachments related list, and clicking on the LeadSignature.png attachment shows the signature image.

When the page is first loaded the canvas is wrapped in a SignaturePad object.

```
var signaturePad = new SignaturePad(canvas);
```

When the user clicks the **Save** button, the signature is converted to a data URI, the form fields are extracted and the controller method is invoked to create the lead and associated attachment:

```
var strDataURI = signaturePad.toDataURL();
strDataURI = strDataURI.replace(/^data:image\/(png|jpg);base64,/, "");

var firstname=document.querySelector('#firstname').value;
    ...
SF1SignHereController.SaveLead(firstname, lastname, company, email,
                       strDataURI, leadCaptured, {escape:true});
```

As JavaScript Remoting calls are asynchronous, a callback function must be provided to handle the controller response, in this case, it is the `leadCaptured` function, which checks the response from the controller, generates the appropriate message for the user and clears the form on success.

```
function leadCaptured(result, event) {
    if (event.status) {
        if ('SUCCESS'==result) {
            document.querySelector('#firstname').value='';
                ...
            signaturePad.clear();
            document.querySelector('#msg').innerHTML='<span
style="color:green;">Lead created</span>';
        }
        else {
            document.querySelector("#msg").innerHTML='<span
style="color:red">An error occurred : ' + result + '</span>';
        }
    }
    ...
}
```

The Apex controller remote method creates the lead record and then creates an attachment containing the signature image.

```
@RemoteAction
public static String SaveLead(String firstName, String lastName,
String company, String email, String pictureBody)
{
    Lead ld = new Lead(FirstName=firstName,  ...   );
    insert ld;
    if (null!=pictureBody)
    {
        Attachment a = new Attachment();
        a.ParentId = ld.id;
        a.ContentType = 'image/png';
        a.Name = 'LeadSignature.png';
        a.Body = EncodingUtil.base64Decode(pictureBody);
        insert a;
    }
    return 'SUCCESS';
    ...
}
```

See also

- The *Capturing the user's location* recipe in this chapter shows how to capture coordinates of the user's current location and store them in a record.

Displaying a location in a map

When a Salesforce record contains geolocation data, a common requirement is to show this location on a map, for example, to allow field service agents to determine the location of their next job or for a sales rep to plan their day visiting prospects.

In this recipe, we will create a Visualforce page that plots the location of a lead record that was created with geolocation information.

 This recipe makes use of the Google Maps API. At the time of writing, the Terms and Conditions of this API provide free use only when your implementation is freely and publicly accessible. In the event that you wish to use this API in a production Salesforce implementation, you will be required to purchase a Google Maps API for Business License. You can find more information at the following Salesforce knowledge article: `https://help.salesforce.com/HTViewSolution?id=188482`. The full terms and conditions for the Google Maps API are available from: `https://developers.google.com/maps/terms`.

Getting ready

This recipe requires that you have already uploaded the Salesforce Lightning Design System version 2.0.2 as detailed in `Chapter 8`, *Force.com Sites*.

This recipe also requires that you have completed the *Capturing the user's location* recipe earlier in this chapter and have captured at least one lead with geolocation information.

How to do it...

1. First, create the desktop version of the page by navigating to the Visualforce setup page by clicking on **Your Name** | **Setup** | **Develop** | **Visualforce Pages**.

2. Click on the **New** button.

3. Enter SF1Map in the **Label** field.

4. Accept the default **SF1Map** that is automatically generated for the **Name** field.

5. Check the box labeled **Available for Salesforce mobile apps and Lightning Pages**.

6. Paste the contents of the SF1Map.page file from the code download into the **Visualforce Markup** area and click on the **Save** button.

7. Navigate to the Visualforce setup page by clicking on **Your Name** | **Setup** | **Develop** | **Visualforce Pages**.

8. Locate the entry for the **SF1Map** page and click on the **Security** link.

9. On the resulting page, select which profiles should have access and click on the **Save** button.

10. Next, add the Visualforce page as a mobile card to the Lead page layout. Navigate to **Your Name** | **Setup** | **Customize** | **Leads** | **Page Layouts**.

11. Click the **Edit** button to the right of the **Lead Layout** entry on the resulting page.

12. Select the **Visualforce Pages** entry from the left-hand palette, drag the **SF1Map** entry to the **Mobile Cards (Salesforce1 only)** area and click the **Save** button.

How it works...

Open the Salesforce1 application and navigate to the **RELATED** tab of a lead record with the Location field populated. The location the lead was captured at is shown on a Google map at the top of the page.

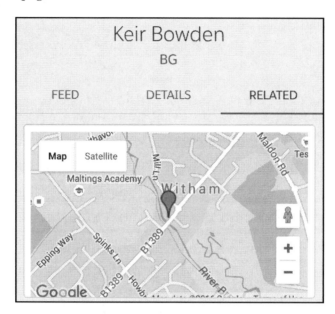

The Google Maps API is used to render a map centered at the lead location with a marker to indicate its exact location. The map is zoomed out to level *15* to display enough information to make the map useful.

```
function createMap(lat, lon){
    // Get the map div, and center the map at the proper geolocation
    var currentPosition = new google.maps.LatLng(lat,lon);
    var mapDiv = document.getElementById('map-canvas');
    var map = new google.maps.Map(mapDiv, {
                              center: currentPosition,
                              zoom: 15,
                              mapTypeId: google.maps.MapTypeId.ROADMAP
    });
```

A marker is then set to indicate the lead location.

```
    // Set a marker for the lead location
    var positionMarker = new google.maps.Marker({
                            map: map,
                            position: currentPosition,
                            icon: 'http://maps.google.com/
mapfiles/ms/micons/green.png'
    });
}
```

See also

- The *Capturing the user's location* recipe in this chapter shows how the geolocation information for a record can be captured at the time that it is created.

Scanning the QR code to access the record

Mobile devices, especially phones, have small keyboards and screens which can make entering page URLs difficult. If the device has a camera, scanning a code to navigate to a page can improve the user experience.

QR, or **Quick Response**, codes are two-dimensional barcodes originally used to track automobiles during manufacture. For more information on QR codes, refer to the following link: http://www.qrcode.com/en/history/.

In this recipe, we will create a Visualforce page to display the QR code of an opportunity. When the code is scanned on a mobile device, this navigates the user to the Salesforce1 record home page to allow them to view the opportunity details.

Getting ready

This recipe relies on the mobile device being able to scan the *QR code* with a custom URL scheme – a free application that provides this capability in iOS is Qrafter, available from the link given as: https://itunes.apple.com/gb/app/qrafter-qr-code-barcode-reader/id 416987?mt=8.

This recipe requires that you have already uploaded the Salesforce Lightning Design System version 2.0.2 as detailed in Chapter 8, *Force.com Sites*.

How to do it...

1. Navigate to the Visualforce setup page by clicking on **Your Name** | **Setup** | **Develop** | **Visualforce Pages**.
2. Click on the **New** button.
3. Enter SF1QRCode in the **Label** field.
4. Accept the default **SF1QRCode** that is automatically generated for the **Name** field.
5. Check the box labeled **Available for Salesforce mobile apps and Lightning Pages**.
6. Paste the contents of the SF1QRCode.page file from the code download into the **Visualforce Markup** area and click on the **Save** button.
7. Navigate to the Visualforce setup page by clicking on **Your Name** | **Setup** | **Develop** | **Visualforce Pages**.
8. Locate the entry for the **SF1QRCode** page and click on the **Security** link.
9. On the resulting page, select which profiles should have access and click on the **Save** button.

How it works...

Opening the following URL in your desktop browser displays the details of an opportunity, including the QR code:

```
https://<instance>/apex/SF1QRCode?id=<opportunity_id>.
```

Here, `<instance>` is the Salesforce instance specific to your organization, for example, `na6.salesforce.com`, and `<opportunity_id>` is the record ID of an opportunity within your Salesforce instance.

Scanning the QR code, with an application such as Qrafter for the iPhone, opens Salesforce1 and navigates to the record home page of the opportunity.

The **SF1QRCode** page generates the QR code via the free API provided by `http://goqr.m e`, available at `https://api.qrserver.com`. The QR code encodes the Salesforce1 custom URL scheme for the opportunity `sObject` view page:

```
<img
src="https://api.qrserver.com/v1/create-qr-code/?size=150x150&data={!URLENC
ODE('salesforce1://sObject/' + Opportunity.Id + '/view')}" />
```

10
Troubleshooting

In this chapter, we will cover the following topics and recipes:

- Avoiding validation errors with action regions
- Errors – harmful if swallowed
- Multiple bindings to the same record
- Reducing view state size 1 – the transient keyword
- Reducing view state size 2 – HTML vs Visualforce components
- Debugging Visualforce
- Logging messages in a Visualforce page

Introduction

Visualforce pages provide a custom interface for users, improving productivity by reducing the number of forms required to create and maintain data compared to the standard user interface, and improving adoption. Non-performant or error-prone Visualforce pages can have the opposite effect, making the user experience frustrating and introducing a *Visualforce tax* on regular activities.

Studies have shown that a user accessing a non-performant application is also likely to believe it is difficult to use, poorly designed, and does not contain useful content, all of which present a barrier to adoption.

In this chapter, we will take a look at solutions to common issues encountered with Visualforce pages. We will then look at techniques for reducing the view state size and how writing information about the internal state of a controller to the Salesforce debug log can help to track down errors.

Avoiding validation errors with action regions

Submitting a Visualforce form without populating a required field causes an error message to be returned to the user. When the user has triggered the submission by clicking on a button, a message of this nature will not come as a surprise. If the submission is automatically triggered, for example, to retrieve fields once a lookup is populated, the sudden and unexpected appearance of an error message is a poor user experience.

In this recipe, we will create a Visualforce page to create an opportunity with a number of required fields. When the user selects the account to associate the opportunity with, the form will be submitted and related fields from the account record will be populated regardless of whether the required fields have been populated.

Getting ready

This recipe makes use of a controller extension, so this needs to be created before the Visualforce page.

How to do it...

1. First, create the controller extension for the Visualforce page by navigating to the **Apex Classes** setup page by clicking on **Your Name | Setup | Develop | Apex Classes**.
2. Click on the **New** button.
3. Paste the contents of the `ActionRegionAvoidValidationExt.cls` Apex class from the code download into the **Apex Class** area.
4. Click on the **Save** button.
5. Next, create the Visualforce page by navigating to the Visualforce setup page by clicking on **Your Name | Setup | Develop | Visualforce Pages**.
6. Click on the **New** button.
7. Enter `ActionRegionAvoidValidation` in the **Label** field.
8. Accept the default **ActionRegionAvoidValidation** that is automatically generated for the **Name** field.
9. Paste the contents of the `ActionRegionAvoidValidation.page` file from the code download into the **Visualforce Markup** area and click on the **Save** button.

10. Navigate to the Visualforce setup page by clicking on **Your Name | Setup | Develop | Visualforce Pages**.

11. Locate the entry for the **ActionRegionAvoidValidation** page and click on the **Security** link.

12. On the resulting page, select which profiles should have access and click on the **Save** button.

How it works...

Opening the following URL in your browser displays the **ActionRegionAvoidValidation** page: `https://<instance>/apex/ActionRegionAvoidValidation`.

Here, `<instance>` is the Salesforce instance specific to your organization, for example, `na6.salesforce.com`.

Create Opportunity				Save	Cancel	
▼ Detail						
Opportunity Name				Close Date		[24/08/2013]
Amount				Stage	--None--	
▼ Account						
Account Name	United Oil & Gas Corp.					
Website	http://www.uos.com			Phone	(212) 842-5500	
			Save	Cancel		

Entering a value in the **Account Name** field and losing focus on the field (by tabbing out or clicking into another field) updates the **Website** and **Phone** fields with the details from the chosen account, even though the required fields of **Opportunity Name**, **Close Date**, and **Stage** are not populated.

The **ActionRegionAvoidValidation** page defines an action region for the **Account** section, which stops the controllers from processing other fields on the page when the automatic submission takes place. The "automatic submission is handled by the" `<apex:actionSupport />` component "nested in the **Account Name** input field".

```
<apex:actionRegion >
  <apex:pageBlockSection  id="account">
    <apex:inputField value="{!Opportunity.AccountId}">
      <apex:actionSupport event="onchange"
```

```
      action="{!accountSelected}" rerender="account, msgs"
      status="stat"/>
  </apex:inputField>
<apex:pageBlockSectionItem />
<apex:outputField value="{!Opportunity.Account.Website}"/>
<apex:outputField value="{!Opportunity.Account.Phone}"/>
<apex:actionStatus startText="Getting detail" id="stat" />
  </apex:pageBlockSection>
</apex:actionRegion>
```

The `accountSelected` method in the controller extension retrieves the related account record and associates it with the opportunity record that the standard controller is managing.

```
Opportunity opp=(Opportunity) stdCtrl.getRecord();

// handle the situation where the account field has been cleared
if (!String.isBlank(opp.AccountId))
{
  opp.Account=[select Website, Phone from Account
    where id=:opp.AccountId];
}
else
{
  opp.Account=null;
}
```

See also

- The *Breaking up forms with action regions* recipe in Chapter 3, *Capturing Data Using Forms* shows how areas of a large and complex form may be submitted independently of each other using action regions.

Surfacing errors

When a form submission results in a rerender of a section rather than refreshing the entire Visualforce page, it is very easy to cause error messages from the controller to be swallowed rather than displayed to the user. In this situation, as far as the user is concerned, the form submission is broken; they click on a button and nothing on the page changes.

In this recipe we will create a Visualforce page to create an opportunity. When the user selects the account for the opportunity, the form will be submitted. The controller then retrieves the account record so that additional fields on the page may be populated. If the opportunity name is not defined, the form submission will fail and an error message will be displayed to the user.

Getting ready

This recipe makes use of a controller extension, so this will need to be created before the Visualforce page.

How to do it...

1. First, create the controller extension for the Visualforce page by navigating to the **Apex Classes** setup page by clicking on **Your Name** I **Setup** I **Develop** I **Apex Classes**.
2. Click on the **New** button.
3. Paste the contents of the `RerenderValidationExt.cls` Apex class from the code download into the **Apex Class** area.
4. Click on the **Save** button.
5. Next, create the Visualforce page by navigating to the Visualforce setup page by clicking on **Your Name** I **Setup** I **Develop** I **Visualforce Pages**.
6. Click on the **New** button.
7. Enter `RerenderValidation` in the **Label** field.
8. Accept the default **RerenderValidation** that is automatically generated for the **Name** field.
9. Paste the contents of the `RerenderValidation.page` file from the code download into the **Visualforce Markup** area and click on the **Save** button.
10. Navigate to the Visualforce setup page by clicking on **Your Name** I **Setup** I **Develop** I **Visualforce Pages**.
11. Locate the entry for the **RerenderValidation** page and click on the **Security** link.
12. On the resulting page, select which profiles should have access and click on the **Save** button.

How it works...

Opening the following URL in your browser displays the **RerenderValidation** page: `https://<instance>/apex/RerenderValidation`.

Here, `<instance>` is the Salesforce instance specific to your organization, for example, `na6.salesforce.com`.

Choosing the account before supplying the opportunity name causes the postback to fail with an error message.

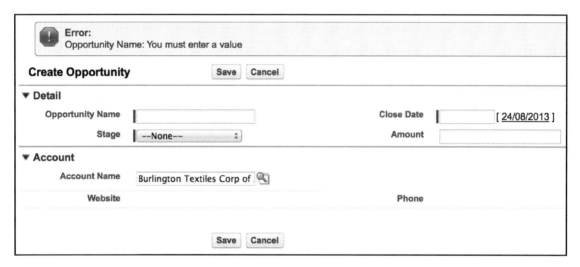

The Account Name input field has a nested `<apex:actionSupport />` component to submit the form and execute a controller method when the value changes.

```
<apex:inputField value="{!Opportunity.AccountId}">
  <apex:actionSupport event="onchange" action="{!accountSelected}"
    rerender="account, msgs" status="stat"/>
</apex:inputField>
```

This component defines the `rerender` attribute, which will result in only the listed standard components being redrawn when the controller method has completed. This list includes an `<apex:pageMessages />` component.

```
<apex:pageMessages id="msgs" />
```

In the event that an error occurs while submitting or processing the form, the account section will not change. Rerendering the `msgs` component ensures that any errors that occur are communicated back to the user.

See also

- The *Adding error messages to non-field inputs* recipe in `Chapter 3`, *Capturing Data Using Forms* shows how error messages can be displayed against input elements associated with controller properties.
- The *Adding error messages to field inputs* recipe in `Chapter 3`, *Capturing Data Using Forms* shows how error messages can be displayed against input elements associated with `sObject` fields.

Multiple bindings to the same record

A very common problem in Visualforce is inadvertently binding multiple `<apex:inputField />` components to the same `sObject` record and field instance. In the following example markup, the **StageName** field of each opportunity record has been bound to two separate input fields – the first intended to display the name of the current stage and the second to allow the user to supply the name of the desired stage.

```
<apex:form >
    <apex:pageBlock >
      <apex:pageBlockTable value="{!opps}" var="opp">
        <apex:column headerValue="Name">
          <apex:inputField value="{!opp.Name}" />
        </apex:column>
        <apex:column headerValue="Stage Name">
          <apex:inputField value="{!opp.StageName}" />
        </apex:column>
        <apex:column headerValue="Amount">
          <apex:inputField value="{!opp.Amount}" />
        </apex:column>
        <apex:column headerValue="New Stage Name">
          <apex:inputField value="{!opp.StageName}" />
        </apex:column>
      </apex:pageBlockTable>
    </apex:pageBlock>
  </apex:form>
```

At first glance, this may seem like a reasonable approach, as the **New Stage Name** input occurs after the current `Stage Name` input. An `<apex:inputField />` causes a setter to be executed on the `sObject` when the records are saved, so it could therefore be assumed that the setter for the **New Stage Name** field occurs last. However, the Visualforce Developer's Guide makes it clear that this is a flawed assumption:

> *Visualforce doesn't define the order in which setter methods are called, or how many times they might be called in the course of processing a request. Design your setter methods to produce the same outcome, whether they are called once or multiple times for a single page request.*

The save process is now subject to a race condition, in that the value saved to the opportunity `Stage Name` field will be that of whichever input field setter is the last to execute. As this is not predictable, it is entirely possible that the Visualforce page behaves as expected during development and testing, and only exhibits problems when deployed to production.

In this recipe, we will create a wrapper class that encapsulates both an opportunity record from the Salesforce database and a carrier opportunity record that is used to capture the new `Stage Name` field value for that opportunity.

Getting ready

This recipe makes use of a custom controller, so this will need to be created before the Visualforce page.

How to do it...

1. First, create the custom controller for the Visualforce page by navigating to the **Apex Classes** setup page by clicking on **Your Name** | **Setup** | **Develop** | **Apex Classes**.
2. Click on the **New** button.
3. Paste the contents of the `OppMultiBindingsController.cls` Apex class from the code download into the **Apex Class** area.
4. Click on the **Save** button.
5. Next, create the Visualforce page by navigating to the Visualforce setup page by clicking on **Your Name** | **Setup** | **Develop** | **Visualforce Pages**.
6. Click on the **New** button.

7. Enter `OppsMultiBindingWrappers` in the **Label** field.

8. Accept the default **OppsMultiBindingWrappers** that is automatically generated for the **Name** field.

9. Paste the contents of the `OppsMultiBindingWrappers.page` file from the code download into the **Visualforce Markup** area and click on the **Save** button.

10. Navigate to the Visualforce setup page by clicking on **Your Name | Setup | Develop | Visualforce Pages**.

11. Locate the entry for the **OppsMultiBindingWrappers** page and click on the **Security** link.

12. On the resulting page, select which profiles should have access and click on the **Save** button.

How it works...

Opening the following URL in your browser displays the **RerenderValidation** page:
`https://<instance>/apex/OppsMultiBindingWrappers.`

Here, `<instance>` is the Salesforce instance specific to your organization, for example, `na6.salesforce.com`.

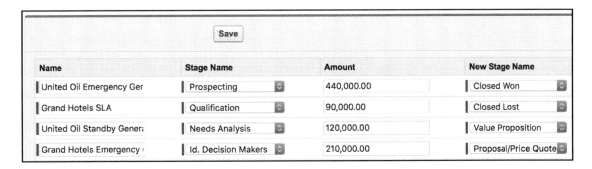

Updates to the **New Stage Name** fields are applied to the associated opportunities when the **Save** button is clicked.

The wrapper class for the opportunity and carrier object is an inner class declared inside the controller.

```
public class OppWrap
{
  public Opportunity opp {get; set;}
  public Opportunity carrier {get; set;}
```

```
   public OppWrap(Opportunity inOpp)
   {
     opp=inOpp;
     carrier=new Opportunity();
   }
}
```

The controller generates a list of wrapper classes in the constructor.

```
public OppMultiBindingsController()
{
    oppWraps=new List<OppWrap>();
    for (Opportunity opp : [select id, Name, StageName, Amount
                  from Opportunity
                  limit 10])
    {
    oppWraps.add(new OppWrap(opp));
    }
}
```

The Visualforce page iterates the wrapper classes, binding the inputs to the encapsulated opportunity or carrier object as appropriate.

```
<apex:pageBlockTable value="{!oppWraps}" var="wrap">
  <apex:column headerValue="Name">
    <apex:inputField value="{!wrap.opp.Name}" />
  </apex:column>
  <apex:column headerValue="New Stage Name">
    <apex:inputField value="{!wrap.carrier.StageName}" />
  </apex:column>
</apex:pageBlockTable>
```

When the user clicks the **Save** button, the list of wrapper classes is iterated and the stage name copied from the carrier object to the opportunity.

```
for (OppWrap oppWrap : oppWraps)
{
  oppWrap.opp.StageName=oppWrap.carrier.StageName;
}
```

There's more …

A variation on this problem is where a separate carrier `sObject` record instance is used to capture the **New Stage Name** value via an extension controller. The carrier object's `Stage Name` field is bound to an `<apex:inputField />`, replacing the second binding to the opportunity record's `Stage Name` field.

```
<apex:form >
  ...
    <apex:column headerValue="New Stage Name">
      <apex:inputField value="{!carrier.StageName}" />
    </apex:column>
  ...
</apex:form>
```

In this scenario, the use of the carrier object may appear reasonable as it is only bound to a single `<apex:inputField />` component. This is not the case, however; the component is inside a repeater component, `<apex:pageBlockTable />`, which means that each row in the table contains an `<apex:inputField />` that is bound to the same `Stage Name` field of the single carrier `sObject`.

As mentioned earlier in this recipe, the order that Visualforce setters will execute in is not defined, so each setter associated with the `<apex:inputField />` updates the carrier `sObject` and overwrites the previous `Stage Name` value. The last setter to execute makes the final update to the field, which is then applied to all opportunity records being managed by the standard controller.

Reducing view state size 1 – the transient keyword

The Visualforce view state is used to maintain the state of a page across multiple requests to the server. If a Visualforce page contains an `<apex:form />` tag, it will also contain a hidden input field with the encrypted view state as its value.

The view state contains the following information:

- All non-transient members of the page's controller (regardless of whether this is a standard or custom controller) and all controller extensions

- The object graph for everything that is reachable from one of the non-transient members detailed in the previous bullet point

- The component tree for the page
- Internal housekeeping data for the Visualforce framework

The maximum size of the entire view state is 135 Kb. Typically, Visualforce developers don't worry too much about the size of the view state until this limit is exceeded. However, as the view state makes a round-trip to the server with every request, reducing the size has a direct impact on page load times.

In this recipe we will create two Visualforce pages:

- The first will store a collection of `SelectOption` records in the view state, even though the options will not change between transactions
- The second will recreate the collection when a user request is processed

We will then use the View State Inspector to examine the overall size and contents of the view state for each page to see the impact that storing the records has.

Getting ready

The View State Inspector, introduced in the Winter 11 release of Salesforce, displays the size and value of all objects in the Visualforce view state, allowing developers to understand exactly how the view state is consumed.

To enable the View State Inspector, navigate to **Your Name** | **Setup** | **My Personal Information** | **Personal Information** and check the boxes labeled **Development Mode** and **Show View State in Development Mode**.

After enabling Development Mode, the development footer is added to each Visualforce page, which contains a tab for the View State Inspector labeled **View State**.

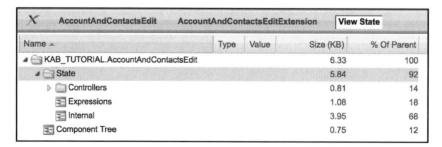

Expanding the view state tree displays the size of the various elements.

 The development mode footer can impact the behavior of the page being inspected – for example, JavaScript navigation via `window.location` does not work and you may encounter problems when embedding iframes in the Sales or Service Cloud consoles.

How to do it...

1. First, create the custom controller for the Visualforce page that stores the records in the view state by navigating to the **Apex Classes** setup page by clicking on **Your Name | Setup | Develop | Apex Classes**.

2. Click on the **New** button.

3. Paste the contents of the `ViewStateLargeController.cls` Apex class from the code download into the **Apex Class** area.

4. Click on the **Save** button.

5. Next, create the custom controller for the Visualforce page that recreates the records for each request by navigating to the **Apex Classes** setup page by clicking on **Your Name | Setup | Develop | Apex Classes**.

6. Click on the **New** button.

7. Paste the contents of the `ViewStateReducedController.cls` Apex class from the code download into the **Apex Class** area.

8. Click on the **Save** button.

9. Next, create the Visualforce page that stores the records in the view state by navigating to the Visualforce setup page by clicking on **Your Name | Setup | Develop | Visualforce Pages**.

10. Click on the **New** button.

11. Enter `ViewStateLarge` in the **Label** field.

12. Accept the default **ViewStateLarge** that is automatically generated for the **Name** field.

13. Paste the contents of the `ViewStateLarge.page` file from the code download into the **Visualforce Markup** area and click on the **Save** button.

14. Navigate to the Visualforce setup page by clicking on **Your Name | Setup | Develop | Visualforce Pages**.

15. Locate the entry for the **ViewStateLarge** page and click on the **Security** link.

16. On the resulting page, select which profiles should have access and click on the **Save** button.

17. Finally, create the Visualforce page that recreates the records for each request by clicking on **Your Name | Setup | Develop | Visualforce Pages** and navigating to the Visualforce setup page

18. Click on the **New** button.

19. Enter `ViewStateReduced` in the **Label** field.

20. Accept the default **ViewStateReduced** that is automatically generated for the **Name** field.

21. Paste the contents of the `ViewStateReduced.page` file from the code download into the **Visualforce Markup** area and click on the **Save** button.

22. Navigate to the Visualforce setup page by clicking on **Your Name | Setup | Develop | Visualforce Pages**.

23. Locate the entry for the **ViewStateReduced** page and click on the **Security** link.

24. On the resulting page, select which profiles should have access and click on the **Save** button.

How it works...

Opening the following URL in your browser displays the **ViewStateLarge** page, which stores the records in the view state: `https://<instance>/apex/ViewStateLarge`.

Here, `<instance>` is the Salesforce instance specific to your organization, for example, `na6.salesforce.com`.

Clicking the **View State** tab shows the size of the view state for the page.

Name ▲	Type	Value	Size (KB)	% Of Parent
▲ 📁 ViewStateLarge			2.05	100
▲ 📁 State			1.94	95
▲ 📁 Controllers			0.81	42
	Page			
▲ 📁 ViewStateLargeController	viewstatelarge		0.81	100
	Controller			
▷ 📁 accountOptions [25]	List<System.SelectOption>		0.63	78

The total view state size is 2.05 KB, of which 0.63 KB is due to the `SelectOption` records.

Opening the following URL in your browser displays the **ViewStateReduced** page, which recreates the records for each user request:

`https://<instance>/apex/ViewStateReduced.`

Here, `<instance>` is the Salesforce instance specific to your organization, for example, `na6.salesforce.com`.

Clicking the **View State** tab shows the size of the view state for the page.

Name ▲	Type	Value	Size (KB)	% Of Parent
▲ 📁 ViewStateReduced			1.5	100
▲ 📁 State			1.39	93
▲ 📁 Controllers			0.25	18
📄 ViewStateReducedController		Page viewstatereduced Controller	0.25	100
📄 Expressions			0.5	36
📄 Internal			0.64	46

The view state size is now 1.5 KB, which shows that removing the records from the view state reduces the size by 25%. In the event that multiple collections of records are stored in the view state, the cumulative effect will start to become significant.

 The figures in the preceding screenshot may not match those of your View State Inspector, but the impact of removing the records from the view state should be similar.

The **ViewStateReduced** controller stores the records in a property marked as transient. The transient keyword indicates that the property cannot be saved and will not be included in the view state. Properties that are only needed for the duration of a single request, rather than storing state across multiple requests, should always be declared as transient.

```
public transient List<SelectOption> accountOptions;
```

 Developers new to Visualforce often avoid uage of the transient keyword where a property is only required for the duration of a request, based on the flawed assumption that it is better to cache the results of an expensive query once it has completed than to re-execute the query for each subsequent request.

This is a flawed assumption as the effect of including this type of data in the view state is typically more expensive than re-querying the data when processing a new request – the overhead of an SOQL query is minor when compared to the full HTTP round-trip time.

The getter method caches the results of the SOQL query, but as this is a transient property the results are only retained for the duration of the request.

```
public List<SelectOption> getAccountOptions()
{
  if (null==accountOptions)
  {
    accountOptions=new List<SelectOption>();
    for (Account acc : [select id, Name from Account])
    {
      accountOptions.add(new SelectOption(acc.Id, acc.Name));
    }
  }
  return accountOptions;
}
```

While the getter for this property could be altered to recreate the collection of options each time it is invoked, this is not an efficient approach in terms of minimizing calls to the database.

The Visualforce Developer's Guide has the following to say about getter methods:

"Visualforce doesn't define the order in which getter methods are called, or how many times they might be called in the course of processing a request.

Thus a getter that executes an SOQL query each time it is invoked may adversely impact the SOQL query governor limit."

There's more ...

Work in progress records are appropriate for storage in the view state as these contain the changes that users have made. When records are stored in the view state, they should contain the minimum number of fields required to represent the user's input.

In a mature Salesforce org where an `sObject` contains several hundred custom fields, or where a number of large text area fields are populated, the impact of not minimizing record sizes on the view state can be significant.

Reducing view state size 2 – HTML vs Visualforce components

Visualforce components contribute to the internal element of the view state. A page with a large number of components, or with a repeating element that contains a number of components, may consume a significant amount of the view state.

In this recipe we will create two Visualforce pages:

- The first will iterate a collection of opportunity records using an `<apex:pageBlockTable />` repeater component with nested standard components for columns and input fields
- The second will iterate a collection of opportunity records using a regular HTML `<table>` element

We will then use the View State Inspector to examine the overall size and contents of the view state for each page to see the impact that storing the records has.

Getting ready

This recipe requires that you have enabled the View State Inspector, as detailed in the *Reducing view state size 1- the transient keyword* recipe in this chapter.

How to do it...

1. First, create the Visualforce page that uses standard components to display the opportunity details by navigating to the Visualforce setup page by clicking on **Your Name | Setup | Develop | Visualforce Pages**.
2. Click on the **New** button.
3. Enter `OppViewStateStandard` in the **Label** field.
4. Accept the default **OppViewStateStandard** that is automatically generated for the **Name** field.
5. Paste the contents of the `OppViewStateStandard.page` file from the code download into the **Visualforce Markup** area and click on the **Save** button.

6. Navigate to the Visualforce setup page by clicking on **Your Name** | **Setup** | **Develop** | **Visualforce Pages**.

7. Locate the entry for the **OppViewStateStandard** page and click on the **Security** link.

8. On the resulting page, select which profiles should have access and click on the **Save** button.

9. Finally, create the Visualforce page that uses HTML elements to display the opportunity details by navigating to the Visualforce setup page by clicking on **Your Name** | **Setup** | **Develop** | **Visualforce Pages**.

10. Click on the **New** button.

11. Enter OppViewStateHTML in the **Label** field.

12. Accept the default **OppViewStateHTML** that is automatically generated for the **Name** field.

13. Paste the contents of the OppViewStateHTML.page file from the code download into the **Visualforce Markup** area and click on the **Save** button.

14. Navigate to the Visualforce setup page by clicking on **Your Name** | **Setup** | **Develop** | **Visualforce Pages**.

15. Locate the entry for the **OppViewStateHTML** page and click on the **Security** link.

16. On the resulting page, select which profiles should have access and click on the **Save** button.

How it works...

Opening the following URL in your browser displays the **OppViewStateStandard** page, which outputs opportunity information using standard components: https://<instance>/apex/OppViewStateStandard.

Here, <instance> is the Salesforce instance specific to your organization, for example, na6.salesforce.com.

Clicking the **View State** tab shows the size of the view state for the page.

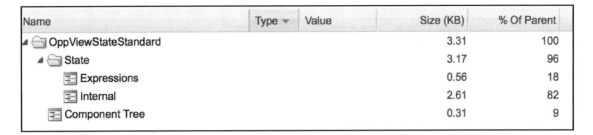

Name	Type ▼	Value	Size (KB)	% Of Parent
▲ 🗋 OppViewStateStandard			3.31	100
▲ 🗋 State			3.17	96
📄 Expressions			0.56	18
📄 Internal			2.61	82
📄 Component Tree			0.31	9

The total view state size is 3.31 KB, of which 2.61 KB is internal.

Opening the following URL in your browser displays the **OppViewStateHTML** page, which outputs opportunity details using regular HTML elements: `https://<instance>/apex/ViewStateReduced`.

Here, `<instance>` is the Salesforce instance specific to your organization, for example, `na6.salesforce.com`.

Clicking the **View State** tab shows the size of the view state for the page.

Name ▲	Type	Value	Size (KB)	% Of Parent
▲ 🗋 OppViewStateHTML			2.8	100
▲ 🗋 State			2.67	95
📄 Expressions			0.56	21
📄 Internal			2.11	79
📄 Component Tree			0.28	10

The view state size is now 2.8 KB, of which 2.11 KB is internal – a saving of 0.5 KB by replacing a standard repeater component with an HTML table.

The figures in the preceding screenshot may not match those of your View State Inspector, but the impact of removing the records from the view state should be similar.

The **OppViewStateStandard** page uses standard components to iterate the opportunity collection and output the details.

```
<apex:pageBlockTable value="{!opps}" var="opp">
  <apex:column headerValue="Id">
    <apex:outputField value="{!opp.Id}" />
  </apex:column>
  <apex:column headerValue="Name">
    <apex:inputField value="{!opp.Name}" />
  </apex:column>
  <apex:column headerValue="StageName">
    <apex:outputField value="{!opp.StageName}" />
  </apex:column>
</apex:pageBlockTable>
```

The **OppViewStateHTML** replaces the standard components with HTML elements, aside from the input/output fields, which generate the appropriate markup for the sObject field type.

```
<table style="width:95%">
  <tr>
    <th>Id</th>
    <th>Name</th>
    <th>Stage Name</th>
  </tr>
  <apex:repeat value="{!opps}" var="opp">
    <tr>
      <td><apex:outputField value="{!opp.Id}" /></td>
      <td><apex:inputField value="{!opp.Name}" /></td>
      <td><apex:outputField value="{!opp.StageName}" /></td>
    </tr>
  </apex:repeat>
</table>
```

 HTML elements will not match the styling of the Visualforce components, so an additional effort will be required if your page must match the standard Visualforce look and feel. Replacing Visualforce input fields with HTML equivalents is not recommended unless you are reworking the entire page to use JavaScript remote methods.

There's more …

Keeping the view state size as small as possible requires constant vigilance. While the individual gains of each technique are small, the aggregated effect of these makes the difference between a performant page that loads without errors and a slow page that regularly breaches the view state limit.

In the event that the aggregation of small gains does not solve a view state limit breach, another option is to make the entire page stateless and manage all server interaction through JavaScript remote methods. However, the re-work required to achieve this is significant for all but the simplest of Visualforce pages, so this should only be undertaken as a last resort.

Debugging Visualforce

When developing all but the most straightforward Visualforce pages, it is highly likely that bugs will be encountered in the business logic, either the Apex controller code or JavaScript executing in the page. In order to identify where in the logic the problem lies, the bug must be reproduced with a mechanism to surface information about the internal state of the page.

The Apex debug log contains a wealth of information about a request to the server, including method entry/exit, database interaction (SOQL and DML), and errors.

 As the Apex debug log has a maximum size of 2 MB, and a Salesforce org is limited to 50 MB of debug logs, a common approach for developers new to the Salesforce platform is to attempt to capture debug information in custom objects. However, custom object instances are only written to the Salesforce database when a transaction successfully completes, which means that when an error occurs and the transaction is rolled back, no information about the error is captured. The Apex debug log is the only way to retain information about a transaction that has been rolled back.

In this recipe, we will create a Visualforce page with a custom controller that generates debug log messages.

How to do it...

1. First, create the controller extension for the Visualforce page by navigating to the **Apex Classes** setup page by clicking on **Your Name** | **Setup** | **Develop** | **Apex Classes**.
2. Click on the **New** button.
3. Paste the contents of the `DebuggingController.cls` Apex class from the code download into the **Apex Class** area.
4. Click on the **Save** button.
5. Next, create the Visualforce page by navigating to the Visualforce setup page by clicking on **Your Name** | **Setup** | **Develop** | **Visualforce Pages**.
6. Click on the **New** button.
7. Enter `Debugging` in the **Label** field.
8. Accept the default **Debugging** that is automatically generated for the **Name** field.
9. Paste the contents of the `Debugging.page` file from the code download into the **Visualforce Markup** area and click on the **Save** button.
10. Navigate to the Visualforce setup page by clicking on **Your Name** | **Setup** | **Develop** | **Visualforce Pages**.
11. Locate the entry for the **Debugging** page and click on the **Security** link.
12. On the resulting page, select which profiles should have access and click on the **Save** button.

How it works...

Opening the Salesforce Developer Console causes debug logs to be captured for a period of time. Open the Developer Console by clicking **Your Name** | **Developer Console**.

The Developer Console is an online IDE that contains a collection of tools to create, debug, and test your applications. As well as providing access to debug lots, it allows you to author Apex, Visualforce, and Lightning Components, as well as execute unit tests.

Opening the following URL in your browser displays the **Debugging** page:
`https://<instance>/apex/Debugging`.

Here, `<instance>` is the Salesforce instance specific to your organization, for example, `na6.salesforce.com`.

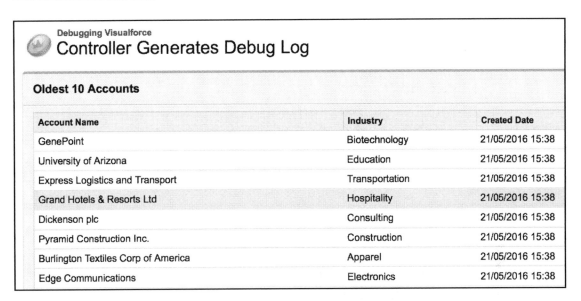

The Developer Console shows the debug log that has been captured for the request.

| Logs | Tests | Checkpoints | Query Editor | View State | Progress | Problems |

User	Application	Operation	Time ▼	Status	Read	Size
Keir Bowden	Browser	/apex/CasesSid...	18/0...	Success	Unread	8.36 KB
Keir Bowden	Browser	/apex/Debugging	18/0...	Success	Unread	14.63 KB

Clicking on the debug log with the **Operation** entry of **/apex/Debugging** opens the debug log for the page. Check the **Debug Only** box to restrict the displayed messages to those generated by the controller's debug logging.

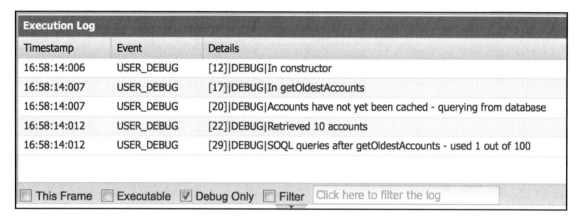

The controller generates debug messages via the `System.debug` method.

```
System.debug('In getOldestAccounts');
if (null==oldestAccounts)
{
    System.debug('Accounts have not yet been cached - querying from
database');
    oldestAccounts=[select id, Name, Industry, CreatedDate from Account
order by CreatedDate asc limit 10];
    System.debug('Retrieved ' + oldestAccounts.size() + ' accounts');
}
else
{
    System.debug('Accounts are already cached');
}
System.debug('SOQL queries after getOldestAccounts - used ' +
            Limits.getQueries() + ' out of ' +
            Limits.getLimitQueries());
```

There's more ...

In order for debugging information to be output to the Apex log file, the Apex log level must be set to DEBUG or higher. In a large and complex Visualforce page with a lot of business logic, this can result in the log file exceeding the 2 MB limit before a key debug statement is reached.

To resolve this, change the Apex log level to ERROR and write debug log entries at the error level:

```
System.debug(LoggingLevel.ERROR, 'Account = ' + account);
```

When using JavaScript or remote methods you may find it necessary to debug your JavaScript code in the client.

JavaScript provides two mechanisms to output debug information.

- The alert() function, which displays a modal dialog to the user and blocks further processing until it is dismissed.
- The console.log() function, which writes a log message to the JavaScript console. The mechanism for accessing the JavaScript console varies, so consult the online help for your chosen browser.

The console.log() method should be used in preference to the alert function as alerts cannot easily be turned off in a non-debug environment, and many alerts on a single page are detrimental to the user experience. The exception to this rule is for fatal errors – in this situation the error cannot be recovered from, so it may make sense to display more information about the error and the current state to the user and ask them to take some action – to reload the page or to raise a case with the development team, for example.

Logging messages in a Visualforce page

In some situations, it is not straightforward to access the debug log messages, for example when debugging Visualforce inside a managed package installed into a subscriber org. In this scenario, the Salesforce platform blocks the messages from being written to the log.

When this is the case, it is useful to write debug information to the page that is being accessed. Clearly, it would not lead to a great user experience to do this in all cases, so a mechanism for generating this on demand is required.

One way to achieve this is to only generate and output the log information if the user passes a specific parameter on the URL – that way, when the page is working as expected, the user doesn't see any extraneous information, but if there are issues, they can simply request the page in a slightly different fashion and capture the debug information to assist the development team's investigations.

In this recipe, we will create a Visualforce page to retrieve the top 10 opportunities by value. If the page is requested with the URL parameter named debug set to true, debug information will be written to the bottom of the page, while if the page is requested with the URL parameter named debug set to false, no additional information over and above the opportunity details will be rendered.

Getting ready

This recipe makes use of a controller extension, so this will need to be created before the Visualforce page.

How to do it...

1. First, create the controller extension for the Visualforce page by navigating to the **Apex Classes** setup page by clicking on **Your Name** | **Setup** | **Develop** | **Apex Classes**.

2. Click on the **New** button.

3. Paste the contents of the `DebugInPageController.cls` Apex class from the code download into the **Apex Class** area.

4. Click on the **Save** button.

5. Next, create the Visualforce page by navigating to the Visualforce setup page by clicking on **Your Name** | **Setup** | **Develop** | **Visualforce Pages**.

6. Click on the **New** button.

7. Enter `DebugInPage` in the **Label** field.

8. Accept the default **DebugInPage** that is automatically generated for the **Name** field.

9. Paste the contents of the `DebugInPage.page` file from the code download into the **Visualforce Markup** area and click on the **Save** button.

10. Navigate to the Visualforce setup page by clicking on **Your Name** | **Setup** | **Develop** | **Visualforce Pages**.

11. Locate the entry for the `DebugInPage` page and click on the **Security** link.

12. On the resulting page, select which profiles should have access and click on the **Save** button.

How it works...

Opening the following URL in your browser displays the **DebugInPage** page containing the 10 most valuable opportunities and no other information:
`https://<instance>/apex/DebugInPage`.

Here, `<instance>` is the Salesforce instance specific to your organization, for example, `na6.salesforce.com`.

Debugging Visualforce
Logging to the page

Top 10 Opportunities by Value

Opportunity Name	Amount	Stage
Test		Prospecting
United Oil Refinery Generators	£915,000.00	Closed Won
United Oil Plant Standby Generators	£675,000.00	Needs Analysis
United Oil Emergency Generators	£440,000.00	Closed Won
Grand Hotels Generator Installations	£350,000.00	Closed Won
United Oil Refinery Generators	£270,000.00	Proposal/Price Quote
United Oil Installations	£270,000.00	Closed Won
United Oil Installations	£270,000.00	Closed Won
Grand Hotels Guest Portable Generators	£250,000.00	Value Proposition
Burlington Textiles Weaving Plant Generator	£235,000.00	Closed Won

Appending `debug=true` to the URL again displays the 10 most valuable opportunities, but this time with debug information about the processing that has been carried out and the limit situation once the processing has completed:

Grand Hotels Generator Installations	£350,000.00	Closed Won
United Oil Refinery Generators	£270,000.00	Proposal/Price Quote
United Oil Installations	£270,000.00	Closed Won
United Oil Installations	£270,000.00	Closed Won
Grand Hotels Guest Portable Generators	£250,000.00	Value Proposition
Burlington Textiles Weaving Plant Generator	£235,000.00	Closed Won

Debug Logs

2016-06-11 05:43:21 : In constructor

2016-06-11 05:43:21 : In getTop10Opps

2016-06-11 05:43:21 : Opportunities have not yet been cached - querying from database

2016-06-11 05:43:21 : Retrieved 10 opportunities

2016-06-11 05:43:21 : SOQL queries after getTop10Opps - used 1 out of 100

There's more

With a slight adjustment, this technique can also be used to display debugging information in Visualforce pages surfaced through the Salesforce1 mobile application. As users do not make direct requests for pages via the URL, a different mechanism is required to indicate that debug information should be generated. One way that this can be achieved is via a hierarchy custom setting instance for the user in question that is evaluated in the Apex controller.

Index

A

action chaining 105, 106, 107
action function
  using 216
action methods
  parameters, passing to 19, 21, 22
  passing, to components 51, 52, 53, 54
action poller
  turning off 13, 14, 15
action regions
  forms, breaking up with 100, 102
  validation errors, avoiding with 308
attachments
  managing 120
attributes
  passing, to components 44, 46
  updating, in component controllers 47, 48, 49

B

bar chart
  creating 178, 179, 180

C

carrier object 154
chart
  customizing 185, 186, 187, 188
  embedding, in record view page 203, 205, 206, 207
charting 177
collapsible list elements 230
component controllers
  attributes, updating in 47, 48, 49
components
  action methods, passing to 51, 52, 53, 54
  attributes, passing to 44, 46
conditional rendering

  in templates 269
confirmation dialog 222, 223, 224
containing page controller
  notifying 71, 74
Content Delivery Networks (CDNs) 216
content
  retrieving, from Salesforce 249
controller extension
  testing 38, 40, 41
controller property
  value, setting into 61, 62, 64
custom components
  about 43, 44
  creating 57, 59, 60, 61
custom controller
  testing 35, 36, 37, 38
custom datepicker ZIP file
  reference 95
custom datepicker
  adding, to forms 94, 95, 97
custom iterator component 57
custom lookup
  adding, to forms 90, 91, 92, 94
custom settings
  managing 123, 125, 126
CustomHeader page 269

D

Data URI scheme
  reference 294
data-driven decimal places 54, 55, 56
data-driven styling 11
Design2Develop, datepicker
  reference 95
Document Object Model (DOM) 216
Dojo
  reference 216

dynamic Visualforce bindings, Apex maps
  reference 169

E

embedded Visualforce
  record details, refreshing from 126, 127, 128,
    129
Enhanced Lookups 90
Enter key
  pressing, to submit 225, 226
error messages
  adding, to field inputs 80, 81
  adding, to non-field inputs 83
errors
  surfacing 310, 311, 313

F

field access 245, 247, 248
field inputs
  error messages, adding to 80, 81
field sets
  using 86, 88
fields
  retrieving 97, 98, 99
  styling 110, 112
Force.com sites 241
form-based searching 141, 142
forms
  about 77
  breaking up, with action regions 100, 102
  custom datepicker, adding to 94, 95, 97
  custom lookup, adding to 90, 91, 92, 94
  lightning 280, 281, 284

G

Google Maps API
  about 300
  reference 300

H

header menu
  adding, to template 260, 261, 262
hierarchy of records
  managing 156, 157, 159

HTML5 279

I

iframe
  reference 15
image
  attaching, to record 115, 116, 117, 118
  saving, when creating record 289, 290, 292
input element documentation, Mozilla Developer
    Network
  reference 284

J

JavaScript 215
JavaScript key codes
  reference 227
JavaScript remoting
  used, for creating record 237
jQuery User Interface
  reference 231
jQuery
  reference 216
junction object 65

L

launch page
  adding 32, 33, 35
lead
  converting 152, 154, 155
line chart
  creating 181, 182, 183, 184, 185
list of records
  managing 148
list
  record, inline editing from 161, 162, 163, 164
location
  displaying, in map 300, 302, 303

M

map
  location, displaying in 300, 302, 303
megapix-image.js
  reference 290
messages

logging, in Visualforce page 331, 332, 333, 334
multiple bindings
    to same record 313
multiple charts
    producing, per page 208, 210, 211, 212
multiple series
    adding 189, 191, 192

N

navigation
    trapping 234
non-field inputs
    error messages, adding to 83

O

onload handler 227
options
    modifying, based on user input 133, 134, 135, 136

P

page layout
    modifying, based on user input 137, 139, 140
pages
    navigating between 274, 275, 276, 277, 278, 279, 280
parameters
    passing, between Visualforce pages 25, 27, 28
    passing, to action methods 19, 21, 22
Please wait spinner 103, 104
pop-up window
    opening 29, 31, 32
Prototype
    reference 216

Q

QR codes
    displaying, to access record 303, 305
    reference 303
Qrafter
    reference 303
Quick Response 303

R

race conditions
    avoiding 219, 220, 222
record details
    refreshing, from embedded Visualforce 126, 127, 128, 129
record parent
    editing 146, 147, 148
record view page
    chart, embedding in 203, 205, 206, 207
record
    about 245, 247
    creating, JavaScript remoting used 237
    editing 146, 148
    editing, in Visualforce 78, 79, 80
    image, attaching to 115, 116, 117, 118
    inline editing, from list 161, 162, 163, 164
    loading, asynchronously 173, 174, 176
reference 168
related objects
    multiselecting 65, 66, 67, 69
report data
    displaying, in Visualforce 169, 170, 172, 173

S

Salesforce knowledge article
    reference 300
Salesforce Lightning Design System (SLDS)
    reference 242
Salesforce Object Query Language (SOQL) 145
Salesforce Reports and Dashboards, via Apex
    reference 173
Salesforce1 273
Salesforce
    content, retrieving from 249, 250
sforce.one object
    reference 275
sidebar
    adding, to template 264
signature
    capturing, when creating record 295
Site.com
    reference 242
site

creating 242, 243
stacked bar chart
  creating 193, 195, 197
standard buttons
  overriding 7, 8
StandardHeader page 269

T

table columns
  styling 113
template
  header menu, adding to 260, 261, 262
  sidebar, adding to 265
third axis
  adding 198, 199, 200, 201, 202
toggle function, jQuery
  reference 234
transient keyword 317

U

URL parameters
  reacting to 22, 24
user location
  capturing 285, 286, 287, 288, 289

V

validation errors
  avoiding, with action regions 308
value

setting, into controller property 61, 62, 64
view state size 1
  reducing 317, 319, 321
view state size 2
  reducing 323
Visualforce components
  versus HTML 323
Visualforce Developer's Guide
  reference 274
Visualforce pages
  messages, logging in 331, 332, 333, 334
  parameters, passing between 25, 27, 28
Visualforce report
  creating 165, 168, 169
Visualforce
  about 15
  debugging 327, 328, 329, 330
  in sidebar 16, 17, 18
  record, editing in 78, 79, 80
  report data, displaying in 169, 170, 172, 173

W

web to lead functionality
  about 253, 254, 256
  reference 253
website template
  creating 257, 260
wrapper class
  using 130, 132, 133